# THE ORPHANED ADULT

# THE ORPHANED ADULT
## Confronting the Death
## of a Parent

Rabbi Marc D. Angel, Ph.D.
*Yeshiva University*
*New York, New York*

**INSIGHT BOOKS**
HUMAN SCIENCES PRESS
72 FIFTH AVENUE
NEW YORK, N.Y. 10011-8004

Printed in the United States of America
987654321

**Library of Congress Cataloging-in-Publication Data**

Angel, Marc.
  The orphaned adult.

  Bibliography: p.
  Includes index.
  1. Death—Social aspects.  2. Parents—Death—
Psychological aspects.  3. Adult children—Psychology.
I. Title.
HQ1073.A53  1987      155.9′37      86-20161
ISBN 0-89885-334-6

# CONTENTS

# FOREWORD

The word "orphan" triggers images of little children— bewildered, defenseless, and suddenly bereft. It is as though society were saying, "Parents are sources of strength and protection for their children. Without them their children are vulnerable and weak. Pity them."

Of course, this is true. But these tragedies in every generation have so riveted us with their lasered focus on weakness that we have ignored adult children, who are strong and independent, but nonetheless bereft. They are bereft of other qualities that emanate from parents—love and compassion and that elusive something called "home," not an apartment or furniture, but mother and father in their own persons.

People often are asked after a parent's death, "How old was she?", as though dying at seventy-five were not a tragedy. The comfort that follows is usually cold: "She lived her life," "You children are all grown up." Someone had to say, publicly and formally: "Grownups suffer their parents' death, too. My mother died at seventy-five. But she is my wonderful mother whom I loved and lost.''

Someone did—Rabbi Marc Angel, and I am very pleased that he did.

I am pleased that a person with his experience coping with the tragedies of others, could document his own ''orphan'' sentiments. Rabbi Angel does it with the wisdom that comes from personal experience, yet he cites authoritative sources; and he does it with understated yet palpable compassion. And more, he writes with clarity about a subject which could become enmeshed in murky sentimentality in a lesser person.

He is to be admired for this. I know this book will be of continuous comfort to orphans of all ages. I congratulate him for undertaking to work through his own bereavement in a way which would alleviate the burdens of others similarly bereaved.

*Rabbi Maurice Lamm*

# ACKNOWLEDGEMENTS

This book owes much of its contents to my late mother, Rachel Angel, of blessed memory. She shared her wisdom and thoughtfulness with us throughout the course of her life. Even during her final illness, she was a source of inspiration, thoughtfulness, and sensitivity. To a large extent, this book is also her book.

I thank my father, Victor Angel; my brothers Bill and David; my sister Bernice; my sisters-in-law, Sharon and Vicki; my brother-in-law, Peter; and all family members and friends who shared their insights with me.

I am grateful to my good friend Alvin Deutsch for his advice and encouragement. I thank Norma Fox, editor-in-chief, and her entire staff at Human Sciences Press, especially Donna Matthew and Brice Hammack.

I am grateful to Rabbi Maurice Lamm for his foreword to this book. I have long admired Dr. Lamm's erudition, sensitivity and lucid literary style and am honored by his enthusiastic evaluation of my work.

11

I express my deepest appreciation to my wife Gilda, whose love and guidance are boundless. To her and our children—Jeffrey, Ronda, and Elana—I convey my gratitude, which is really too deep for words.

## CHAPTER 1

# ADULT AND ORPHAN

In February 1983, I received a telephone call from my father in Seattle. Almost everyone reading this book has received, or will receive, such a call. My father's voice was broken and somber.

"Mom is in the hospital. Her cancer has spread. The doctors offer little hope. I think you had better come home to see her."

Mom had been fighting cancer for several years and we had hoped she was winning. She was a strong woman, sixty-eight years old. She had a good husband, three sons and their wives, a daughter and her husband, 10 grandchildren, and a large extended family of siblings, nephews, and nieces. She was active in her community and had many interests. She was always in the midst of knitting slippers, sweaters, or afghans for her family. She had much to live for.

Although we live in New York—I have been here since 1963 when I came to attend Yeshiva College—we had always maintained a close relationship with my parents. Every summer, my wife and I travelled to Seattle with our children, and we lived with my parents in their house for a month or so. And they visited us in New York. In between visits, we spoke by telephone regularly.

The call from my father caused a dull sensation within me. It was as though the circuits of my brain had overloaded. I did not want to think about my mother being ill. I did not want to believe that this was anything more than an unpleasant, and quickly passing, dream. My wife and children, who were very close to Mom, wished me a nervous goodbye as I left for the airport the next day.

On the airplane, I closed my eyes and visions of my mother filled my mind. I remembered all the good times together, the family gatherings, the special quiet moments of private conversation. And I thought of my own wife and children and of their links with Mom. Mom's illness and possible death would create a rupture in our pattern of life. We had somehow taken it for granted that everything would always stay the same.

Ecclesiastes teaches: "A generation comes and a generation goes, and there is nothing new under the sun." Everyone recognizes the universal rhythm of life and death; everyone knows that generations come and go, that each person who lives will also die. Yet when this truth confronts a person directly, it seems new and unique, as if only now discovered for the first time. I was not the first child on the way to visit a dying parent. But for me, the experience was without precedent or parallel.

When I arrived in Seattle, my father met me at the airport. His normally jovial face was ashen and drawn. He shook my hand as though he were now a stranger to me. And in some special way, he had now become a stranger. He was afraid of being alone, afraid of thinking what would become of him if Mom were to die. They had been married for nearly 44 years. His life was bound to hers.

We went directly from the airport to the hospital. I

asked my father to let me enter Mom's room alone. I wanted that first meeting with my dying mother to be private and personal.

She was sitting up on a chair adjacent to the hospital bed. When I entered the room and greeted her as calmly and easily as I could, she turned her head to me with a relieved expression—and then began to cry. Her crying wrenched my heart, since I could hardly remember having heard her cry before. She had always been a strong, restrained person, reluctant to show extreme emotion. "I'm going to die," were her first words to me on that visit. She took my hand and sobbed uncontrollably. She had already begun to mourn her own impending death.

That was the first in a series of monthly visits. I came to Seattle as frequently as I could, for stretches of 4 to 6 days. With each visit, I noticed the continued deterioration of her physical condition. Chemotherapy had robbed her of her beautiful head of hair of which she had been so proud; she wore a head scarf now, and pretended not to mind it. Radiation therapy weakened her. The medications and pain killers played on her moods. The physical therapy, where the nursing home staff tried to help Mom to walk, had gradually been phased out. There was no point to it. Mom was getting weaker, and would never walk again.

With each visit I found her weaker and closer to death. By April she hardly had the strength to push the button to signal for the nurse. She would concentrate all her mental and physical ability to push that button. After a long while of concerted effort, she would sometimes succeed—and beam with pride and satisfaction. By May, she never succeeded with the button, no matter how hard or how long she tried.

The cancer spread relentlessly. In her period of physical and emotional pain, we could only stand on the sidelines and watch helplessly. We tried to encourage her, to tell her about the family, to listen to her own words. We watched her, we prayed, we nagged the doctors and the nurses. We read books to learn more about cancer and about its cures. But the situation was really hopeless. We were in the midst of a family crisis in which Mom was the central figure, and which would inevitably end in her death.

I visited her during the last week of May. It was a special week for me, for Mom, and for the family. Mom seemed radiant, in very good spirits. She spoke candidly and lovingly to all of us. When I visited her on Thursday morning, I fed her breakfast, kissed her goodbye, and told her that I would be returning to New York that afternoon. But, I assured her, I would be back with my wife and children in just a few weeks and we would all be able to spend some time together. She nodded her head with a Mona Lisa smile on her face, and a distant gaze in her eyes. We embraced. I left.

That Saturday night, I received another call from my father. Mom had died. On Sunday, I again travelled to Seattle, this time for the funeral.

Being a rabbi, I participated in the funeral service and delivered a eulogy for Mom. The chapel was filled with relatives and friends. In the course of my eulogy, a thought forced itself into my mind: I am an orphan.

An orphan? I was thirty-eight years old at the time. I had a wife and three children of my own. I was well established in my position as rabbi of a large and distinguished congregation. Being a self-sufficient adult seemed to exclude the possibility of considering myself to be an orphan. But the thought persisted. And persists.

## Adult and Orphan

In the normal course of events, almost everyone will lose his parents. In some sense, all humans are destined to be orphans. Being an orphan does not necessarily mean being helpless or forlorn. But it does mean dealing with life without the direct relationship of a living mother and/or father. And even adults will find that their lives have been changed by the death of their parent(s).

Reactions to the death of parents will vary from person to person, depending on the kind of relationship which existed during the parent's lifetime. Where the parent was a dominant force in the child's life, "orphanhood" may be painful and disorienting. Where the bonds between parents and children had been tenuous, "orphanhood" may be less of a crisis. Where there had been a very bad relationship between parents and children, the new adult orphans may find themselves somewhat relieved that their parents are dead. And they may also feel guilt. No one can be completely untouched by the death of a parent, even if the parent died in advanced old age after a period of incapacitation.

There has been considerable study of how young children react to the death of a parent. Since children are so dependent on their mother and father, the death of either or both is usually traumatic. The children's lives are greatly disrupted. They tend to be angry at the dead parent for having abandoned them. They may feel guilt, believing that they may in some way have caused the parent to die. Or they may fantasize that the parent may one day return. These young orphans must cope with a particularly difficult reality. It is certainly about such orphans that the Bible commands our compassion. Since they are "helpless," it is a virtue to help them.

But very little attention has been given to the reaction of adults to the death of their parent(s), to adults who are "orphans." Of course, adults who lose parents are not at all in the same predicament as young children who lose parents. But this does not mean that adults absorb their "orphanhood" without undergoing many crises, practical and philosophical. Adult orphans generally experience less extreme conflicts than young orphans; but their reactions may be more subtle, intellectually challenging, and introspective. Since almost all adults have experienced orphanhood throughout history, this life crisis has played—and continues to play—a significant role in how adults deal with death; and with life. For the death of one's parent cannot be seen merely as a private matter in the experience of one family. On the contrary, the rhythm of the passing of the generations is a characteristic feature of human existence.

In the normal course of events, a person will first confront death seriously when his grandparents or elder uncles and aunts die. This confrontation often occurs when the person is still a young child or a teenager. At that time, death may seem ugly, cruel, horrible; the mourning process may be muted by anger or by lack of real understanding about death. The reality of death is integrated into the child's experience, but is filtered by the child's own inexperience and intellectual limitations. And the child is generally removed from the one who died, even if he loved the deceased with the intensity of a child's love.

The first very close person whom one normally loses to death is a parent. The child has spent many years in the same house with that parent, has had his personality shaped by that parent. There are strong bonds of love, respect, and obligation towards that parent. The death of a parent marks the loss of one's first deep human relationship. Even if the "child" is now an adult living on his own, the parent's investment of years in his life cannot be ignored or erased. A parent, after all, is part of the child. When mother or father dies, part of the child has also died.

Adults and their parents operate on a different level of relationship than that of young children and their parents. In the case of youngsters, parents are recognized to have authority over them and responsibility for them. Even when the children are rebellious, there is a general acknowledgement that parents are the authority figures in their lives. They reject the authority, so they rebel. But they are still conscious of the inequality in their relationship with their parents.

Adults, by contrast, have (or should have) a more equal relationship with their parents. They must still respect their parents, and have patience with them beyond what they might have for other people. Yet, since they are adults— and since their parents recognize them as such (or should recognize them as such)—they need not see themselves as being dependent on and subservient to their parents. How adult children and parents interact—how they respect each other's independence—will have a definite impact on how adults will deal with the death of their parents.

Peter DeVries (1965), in his novel *Let Me Count the Ways,* observes: "That you can't go home again is a truth inseparably linked to the fact that neither can you ever get away from it" (p. 176). It is the nature of children to grow up, to become independent, to leave the home of their parents. Good parents encourage this process, even if there is a poignant melancholy in watching their children grow more independent. Yet, no one can ever fully get away from his parents' home. The memories, the experience of childhood, form an integral element of our personalities. An adult child is an adult: but also a child. And for the child, the parent is the central character outside himself.

## Parents as Symbols

Parents are not just providers, guides, friends. They are not merely those two human beings who have bequeathed to us their genes and who have considerably determined the context of our early lives. They are also symbols. They are our link with times past, with the generations before. Their memories span back to the generation before our own birth; they tell us their stories and experiences; they convey to us the stories they had heard from their own parents and grandparents. They are the repositories of the history of our family, and therefore give us the historical context of our lives.

When our parents are alive, we always feel that we have access to their memories and traditions—even if we don't ask them to relate them to us, even if we don't listen too carefully when they do tell us about days gone by. But when they are dead, that living link with our past is irretrievably gone. We are now catapulted into the position of being the "older generation," a position we may or may not be prepared to accept.

We become acutely aware of the symbolic, historical role of parents when we are confronted with the prospect of their dying. In some subtle way, we feel the hours ticking away; not only do we sense the impending death of the physical parent, but we become uneasy about the coming loss of the symbolic parent. Did we fully understand the meaning of the life of our dying mother or father? Did we listen carefully enough to them? Do we have any last questions to ask, any last memories to elicit? Upon looking at a dying parent lying in a hospital bed, we may discover for the first time how little we really know of the life of the parent. We never took the time to learn about their real selves—or at least, not enough time. Everything has to be squeezed in now, before it is too late, before death forever takes that parent from us.

When my mother was dying, I bought a tape recorder and a supply of tapes and brought them with me to the nursing home where Mom was living. Whenever Mom felt strong enough, I "interviewed" her. I asked her questions about her childhood, about her experiences with her own parents. And I asked her to tell me whatever she could remember having heard from her parents about *their* parents, their life in Turkey. No detail was unimportant. As ill as she was, she delighted in these taping sessions. She laughed as she recalled one incident after another. She listened eagerly as I replayed each tape for her. "But all these things aren't important," she said after one of the "interviews," but without much conviction. "They are very important, Mom," I reassured her. And she knew very well that I was right.

My mother had a dramatic life story to tell, as I suppose all parents have. Her parents had come to Seattle from villages in Turkey, early in the twentieth century. They were only teenagers themselves at the time. They came penniless, with no knowledge of English, with nothing but the ambition and courage to make a new life for themselves in America. They had met in Seattle and were married there, and in fairly short order they had seven children—of whom my mother was second. They spoke Judeo-Spanish, the language of the Sephardic Jews who had come to Turkey from Spain during the fifteenth century. My mother, born in Seattle, spoke only Judeo-Spanish until at the age of five she went to public school. She learned English there.

Throughout her life, she saw herself as being part of a transition generation—linking the immigrants who were born in Turkey with the following generation of thoroughly Americanized children. Her parents spoke Judeo-Spanish almost exclusively. Her children spoke English almost exclusively. And she spoke Judeo-Spanish to the elders and English to the youngers. She was a blend of cultures.

She had to quit high school at age sixteen in order to take a job to help bring in some money for the family. She told us how one of her teachers had cried at learning of her need to leave school. Mom was a bright student, with a great potential. But for her time and place—and since she was "only" a girl—work seemed more important to her family than her further education. But Mom was an avid reader throughout her life, and was an autodidact of the first caliber. There was hardly any important world literature that she did not read. Reading and knitting were her two most satisfying hobbies.

Mom often reminisced about the dramatic material changes that had occurred during the course of her lifetime. She spoke of gathering the fuel for the wood and coal stove in her parents' home, of helping the iceman bring large bricks of ice into their icebox. She told of her fascination at first hearing a radio, of first riding in an automobile, of first getting an automatic washing machine. She was awed by the space age, by how far technology had advanced in so short a time. And the more she spoke of these feelings, the more we felt connected with her past—with *our* past.

During our taping sessions, Mom frequently reverted to using the language of her own childhood, Judeo-Spanish. In approaching the physical end of her life, she was emotionally returning to the beginning of her life. It was as though life was a circle, the end connecting itself with the beginning. She noticed, for example, that her room number in the nursing home was 214, exactly the number of the address of the home of her parents, the home of her childhood. Life had come full circle.

My brother, who was present in the hospital room when my mother died, said that he felt a tremendous emotional experience at that moment, one akin to the feeling of being in the presence of the birth of a child. It was an interesting analogy. It underscored the circularity of the human condition, where the end converges with the beginning, where the beginning already foresees the end.

A dying person may learn deep wisdom from the process of dying, and may convey that wisdom to the children. Being face to face with certain death necessarily changes one's perception of reality, of what is important and what is trivial. No one knows the meaning of time or of pain or of fear in the same way as the person who is dying. Suffused with this special wisdom, the dying parent can be a profound teacher and inspiration in a way qualitatively different from what was possible when that parent was in good health.

As my mother was dying, becoming physically more and more helpless, she was also radiating a deep, silent wisdom; she was becoming more and more philosophical. She was in great pain and discomfort for most of the time. More than once she said that she was ready to die, that she wished it was all over. One time I responded to her: "I can't offer you any consolation on your suffering. You are going through it. I am on the outside. But I can say this: as long as you live, you give us added strength and wisdom. Your life means a lot to us." Even holding on to those last moments was important.

## Reacting to a Parent's Death

When the parent dies, the adult children find themselves in a new situation. Orphanhood has become a reality.

There are practical and philosophic aspects accompanying orphanhood for adults. How do you relate to your surviving parent? Or, how do you adjust to the new reality of not having any living parents? How do you deal with your anger, frustration, guilt? How do you compensate for the loss of your mother's constant words of encouragement, for your father's guidance and pride? How do your dead parents continue to live within you, so that you sometimes think you can actually hear their voices? How does the family structure maintain itself after the parents have died? How do you deal with your siblings in dividing up the estate? How do you avoid antagonistic relationships with siblings from developing in the absence of a conciliating parent?

There are philosophic questions involved, too. What is the meaning of life and death? As an orphan, do you now have a different sense of your own mortality? A different relationship with God? How we face the reality of death, how we mourn and remember—these are underpinnings of our philosophy of life. In contemplating the mystery of the generations, we reflect on basic ideas relating to the meaning of our lives in particular, and human life in general. The death of a parent makes us philosophers, whether we like it or not.

In coping with these problems, the adult orphan needs to be thoughtful and patient. His emotions are raw; he must deal with new, sometimes conflicting, feelings. Sometimes the mourning is "normal," causing minimal disruption in one's life. Sometimes the mourning is overly deep, and the adult orphan may want to seek professional counselling from a clergyman or mental health professional.

There are a variety of factors which play a role in how adults deal with their status as orphans. Each must be carefully considered and evaluated if one is to deal with the situation with understanding.

1) How much was your parent really a part of your life? Was your mother or father living in an old age home, or senior citizen center? How often did you see, or communicate with this parent? Do you feel guilt at not having been as close to mother and father as you should have or could have been? What was the quality of your relationship?

2) Has your parent's death created new strains in your family, or has it brought the family closer together? How did your parent face death, with courage or with dread? Did your parent die suddenly, unexpectedly, or after a long illness? Is the death actually a relief to you, since you no longer have to disrupt your life with constant hospital visits and telephone calls?

3) Did you say a final goodbye to your dying parent? Did you and your parent say everything that had to be said, so that you feel no lingering sorrow that the relationship

ended without your having a chance to wrap it up neatly? When you envision your parent, do you only see him or her in the dying phase; or do you remember your parent in health and vigor? Do you feel pangs of yearning to talk with or to see your parent to bring the relationship into a smooth conclusion?

4) Does your being an orphan make you think of your own death more vividly? How does our society influence our attitudes on aging and dying? What are your concerns about mortality and immortality?

5) Is your mourning "normal" or "abnormal"? How do traditional mourning rituals relate to your existential situation? Have you visited your parent's grave? What feelings have surfaced at the gravesite?

6) Do you find that your parents continue to influence your life, even though they are now dead? Do you try to do things that would please them? Do you avoid doing things that they would not have approved? Or do you now feel free of their control? What are the psychological and emotional elements that transcend a parent's death and continue to exert a pull on our own lives?

7) With the death of your parents, do you find yourself becoming more conservative and traditional? Have you given more effort to tracing family roots, hunting up old photographs? Are you more nostalgic, more interested in memories, than you had been previously?

8) Are you now taking over the role of your parents by becoming the matriarch or patriarch of your own family? Do you find new responsibilities coming your way? Has your relationship with your siblings changed? Did the family squabble over a will, or over how to divide souvenirs of property owned by the parents? If you have a surviving parent, how does he or she fit into your life? How have your children dealt with the passing of their grandparent(s)?

9) What is your concept of the meaning of life and

death? How does being an orphan heighten your sensitivity to the eternal rhythm of history?

We are a society of orphans. We have either lost our parents or will lose them. This is a complex reality which adults need to understand and evaluate. Adult orphans, being adults, bring reason, experience, and strength to their confrontation with this life crisis. Adult orphans, being orphans, bring anxiety, emotional conflict, and weakness to this life crisis. Adult orphans are wise and ignorant, strong and weak, courageous and frightened.

We are a society of orphans.

## CHAPTER 2

# THE DEATH OF A PARENT
## Some General Issues

*Traditional Death Scenes*

The Bible tells that when the patriarch Jacob was about to die, he called his family together and gave them his last message. The death scene is described in a simple, matter-of-fact way, without tears or grief. The father knows that his life is slipping away, and he wants to leave parting words to his children. The children, adults themselves, understand that their father's death is inevitable, and they stand at his bedside respectfully.

A rabbinic tradition has it that Jacob used these closing moments of his life to determine whether his children had fully committed themselves to his teachings about the uniqueness and oneness of God. Just before he died, his sons assured him that they believed that the Lord was their God, the Lord was One. And so, the patriarch died with a feeling of contentment and satisfaction.

This biblical death scene was, for centuries, characteristic of the way families dealt with the death of a parent.

Since everyone knew the parents would die, and death was considered a perfectly normal part of life, the dying parent would let his children know when he or she was dying. They would gather around the parent and listen to the last messages, and offer comfort and assurance that the family would carry on with its traditions.

This style of death scene seems to have prevailed throughout the premodern world. Philippe Aries (1974) in his classic study, *Western Attitudes toward Death,* has coined the phrase, "tamed death" (p. 12). By this, he means that people usually knew that death was coming and prepared for the event. An important part of that preparation was calling the family together. Children were brought in the room in which the parent was dying. Until the eighteenth century no portrayal of a deathbed scene failed to include children. This is a far different attitude from a popular modern idea to keep children away from death.

Indeed, it was normal for death to take place in the midst of kin, in one's own home. It must have been a comfort to the dying person to be in familiar surroundings, together with the people most important in life. The deathwatch was a family experience, involving the dying person, the spouse, the children, and other loved ones.

In former generations, when life expectancy was far lower than it is today, it was not uncommon for parents to die while they were still in their thirties, forties, and fifties. Thus, their deaths created severe disruptions in the pattern of life of their family; their children may very well have still been economically dependent on them. In traditional societies, where parents served as authority figures for the family, their death led to a reorganization of the family hierarchy. Death, by its constant nearness, reminded parents and children of the tenuousness of life, of the need to stay together and advance the position of the family.

The "tamed death" was accepted as a normal feature of existence. In spite of the grief and problems it engendered for the survivors, it was something that had to be dealt with in a straightforward way. Children, being important elements in the life of the parents, were also expected to attend the parents' deaths.

## Modern Death Scenes

For millennia, people died calmly, without theatrics, without lavishly emotional death scenes. In the words of Aries: "With little difficulty the man of traditional societies, the man of the first Middle Ages . . . became resigned to the idea that we are all mortal" (p. 52). But the subtle change in attitude began to insinuate itself in Western society in the late Middle Ages. People started to view death not merely as part of a normal, impersonal process; but as a specific, private crisis of the individual person who was dying. Aries has noted that since the High Middle Ages Western man has discovered his personal death.

In fact, the "tamed death" is a notion that moderns may have difficulty understanding. Aries (1981) has noted in *The Hour of Our Death* that "it has by now been so obliterated from our culture that it is hard for us to imagine or understand it. The ancient attitude in which death is close and familiar yet diminished and desensitized is too different from our own view, in which it is so terrifying that we no longer dare say its name (p. 28). The conditions of death and attitudes toward death have undergone dramatic changes, especially over the past 50 years. Between 1930 and 1950, a general revolution occurred in Western countries: people no longer died at home among family, but in hospitals, among strangers.

It is estimated that about three-quarters of the deaths in the United States occur in institutions, although many people say they would prefer dying in their own home among family. Ruth Gale Elder (1976), in an article, *Dying and Society,* has observed that "the dying phase of life usually occurs in surroundings unfamiliar to the persons concerned. Dying is now likely to be managed by strangers, institutional personnel, rather than the family, and in some cases the family is not present at all'' (p. 4). The traditional deathbed scene, where the dying parent rests comfortably in his or her own bed and is surrounded by the children, is something more and more removed from contemporary experience. Few families today follow that pattern.

In my 16 years in the rabbinate, I can remember only a tiny number of instances where a dying parent was able to die at home. Usually, dying people have been in hospitals, plugged into sophisticated medical equipment, with tubes in their arms or throats or noses; or have been in frail condition, so that the hospital staff (and family) have been afraid to move them home. It is generally assumed that the hospital can provide far better care for the dying person than could be provided at home. The kind of total care required by such a person would place an enormous strain on the family at home—emotional, physical, and financial. Our modern upbringing has led us to a different way of dealing with the death of parents than had been the case in previous eras.

Another factor that must be considered is that parents today tend to live longer than the parents of past generations. The phenomenal advances in medicine have significantly increased life expectancy. Moreover, medical technology is able to keep people alive in situations where they certainly would have died in previous generations.

So most parents today die in hospitals or nursing institutions: and most die when they are elderly—when their own children are adults with families of their own. Both factors affect the "orphanhood" of the children.

Aries (1974), in *Western Attitudes Toward Death,* has described death in the hospital in rather strong terms: Such a death is no longer a ritual ceremony over which the dying person presides, while his relatives and friends surround him. Rather, death has become a technical phenomenon resulting from a cessation of care, generally determined by a decision of the doctor and the hospital team. In the majority of cases, the dying person has already lost consciousness. "Death has been dissected, cut to bits by a series of little steps, which finally make it impossible to know which step was the real death, the one in which consciousness was lost, or the one in which breathing stopped. All these little silent deaths have replaced and erased the great dramatic act of death, and no one any longer has the strength or patience to wait over a period of weeks for a moment which has lost a part of its meaning (pp. 88–89).

The dying parent in the hospital or nursing facility is often viewed as a helpless victim, and may so view himself. Such a parent may well lose a sense of being a parent—a respected person with authority in the family. Rather, the parent becomes a child, at the mercy of the doctors, the machines, the nurses. Adult children who visit their dying parent may stay for only a short while, offer some kind words, and express confidence in the medical staff. In the hospital, the parent is a stranger; the children are strangers. It is not *their* domain. They are subject to the world of a medical officialdom. The hospital room just doesn't have the same feeling of warmth and security as a room of one's own home.

## Coping with Guilt Feelings

Institutionalized death has transformed the way people die in modern society. It has also transformed the way adult orphans respond to the death of their parents. One issue now is guilt feelings. Did we do enough to help Mom? Did we get the best medical advice available? Could we have brought Dad back home for his last few weeks of life, as he wanted us to do? These and similar questions may haunt adult orphans for the rest of their lives. They need to be dealt with directly and without self-deceit.

Very often, adult children *did* do all that they could reasonably have been expected to do. If they will verbalize their guilt feelings to each other, to a trusted loved one, or to the clergy, they will be able to clarify for themselves that there is no reason to feel guilty. Given the reality of modern society, given the medical needs of the dying parent, all that could be done was done.

If the adult orphan has recognized intellectually that he did well by the parent, and yet still has a lingering sense of guilt—he needs to be reminded that death is a natural feature of life. The values of the "tamed death" need to be brought to mind. Death is not proof that we have failed our parents in some way. It does not mean that the medical care was inadequate, or that we were delinquent in doing what we could to save the parent's life. Death is the natural end of everyone. Even where we have really done our best for our parent, that parent may still die. And there is no blame for this death. It is simply part of the rhythm of the generations.

Several years ago, two brothers came to my synagogue in despair. Both were professionals in the health field, both were adults, both were unmarried. Their mother had just died of cancer. They had been very attached to her, and almost worshipped her as a model of motherly perfection. During her illness, they had acted heroically to save her life. They contacted the best specialists; they obtained the best medications and treatments. They took off work in shifts, so that at least one of them or their father would constantly be at their mother's side in the hospital. It happened that one night, while one of the men was on his vigil of care for his mother, the mother's condition worsened. The son did his best to relieve her pain, and called the medical team to assist. The mother's condition then seemed to stabilize. The son remained in the room alone with the mother. But late into the night, he dozed off. And while he was sleeping, his mother died.

When he awakened, he found her dead. He immediately blamed himself. If only he had remained awake, she would not be dead. If only he had not yielded to fatigue, he could have saved her.

The brothers were disconsolate. I spoke to them of the need to face reality. Their mother was dying from a deadly disease. Every doctor involved in the case knew she was terminal, and would die relatively soon. None of the medications or experimental treatments had proven effective, although it was noble of the sons to have done so much to try to save their mother's life. That she happened to die at the moment when the son was sleeping was an unfortunate coincidence; but she would have died anyway, even if he had been awake. And even if he could have prevented her death at that moment, which was by no means certain, she would certainly have died within a day or two. "God gives life; and God takes life away," I told them. "That is the reality of the human condition. You are not to blame for your mother's death. You did everything possible for her, and certainly a lot more than many others would have done for their parents." They gazed at me in wonderment. This very elementary observation had not occurred to them! It took a few months of reenforcing this idea before the brothers seemed to have accepted the fact that they were not guilty of their mother's death.

This is an extreme case. Yet, even in "normal" cases adult orphans need to be helped to overcome unjustified feelings of guilt. Such guilt is saddening, even crippling; and it must be controlled by a reasonable evaluation of the causes of the parent's death, and by a wise understanding that death is natural and cannot be forever put off.

On the other hand, sometimes the guilt is warranted. Why didn't we pay more attention to Mom when she complained about her symptoms? Why didn't we get better medical attention for Dad? Why didn't I visit the hospital more often, or spend more time with Mom? Why didn't I do that little favor Dad asked from me? But though the adult orphan may feel legitimate guilt for carelessness or inconsiderateness, carrying the guilt throughout life is destructive. One should atone for one's sins, and go on with life in a positive and creative way.

But how can one atone? The parent is now dead, and communication is terminated. How can one ask for forgiveness, and how can one know if the parent has forgiven? One may go to the parent's grave and pour out his heart; and one may thus purge the feelings of guilt, in the belief that the parent is, or was, a forgiving and loving person. One may devote some time as a volunteer for a hospice or a hospital, as a way of demonstrating that a lesson has been learned: people must be sharing and caring. One may be more considerate of the surviving parent or elder relatives. The point is that it is essential to face the guilt feelings directly and find an appropriate way of relieving them.

Often, guilt feelings do not stem only from the few months surrounding the parent's death. Rather, they go back to a period of years when the parent had been relatively neglected. The relation of elderly parents with their adult children needs to be considered.

## Generations Together, Generations Apart

Margaret Mead (1970), in her book *The Generation Gap*, delineates three different types of societies. A "postfigurative" society is one in which the elders are venerated as the authorities. In these traditional societies, the pattern of life is established and fixed. One can predict from the time the child is born how his life will unfold, what occupation he will engage in, what role he will play in the social structure of the community. Since the elders know the traditions best, they are in control of the younger generations. They are the teachers, guides, authorities. In postfigurative societies, the death of a parent created a definite void in the social scheme. A person upon whom one depended was now gone. A vital force in family and community life was dead.

A "cofigurative" society is one where the parents have lost much of their authority. The children no longer wish to be bound to the old traditions of which the elders are the masters. An example of a cofigurative society is one in which the parents are immigrants in a new country. To the children, the parents represent the old world, the old language, the old style. The children would rather adapt to the new land in which they are now living. They draw their authority figures not from their parents and elders, but from their contemporaries. They want to be like others of their own age who are from the adopted country.

In a cofigurative setting, there are serious conflicts between the values of the parents and the children. When the parent dies, the child does not feel the loss of a venerated authority figure. Rather, he may feel a mixture of emotions—guilt, nostalgia, relief, shame. A sensitive child will have conflicting emotions regarding the death of a parent in a cofigurative society.

Postfigurative and cofigurative societies have existed throughout history. Elements of both exist in almost everyone's experience. But Margaret Mead argues that our contemporary society fits into neither of the above categories. Instead, we live in a "prefigurative" society. In this kind of setting, parents and children are equally lost. No one is an adequate authority; not the elders, not the contemporaries. No one seems to know for sure what the future will bring, what is the right course to follow. Technological changes make life subject to rapid and constant changes.

Children born today may very well be working in occupations that have not yet been created. The elders and the young are equally unable to control nuclear energy; war; social injustice; prejudice and hatred. No one seems to have the right set of rules, which, if followed, will result necessarily in a good society and a safe world.

In a prefigurative society, parents and children need to understand how dependent they are on each other. In an uncertain world, they must find in each other the stability and love which will help them to live happy lives. A parent's death, in the ideal prefigurative setting, represents the loss of a partner in life, one who shared much with the child.

Margaret Mead's analysis of societies is helpful in our evaluation of our own relationship with our parents. It places specific children-parent relationships into a general social context. Yet, our modern situation—even if it is prefigurative—has additional complications that need to be studied.

## The Challenges of Longevity

As was noted earlier, parents today tend to have much longer life expectancies than parents of former generations. It is no longer uncommon for parents to live well into their seventies, eighties, and even nineties. Since the parent's role as authority and central figure in family life is rarely evident in our society, the parent may become more and more extraneous to the family as he or she grows older. The adult children have families of their own and concerns of their own. The elderly parents can become a nuisance at best and a burden at worst.

In his study of the effects of death upon the family, Richard Kalish (1969) has noted that our society does not highly value the elderly; therefore, their death is the least disturbing to our family life. The elderly are generally separated from their children. Children tend to have nuclear families, where the elderly parents are on the outside. Parents seldom serve as the patriarchs or matriarchs to whom the youngsters come for advice. Moreover, parents are often separated from their children by many miles. Retirement communities also serve to separate the elderly. As parents grow older, they become less important to the well-being of their family—generally the children are better educated and better off financially.

Children may resent the financial burden of caring for aged parents who are terminally ill; and at the same time they may feel guilty for their angry feelings. Or, children may place parents in nursing homes, assuring themselves that this is in the parents' own best interests. After all, the nursing home can provide a clean room, meals, companionship, medical services—whatever the elderly parent needs. Except the feeling of being loved and needed!

Kalish reports that he once asked a group of Cambodian students in their mid-twenties whether they would save the life of their mother, their wife, or their daughter if only one could be saved. All responded immediately that they would save their mother. Their tone of voice implied that only an immoral or ignorant person would even ask such a question. Kalish doubts whether 10 percent of a comparable American group would give that response. There is no question but that elderly parents in our society are generally not considered central or vital to the lives of their adult children. They may be loved and respected; but they are not always "needed".

Kalish notes: "It is easy enough . . . to rationalize the death of an elderly person and even to rationalize one's wishes that the death would occur: he had lived a long, good life; or his life was long and wretched and he is better out of it; or how fortunate that he did not suffer any pain or any more pain or was able to gain release from the terrible pain. In giving these hypothetical quotations, I do not intend to belittle their validity, but merely to describe experiences we have all observed'' (p. 90).

If elderly parents are peripheral to the lives of their adult children, their deaths will not create a significant disruption among the survivors. But if they are very important, their deaths will result in more intense mourning on the part of their children. It is difficult to measure "importance" with mathematical accuracy. Sometimes parents live far away from the children and have little direct contact with them; yet there is a strong emotional bond which ties them together. Each child and each parent will evaluate "importance" by their own set of standards.

## When Children Become Parents

It is normal and desirable for children to become independent adults, and to leave the home of their parents. It is also normal and desirable for adults to love people other than their parents. A Talmudic sage, Rabbi Yose, observed long ago: "Isaac mourned his mother Sarah for three years. At the end of three years he married Rebecca and stopped mourning his mother. Thus we see that until a man takes a wife, he directs his love toward his parents. Once he marries, he directs his love towards his wife" (*Pirkei de Rabbi Eliezer,* Chapter 32).

Another Talmudic sage, Rabbi Hunna, once found a juicy date which he took and wrapped in his mantle. His son, Rabbah, came and said to him: "I smell the fragrance of a juicy date." The father praised his son and gave him the date. Meanwhile, Rabbah's son, Abbah, came. Rabbah then took the date and gave it to his own son. Rabbi Huna said to Rabbah: "My son, you have gladdened my heart (with your purity) and blunted my teeth (by loving your son more than you love me)." That is what the popular proverb says: "A father's love is for his children; the children's love is for their own children" (Sotah 49a).

No doubt, adult children must naturally turn their main attention to their own spouses and children. The parents may retain their importance, but lose their centrality in the lives of their children. But though this process is normal, it need not lead to the parents' feeling extraneous and unwanted. Adult children, though loving their own families, can also love their parents and be devoted to their well-being.

## The Aging Process Today

A problem in our society is that the aging process is popularly identified as a negative phenomenon. People are afraid to grow old, or at least to appear to have grown old. Billions of dollars are spent each year on cosmetics, medical procedures, hair dyes, etc.—all with the goal of making people appear younger than they actually are. Old age is not highly respected in our culture. Modern science has enabled people to live much longer but has not been able to give older people a sense of the value of their lives. On the contrary, there is a popular notion that the elders are unproductive members of society. They are a burden on the taxpayers, on their families, on the nation's medical institutions.

I have often visited people in homes for the aged. Many are seldom visited by their children or other relatives. They live in an artificial world, segregated from people of the younger generations. I have learned much from the elderly residents of such homes.

One octogenarian showed me a tile tray he had made in the "arts and crafts" department of the home for the aged of which he was a resident. He asked me what I thought of it. I politely told him that it was very nice. He frowned, his eyes becoming watery. "No," he said, "it is not at all nice. It is a clumsy piece of work. I had a stroke last year and can hardly control my hands. It took me many hours to make this little tray of tiles; and it is still a very poor job. I used to be a nuclear physicist. Now I make clumsy tile trays." He restrained himself from weeping, but waved me away. I learned from a member of the staff that this gentleman had indeed been a noted scientist, that his children lived in a city far away, that he was seldom visited by anyone. And that his situation was fairly common.

One elderly resident of a nursing home told me that she feared to strike up new friendships. "It can only lead to loss," she confided to me. "How long can any of us expect to live? Why come close to a person when you know the relationship can only end in tragedy?" She was not only cut off from her children, who visited her only on holidays, but even from the other residents of the home.

And another elderly man, formerly an owner of a garment factory, told me that his whole purpose in life now was to die an easy death. "They (his children) have put me in here to get me out of their way. I understand. They have lives of their own. So let me die quietly, without much pain. That's all I ask. I'll be out of their way for good."

Barbara Myerhoff (1978) reported her research in a senior citizen community in California. Her book, *Number Our Days,* is a powerful story of the lives of elderly people and how they deal with their lives. Myerhoff describes a visit she made to a convalescent home to see an elderly woman who had just gotten over a stroke, but who was completely blind. Her wit was sharp, her mind was lucid. She was furious about her situation. "They told me that toward the end of life you get dim, sort of fade out, peaceful-like. Look at me. I'm completely awake. My body is strong. I'm ninety-one. Why has God cursed me to keep on living this way?'' She had been expecting to die imminently for months. Her children had already sold her possessions. A small aluminum table with one drawer beside her bed in the bare room she shared with two other women contained all that she owned. '' 'Darling,' she said, 'I will be honest with you because I love you. Never trust your children. No matter how much you love them. Never give them control over you. It asks too much of both of you.' Her family had not visited her for months'' (p.278).

Growing old is not easy in our youth-centered, productivity-oriented society. Adult children may simply believe themselves too busy, too involved with their own lives and careers to be able to devote significant time and emotional energy to their elderly parents. It is so much simpler to have them tucked away safely in a home for the aged or a retirement community. When this is the case, the parent's death may come as a relief. In a certain sense, the death removes a child's guilt feelings about not attending to the parent's needs more conscientiously. But in another way, the death may generate new feelings of guilt: why didn't I do this or that, why didn't I visit more often? And another sensation may emerge: Will the same thing happen to me when I get old? Will my children abandon me?

## Quality of Parent-Child Relationships

An adult orphan's mourning will be correlated to the quality of his relationship with the deceased parent. An adult who feels no sense of loss at the death of a parent must have had a peripheral connection. He already had disengaged himself emotionally from the parent. An adult who grieves inconsolably for a parent has been overly attached emotionally to the parent. Such an adult has not been able to act as an independent person, but has rather been at the mercy of the parent.

An adult who had a loving and respectful relationship with his parent will mourn his parent's death, recognizing a real loss to the fabric of his life. Yet, his mourning will be tempered with the wisdom that death is part of the human condition, and that he was fortunate to have had a loving, respectful relationship with his parent. Mourning too little and mourning too much are signals that there was something wrong with the parent/child relationship during the parent's lifetime.

Modern society presents many serious challenges to the quality of parent-child relationships. Families are generally not as close together, either physically or emotionally, as had been the case in postfigurative societies. Growing old is often a difficult process, especially when one becomes more isolated from his family.

Yet, it can be fairly stated that most adult orphans do feel that their lives have been ruptured by the death of a parent. The intensity of the sense of loss is correlated to the conditions discussed above. In fact, the reactions of adult children to the death of their parents is a good barometer of the quality of the parent-child relationship.

The sense of being in some way an orphan is a reflection of the importance the parent played in the child's life. The stronger the family structure, the greater the awareness of orphanhood. The closer people are to each other, the more they will miss each other when they are separated.

## CHAPTER 3

# THE DYING PROCESS

Sometimes death comes suddenly, without warning. A person may succumb to a heart attack or be killed in an accident. Such a death, though it does not involve a prolonged period of suffering, deprives a person of the opportunity to prepare for death. And it comes as a shock to the survivors, who did not have the time to adjust their own thinking to the possibility of the unexpected death.

In the case of a sudden death, the death is not experienced as a process but as a singular event. Orphans who must deal with the unexpected loss of a parent have a different kind of mourning to undergo than those who have lost parents after a prolonged illness. We will discuss "sudden orphanhood" later in this book.

## Natural Warnings of Death

There are times when the death of an elderly parent *seems* sudden. More than once I have heard adult orphans lament: But Mom died so suddenly; we didn't expect Dad to die just yet; but Mom just had her hair done yesterday; but Dad just got a clean bill of health from the doctor. And these adult orphans were referring to parents in their seventies, eighties, and even nineties. To be sure, the death was not expected at the time; yet, it could have been foreseen, at least theoretically.

A story goes that there was a young man who had a dream. In the dream the Almighty appeared to him and gave him one wish. The young man thought a bit and then responded: "I don't want to die suddenly. My wish is that you give me fair warning before I die." God agreed to fulfill this wish.

Years passed. The young man had now grown into an old man. His hair was all gray, he walked with a stoop, his youthful strength was gone. One night he went to sleep: and he died.

When he arrived in heaven, he was furious and demanded a meeting with God, who was pleased to oblige. "You did not keep your promise," the man accused God. "You granted me my wish that I would not die suddenly, without fair warning. But here I have died in my sleep without having been warned at all."

God replied: "I have kept my promise. I have given you fair warning. Actually, I have given you many warnings."

"That is not true," the man objected vehemently.

"It is very true. Look at the color of your hair. It is gray. That was a warning. Look at the way you stoop over when you stand up. That was a warning. Look at your wrinkled, tired and weak body, sapped of its youthful strength. That was a warning. I gave you warnings: you simply did not pay attention to them." The man bowed his head in the presence of God's truth.

As people become elderly, they are given plenty of warnings of their impending death. But many prefer not to notice the warnings, to pretend that life will go on indefinitely. Our society generally prefers to camouflage the warnings with dyes, makeup, plastic surgery, and other techniques. There is a tendency to deny (or to ignore the reality of) the warning signals. So when a parent, aged seventy-five or eighty "suddenly" dies, the death was not sudden at all. It was the culmination of a long aging process whose only conclusion could have been death.

In societies where the "tamed death" existed (or still exists), an elderly individual recognizes realistically that he is approaching death and plans accordingly. The family is also aware of the fact that the elderly are living "on borrowed time." Death is a presence in their lives, is thought about and planned for openly and candidly.

In our society, though, it is preferred to avoid the topic of death. An elderly parent, who might very much want to talk about his or her inevitable death, may feel reluctance in opening up the topic with the children. Adult children may often relate to their elderly parents in unrealistic terms. "You are looking younger and younger every day." "Don't worry. You'll get over the illness. You'll be just fine in no time." "Don't talk about dying. You've got a lot of good years ahead of you." These and similar statements may be very well-intentioned; but they prevent the parents from sharing their deepest feelings with the people they love most.

Elderly parents and their adult children need to be candid with each other, need to be free to discuss death openly and without inhibition. This does not mean that they should become morbid and solely concerned with death. On the contrary, they should be able to discuss aging and dying in a natural way, exactly so they will not have to be preoccupied with it. Too often, the image of death is a shadow hovering over family relationships. If it is dealt with honestly and directly, it will free the parent-children relationships, removing the dreaded shadow of death with the light of openness and love.

Confucius taught: "The parents' ages must always be

known, both as a source of joy and as a source of dread."
It is the responsibility of adult children to be sensitive to
the inner life of their parents. Long life is a source of pride,
but also contains within it the seeds of impending death.

Elderly people receive "warnings" in the physical
changes in their bodies. The mind might be very alert, the
person might feel that he is still the same person that he
was 20 or 40 years ago. Yet no one should be able to delude
himself into thinking that aging has not brought definite
changes in his personality, in his thinking patterns, as well
as in his physical condition.

Since many of the elderly are retired from their work,
they have much time on their hands. They may take a greater
interest in their religion. They may seek pastimes to keep
them occupied. They may do volunteer service at the local
hospital or social service agency. And they certainly spend
time thinking about their lives, their families, their past. And
their future. How do people face their future when they do
not anticipate too many more years to live? Young and even
middle-aged people seldom stop to consider the feelings of
the elderly toward the future. It seems a problem which
only concerns "them," the elderly. Younger people are too
busy to give the matter serious attention. They may not adequately empathize with the existential issues confronting
their elderly parents. How, then, do elderly people deal with
the future?

The most comfortable way is *not* to think about the
future in the long term. Rather, take things day by day, event
by event. By not directing one's attention to where he might
be in 5 years, or 10, one can avoid the confrontation with
death. But it is inevitable—and desirable—for an elderly
person to think deeply about death, and even plan for it.
The future reality cannot be completely blocked from one's
consideration. Nor should it be.

We need to give some attention to the aging process,
how people deal with their advancing years. Everyone

knows that each day lived is one day closer to death. Though an elderly person should not be obsessed with this fact, it does play a role in the way he deals with life.

Some writers have described the "disengagement theory of aging." The theory is that as people grow older, they disengage from activities that used to occupy their whole lives. Since they realize that time is running out, they want more time for what they want to do. They are more selective in how they use time. Robert Kastenbaum (1977) has written: "Death is the ultimate disengagement. But there may still be much time ahead before the final separation. During this time, the individual is likely to go through a process of altering his relationship both to society and himself. . . . Meanwhile, the aging individual has more time to devote to his own thoughts, feelings and interests" (p. 147).

Robert Butler (1963), in his psychological study of the nature of aging, has observed that as people grow older, they review their lives. If reviewing makes them happy, they can face death without much fear. But if reviewing leads to feelings of regret and distress, the idea of death will seem hard to endure (pp. 721–728).

However we theorize about the psychological aspects of growing old, the fact is that adult children have a special responsibility to be aware not only of physical "warnings" which are being given to the parents, but also of the emotional and intellectual warnings. Sensitivity, patience, and understanding are needed. The elderly parents themselves need to understand the signals, the changes, the process.

Every older person should certainly want to set his spiritual life in order. Just as wills are drawn up to handle the financial matters, so spiritual wills should also be drawn up to convey one's values to his heirs. These spiritual wills may or may not actually be written. But elderly parents have gained much wisdom and insight from their experiences in life; they need to reevaluate the lessons they have learned and share their feelings with their children. If parents are

reluctant to do this, the adult children should ask for a spiritual will, or an ethical will. They can thus help the elderly
parent gain a sense of self-worth; and probably learn something about their parent which they had not previously
understood.

## The Stages of Dying

When a parent is afflicted with a fatal disease, there is
usually a period of time that elapses before death comes.
This period is a difficult one both for the individual and his
or her family.

Dr. Elisabeth Kubler-Ross did the pioneering research
on how the dying person faces death. She devoted much
time to interviewing dying people, to eliciting their thoughts
and feelings. She learned that the dying person goes through
various mental stages during the struggle with death.

When first diagnosed with a fatal illness, a person's first
reaction is to deny it. The diagnosis is wrong. Let's consult
another doctor. Let's keep seeing different experts until we
find one who will give a more positive diagnosis. The person
may claim that he feels fine, that the doctors are wrong.
Generally, denial is a short-lived reaction stemming from
the initial shock of the serious news. Once a person understands that the illness is real, the tendency to deny the
condition diminishes. Dr. Kubler-Ross has found that only
a tiny minority of her patients carry their denial throughout
the illness, even to the point of death.

Once a person can no longer deny the illness, the next
stage is anger. Why did this happen to me? There are so
many bad people in the world—it should only happen to
them! What did I do to deserve this? A person in this stage
may express anger at God (who should not have allowed
him to be afflicted with the illness); at loved ones (who
should have taken better care of him); at himself (who should
have taken better care of himself).

A stage of bargaining then follows. The person pleads with God and his own conscience: If I recover from this illness, I will be a better person. I will do good things for my family and for society. I will be charitable and kind. If I can just be given a few more years of life I will make them very worthwhile and meaningful.

As the illness progresses, the person sinks into a state of depression. In a real sense, he begins to mourn his own forthcoming death. He may become despondent, unwilling to talk too much to others, even to loved ones. In fact, he might prefer to be left to his own broodings and not be disturbed by the idle chatter of visitors. He is mourning his own death: Why should he want to hear artificially cheerful voices talking to him about the weather, the coming elections, the activities in the community? During the stage of depression, a person may prefer to be silent.

The final stage is acceptance. The person fully realizes that he will die, understands this reality to the core of his existence. And he accepts it. There is no more point to denial, anger, bargaining, or depression. Death is coming. The person accepts this, and even welcomes it. In achieving acceptance, the person has come to peace with himself. The fight is over.

The family of the dying person undergoes a similar pattern of stages. They, too, naturally try to deny the illness at first. They, too, encourage the person to shop around for other doctors in the hope of coming up with a better diagnosis. They start to learn more about the illness, read about new cures, miracle drugs, etc.

The family expresses its anger. "Why did this have to happen to Mom? She never hurt anyone in her life." "Why did Dad get cancer? He never even smoked." "Why should he (she) go through so much suffering? They didn't do anything to deserve this."

The family, too, has its own way of bargaining. "Just let Mom live to see her grandchildren married." "If only

Dad could have a few more years so he can see his grand-child graduated from college.''

The level of depression will vary among family members, depending on their closeness to and identification with the dying person. The heaviest depression will generally be shared by the spouse. Adult children may feel depressed, but not sink into a real depression.

Acceptance is the stage in which the family member has come to terms with the person's impending death. This stage is surprisingly peaceful. When the dying person and the family reach the stage of acceptance together, this is actually a happy and beautiful period of time.

When my mother was dying, she (and we) did go through these stages. Some problems came up from time to time since not every family member was going through the process in the same way, at the same rate. Some carried the denial stage much longer than others. Others seemed not to have gone through a serious stage of depression. These stages, of course, are not neatly defined packages that can be precisely defined and dissected. Very often, they overlap with each other. One may have elements of depression and acceptance simultaneously, for example.

During the month before Mom's death, she was obviously depressed but was grappling with acceptance. She knew full well that she was not going to recover, and did not want to hear people telling her that she was going to get better—as some people told her with the best of intentions. During my last visit to Mom, the last week of her life, Mom had definitely reached the stage of acceptance. Her face glowed with peace. She was actually happy. Her attitude was noticeably different than it had been when she was still struggling with depression. All of us who shared that last week with her were fortunate to benefit from her serene wisdom, her unlimited love. There were no more artificial barriers between us, no more games to play. Mom, though too ill to move from her bed, was spiritually and emotionally free.

## Achieving Acceptance Together

When a parent is dying and has reached the stage of acceptance, the adult children need to share in that acceptance. Feelings of guilt, or overdependence on the parent, may prevent the child from attaining acceptance of the parent's death. He may continue to lie to himself, and to the dying parent, that there is still hope, that a miracle will happen. He may want the parent *not* to be accepting of death, not to give up without more fighting for survival.

On the other hand, there are instances where the children have made peace with the fact that the parent will die, but the parent continues to resist acceptance. Fear of death, fear of leaving his position in life may delay the parent's reaching the stage of acceptance. The parent, seeing that the children seem resigned to his or her death, may interpret their acceptance as a tacit wish for death to come. The parent may feel angry at the children for not encouraging him or her in the battle against death, a battle which the parent still thinks can be won.

Another scenario is when both the dying parent and his family have reached the stage of acceptance, but don't tell each other. They try to pretend there is still hope. The parent feigns a smile and an optimistic attitude. He does not want the family to feel sad, without hope. The spouse and children pretend to be cheerful, offering words of hope and encouragement in order to prevent the parent from "knowing" how serious the situation is. Actually, a dying person knows his real situation far better than anyone on the outside could know.

When the dying person and the family do not achieve death-acceptance together, they live in an artificial relationship. They do not share with each other their deepest feelings and knowledge. Rather, they squander the last days of a person's life with empty talk, with circumlocutions, with make-believe dialogues.

Dr. Kubler-Ross reports a case where a dying husband told her: "I know I have only a short time to live, but don't tell my wife, she could not take it." But when Dr. Kubler-Ross later was speaking with the wife in a casual conversation, she volunteered almost the same words. They both had accepted the same reality: but were reluctant to tell each other in order to spare the other's feelings. Once they both were made to realize that they shared the same feeling, they felt greatly relieved that they no longer had to continue with their deceitful game.

It is difficult in our society for a parent to tell his family that he is prepared to die. To our ears, this seems like an admission of defeat, of giving up. It is also difficult for a child to tell his parent that he has accepted the parent's approaching death. This seems callous, unfilial. Yet the communication should take place. The parents and the children need to reach the stage of acceptance. It is a tremendously meaningful part of life and is infused with profound love, wisdom, understanding.

## The Responsibility of a Dying Parent

A parent who has reached the stage of acceptance needs to tell his family what he has come to think and feel. This need not be in the form of an abrupt statement: "I am going to die." Rather, he can convey the acceptance of death calmly and easily, assure the family that he/she is ready to die, and that his/her blessings are with the family. Dr. Kubler-Ross (1975) has written: "I think the dying person can be of great help to his relatives in helping them meet his death. He can do this in different ways. One of the ways is naturally to share some of his thoughts and feelings with the members of the family in order to help them do the same. If he is able to work through his own grief and show his family by his example how one can die with equanimity, they will remember his strength and bear their sorrow with more dignity'' (p. 142).

A dying parent is in the unique position of being free to express his feelings to the family. Out of sympathy, respect, or love, they will pay close attention to the words and wishes of the dying parent. A wise parent can use this opportunity at the end of life to impart to the family his feelings of love for them, his respect for them. If the parent has loved a child, but somehow never found the right way to express this feeling, then this love should be expressed now, before it is too late. If the parent had a grievance with a child or relative, this is the time to offer forgiveness openly and freely. If he feels distressed about some dissension among family members, then let him express those feelings now. In the face of death, one can bring a more profound perspective to life for the family members. One can bring the family closer together, explain to them the foolishness of petty disagreements, convey to them the healing power of love. The time of a parent's death can also be a time of reconciliation for family members.

One cannot overstate the importance of the parent sharing these thoughts and feelings with the children. An adult orphan who shared the experience of death-acceptance with his parent will better be able to cope with mourning. The image of the parent will provide inspiration and guidance. An adult orphan who was deprived of this experience with the dying parent will have more problems to work out during the period of mourning and thereafter. The parent-child relationship had not come to a mutually accepted conclusion.

## The Responsibility of the Family

When a parent is dying, the family has a responsibility to help in achieving an honest and open relationship. They need to reassure the dying parent that they will be all right, that they will continue to live according to the parent's example, that the future of the family will be planned for. If there is a surviving spouse, the dying parent needs to be assured that he or she will be cared for.

Needless to say, these conversations ought to be gentle and thoughtful. Both sides need to understand that they have both reached the stage of acceptance. This stage cannot be forced on anyone, nor can it be feinged. Where the parent takes the lead and guides the family, the optimal situation takes place. But when the parent is not ready to share his feelings, family members can be helpful in gently eliciting those feelings. Family members need to listen carefully to the dying person's words, to try to find the right opportunity to open up the conversation.

## Orphanhood as a Process

When a parent dies gradually, the children become orphans gradually. They have the immediate concern of seeing to it that the parent receives the proper medical attention. They have to fill the needs of the ill parent, and also those of the well parent if there is one. At the same time, they have to conduct their own normal daily activities with their own families, their businesses, their social responsibilities. The illness of a parent causes disruptions in their practical pattern of life, and also in their internal life. They have now to deal with the anxieties that go with the illness of a parent; with thoughts of the parent's possible death and the further disruptions to the family that that will bring.

In such cases, orphanhood does not simply spring on

the child as a sudden new reality. Rather, the child has the time to think through the implications of the parent's impending death. The child goes through emotional stages along with the dying parent. Orphanhood itself may be viewed as a process, an experience.

To a certain extent, an adult child can prepare for orphanhood. Though the actual death of the parent will generate grief and mourning, the preliminary grieving and acceptance of the parent's death will greatly aid the orphan in dealing with his new situation.

## CHAPTER 4

# THE FINAL GOODBYE

Separation is at the root of the deepest human sadness. Throughout life, we deal with many forms of separation— some fairly mild, others quite painful. There are physical separations that cause loved ones to be far from each other's company. A parent lives in one place, the child has moved to another location. One family member resides in one part of the country, another lives in another part, or even in another country. The difficulties of physical separation can be assuaged somewhat by telephone communication, by written correspondence, by periodic visits. The separations, though containing elements of pain and sadness, are not final. Sometimes they are even brought about for happy reasons—a child going off to college, a relative moving to another town for a better job.

There are also emotional separations that affect people's lives. When a child goes off to college, he is not only leaving the physical presence of the parents, but also is moving away emotionally. Likewise, when a child is being married, parents tend to cry. Their tears are not of unalloyed happiness; they also stem from a deep sadness, an awareness that their child is no longer dependent on them as in the past. An emotional separation has taken place.

The most complex and painful form of separation is death. The loved one who has died is now separated from the survivors, and will not return. The physical separation, for all practical purposes, is final. The separation of death precludes further mutual communication.

Death also brings emotional separation. The survivors will feel keenly the absence of the one who has died. They will miss the deceased's love, friendship, encouragement, criticism. A human being who played a role in the emotional life of the survivors is now gone. A gap has been opened.

When people know that a separation is coming, they plan for it in some way. They have a farewell party; or they give a present to be remembered by. They adjust themselves emotionally to the coming change. They embrace, they cry, they wish each other well. They encourage themselves that they will be seeing each other again sometime, perhaps soon. They create a "bridge" to link them together in spite of the physical and emotional separations they face.

The separation of death is different. While it is sometimes possible to prepare for the death, to have a farewell meeting, everyone knows that this separation will be in a separate category from the other separations of life. This is a deeper experience. It is clear to the people involved that their relationship is now coming to a conclusion; the relationship is irretrievable; there is no coming back. A dying person who is saying goodbye is operating on a different level from someone who says goodbye to friends upon moving out of town. A person saying goodbye to a dying person is experiencing something different from someone saying goodbye to a child going off to college.

It seems to be a universal truth that people pay close

attention to the words of a person who is about to die. We attribute special meaning to someone's last words. We look for *hidden* meanings, for answers to unasked questions. The final meeting between a dying person and those who will survive is an emotionally loaded event. Since death is a mystery to us, and since it is so conclusive, the dying person's last words leave an echo in our memories.

In the classic death scenes described in Chapter 2, parents who felt that they were about to die called their families to surround them. They gave their last messages to the family members; their blessings; sometimes, their curses. And the family members bid their farewell to the dying patriarch or matriarch.

In a less formal fashion, this process of saying goodbye still functions for many people. Often, a parent does know within himself that death is approaching. The father or mother does impart final messages to family members, if not in a group, then individually. The goodbye scene between a dying parent and the children continues to be replayed in the mind of the orphans throughout their lives. (Indeed, the goodbye scene between a dying person and any loved one will leave an indelible impression on the survivor.)

Three psychiatrists, Dennis Malinak, Michael Hoyt, and Virginia Patterson (1979), made a study of adults' reactions to the death of a parent. They interviewed 14 people—10 women and 4 men, aged twenty-two to forty-two years old. Nine of them had lost a father; five, a mother. Nine deaths followed illness and were expected; five were unexpected. At the time of the interviews, the subjects appeared to be relatively normal and were functioning properly; the mean amount of time since the death of the parent was 11 months. In 12 of the 14 cases, the other parent was still alive. The majority of the subjects had at least a college degree. The interviews, which lasted about 90 minutes each, took place at the University of California Medical Center.

Several major themes emerged from this study, including the "importance of the last meeting with the parent and events at the time of death." A number of the subjects assigned special significance to their last meeting with their parent. "These reports were retrospective, of course, and often seemed to serve as a kind of condensed 'screen memory' for many of the aspects and issues of the parent-child relationship" (p. 1153).

## When the Final Meeting Goes Well

The final meeting between parent and child does not necessarily take place just before the parent dies. It may occur before a parent falls into a coma. In a case where a child lives in another town from the parent, the final meeting might happen during the child's last visit to the parent. It sometimes occurs that both the parent and the child feel intuitively that this will be their final goodbye, that they very likely will not see each other alive again. Against this emotional backdrop, this meeting will take on a special significance and poignancy. Quite often, though, it is not clear at the time that this will be the last meeting. The child, in reviewing that conversation in retrospect, may only later discover the signs that the parent knew it was the final goodbye. Malinak, Hoyt, and Patterson (1979) report the case of a woman who normally saw her father several times a year when he came through San Francisco (where she lived) on business. "She recalled a sense of urgency during his last stopover; she felt that she had to see him. It was a good visit but he looked tired and older than usual. She tearfully remembered prolonging their last hug" (p. 1153).

In the instance of my last meeting with my mother, I did not fully realize that it was the final goodbye until after Mom had died. Then, in thinking over the events, I came to realize that Mom had known that she was about to die, that she would never see me again. I spent that Thursday

morning with her in the nursing home, and left from there
for the airport to return to New York that afternoon. We
had a wonderful conversation about many things, including
each member of my own family—my wife and three children. She expressed her love for all of us in a sincere and
moving way; she gave all of us her blessings. When the time
came for me to leave, Mom asked me to kiss her. The request struck me as unusual, since I could not ever remember
Mom asking me to kiss her since I was a little boy. I kissed
her, said goodbye, and left her room. As I walked out of
the building, I felt tears running down my cheeks. Looking
back now, I guess that I, too, intuited that that goodbye
was forever.

In speaking with congregants and friends about their
final meeting with their dying parents, I have found that
many people report similar experiences. The parent gave
them some signal that this was goodbye. An unusual gesture,
some cryptic words, a longer than usual embrace—the parent had given a sign of foreknowledge of impending death.
The parent knew that this was the last farewell.

When the final meeting goes well, the adult orphan carries a special memory of the parent. It somehow seems easier to reconcile oneself to the parent's death if the relationship had come to a meaningful conclusion. In thinking over
the last meeting, the orphan's sadness is mixed with a certain
pride in the parent. The parent demonstrated courage, wisdom, foresight. The parent was ready to die and imparted
a personal blessing. The remembrance of the final goodbye,
although it will always evoke feelings of sorrow, will also
evoke an inner peace and gratitude.

That final meeting can be a time of reaffirmation of love
between parent and child. It can be an intense, profoundly
moving event. With the shadow of death in the room, the
true value of human relationships can emerge with surprising
clarity and force.

The last meeting can also be a time of forgiveness and reconciliation. A parent who has acted badly toward a child can use the last moments together to set things straight, to apologize, to express love without reservation. A child who was neglectful of the parent, or who had otherwise not acted well towards the parent can use these moments to express feelings of regret, to ask for forgiveness.

When the final meeting between parent and child goes well, the parent may die peacefully, and the child may go on living with a positive attitude. When the parent and child say goodbye, they do so with an outpouring of love and respect. The memory of this final meeting serves as a consolation and strength to the child.

Seeing a parent shortly before his death makes a deep impression on a child. This person who brought you into this world is now on the verge of passing out of it. This mother, or this father, was once at the center of your life; guided your childhood, provided for you, worried about you. This parent loved you and your children, enjoyed spending time with you and your family, helped you in so many ways. This is the end of a human life, a parent's life; this is the past, the present, and the future. This is human destiny.

Max Lerner (1974) wrote a moving article describing his reactions to the death of his father. Though the parent was eighty-seven years old, "even an old man leaves a gaping hole when he breaks through the skein of life and hurtles into no-being." Lerner describes his last meeting with his father. "When I last saw my father, just before he died, he seemed so shrunken and wasted that I fear I broke down shamelessly and wept. It was for more than my father that I wept. It was for death which shows up the final helplessness of life, and for the crazy, tragic absurdity of the whole human condition" (p. 157).

One need not arrive at the same overwhelming conclusions that Lerner did; but one will be brought to meditate on the ultimate significance of life. Religion is often in the thoughts of people who confront death. And what is religion if not a quest for the ultimate meaning of life?

The final goodbye, then, brings an important relationship to a close. In a practical sense, it allows parent and children to come close together in a unique spirit of love. In a philosophic sense, it dramatically opens the child's mind to thoughts of the meaning of death, the meaning of life. Just as the parent had brought the child into this world, the parent has brought the child to a deeper analysis of the meaning of this world.

## When the Final Meeting Goes Badly

What happens when the final meeting between the parent and child goes badly? What if the conflicts in the relationship have not been dealt with or resolved? What if either or both expressed hostility or harsh criticism? What if the child, not realizing that this was indeed the last meeting with the parent, did not have the patience to hear the parent out, but rather spoke only of superficial matters, or cut the meeting short?

The tendency to review and even relive the last meeting is very common among orphans. If that final dialogue was not satisfactory, feelings of anger, shame, and guilt will likely arise.

In my own interviews with adult orphans over the years, I have found that some have continued to be negatively affected by an unhappy last meeting. One prominent communal worker, now in his sixties, still expresses strong regret over the fact that he rushed away from his dying father in order to go on a date with his girlfriend. He obviously did not think his father would die that evening; he was so preoccupied with his own personal life that he was not receptive to his father's need at that meeting. "How could I have been so selfish and insensitive?" he asked me. "Why didn't I realize that my father was going to die, that he wanted to talk to me while he still had time?'' His father died 40 years ago, and yet the son continues to blame himself for his behavior of so long ago, and still grieves over it.

A woman educator, now in her midfifties, told me that her mother used the last meeting to condemn her for being divorced, for not raising her child properly. The mother blamed the daughter for not being a good person. The woman has continued to mourn over this bitter memory, one that damaged her self-esteem and integrity. Her mother, through her hostile last words, has left her daughter an unhappy legacy.

These and similar examples reflect the pain perpetuated by an unsatisfactory last meeting. It is difficult for a person to remember that the final words of a parent were hostile and ungenerous. It is difficult for a person to overcome feelings of guilt for not having appreciated the significance of the event when it was happening.

Yet, when the final meeting does go badly, children must live on with the unpleasant memory. How can they do so without giving in to feelings of anger or hatred towards the parent, or to shame and guilt?

It is fruitless to let an unsatisfactory last meeting with a parent plague one. The event is over and done, and cannot be undone. Grieving over it will not change it. This will only serve to depress the adult orphan and increase the pain and unhappiness.

The orphan needs to evaluate the last meeting with the parent in the context of the general parent-child relationship that had existed before the parent's death. Was the relationship always a stormy one? Was the parent an angry, jealous, or vindictive person? Was the child guilty of neglecting the parent, leading the parent to become filled with anger and despair? Did the parent's last words really reflect the life-long relationship between parent and child, or was it imbued with bitterness stemming from the pain of illness, loneliness, and isolation? By placing the last words in the context of the overall relationship, the adult orphan can hope to understand what weight to give those words. We do not internalize words spoken to us in irrational anger to the same extent that we internalize calmly reasoned, harsh criticism. If the orphan can come to understand that the parent's closing remarks did not reflect deep-rooted feelings, but were rather the result of internal confusion, pain, and anger, then the child can discount the significance of the final meeting.

If the adult orphan feels guilt at not having been sympathetic enough to the parent, at not having realized the full meaning of that final meeting, he needs to remember that human beings are frail and prone to unintentional errors in judgment. The orphan must come to forgive himself, and to feel that the parent would also be forgiving. After all, if the relationship had been good throughout the parent's lifetime, it is not unfair to imagine that the parent would not wish to burden the child with guilt. If the parent would forgive the child, then the child should certainly forgive himself. If the parent would not have been forgiving, there was some deep-seated problem with the parent. An adult orphan should not carry excessive guilt feelings caused by an unforgiving and troubled parent.

Sometimes the last meeting may go wrong, although neither the parent nor the child has done or said anything overtly problematic. The opportunity for a final exchange of love and blessing may be precluded by an unspoken lie, a social pretense that blocks honesty between the dying parent and his children. Philippe Aries (1981) writes of the pious game where the dying person and the loved ones try to "protect" each other from the seriousness of the situation (p. 566). Neither wants to admit to the other the reality of imminent death, seeking to spare painful feelings. The dying person tries to conceal his real condition; the loved ones pretend that they do not realize how serious the condition is. Since both sides are involved in a "loving lie," the last meeting may pass without either being able to break through the barrier of the lie. They may speak of trivial things, being afraid to express their true feelings. It is painful for an orphan to think back to the last meeting with a dying parent and to realize that all they could talk about was the weather, the efficiency of the doctor, the latest political news. They were together; they knew the truth; they pretended they did not know the truth; they lost their special moment forever.

Aries (1981) has written: ". . . In the nineteenth century, death, by virtue of its beauty, had become an occasion for the most perfect union between the one leaving and those remaining behind. The last communion with God and/or with others was the great privilege of the dying. For centuries there was no question of depriving them of this privilege. But when the lie was maintained to the end, it eliminated this communion and its joys. Even when it was reciprocal and conspiratorial, the lie destroyed the spontaneity and pathos of the last moments" (p. 612).

Again it becomes clear that the dying parent and his family must be honest with each other. The well-intentioned game of the loving lie is actually a source of anguish: anguish for the dying person, who cannot speak his mind freely; and anguish for the survivors, who trivialize their experiences with their dying loved one and are left with a feeling of emptiness.

If an adult orphan, in reviewing the final meeting, recognizes that the loving lie prevented a full and open relationship with the dying parent, he should learn from this new awareness. One can determine where the errors were made, why they were made, how good intentions can sometimes cause unintended barriers between loving people. And one can apply this knowledge to future relationships. By understanding and discussing the loving lie, one can make a determination to avoid a similar mistake in the future.

## Sudden Orphanhood

If a parent dies suddenly—a heart attack, accident, possibly even suicide—the survivors find themselves in a state of shock. The death was not foreseen. There was no opportunity to prepare oneself for the death, to have a final meeting where either side realized that it was, in fact, the last meeting.

An adult orphan in this situation does not have the comfort of having had a fulfilling last meeting with the parent; nor even the bitter memory of having had a terrible final encounter. Rather, the survivor has to deal with a kind of emotional void.

If the parent-child relationship had been good, the orphan may find solace in the positive memories of the parent. The trauma of a sudden, unexpected loss is softened by the passage of time. Once the initial shock has passed, the healing process of mourning may begin.

But if the parent-child relationship contained unresolved conflicts, guilt feelings, and anger, the sudden death of the parent now precludes the possibility of direct reconciliation. The relationship is cut off abruptly. Neither the parent nor the child had the chance to try to work out the problems in their relationship. And now it is too late.

The psychiatrist, Howard M. Halpern (1976), discusses how to cope with the death of a parent when no occasion offered itself for the final goodbye. How can the orphan bring his relationship with the parent to an integral conclusion, when the parent is no longer among the living?

Halpern describes a technique known as "the empty chair" dialogue, used prominently in gestalt therapy. The person talks to an empty chair, as though the parent is actually there. After he poses questions or says what he wants to say, the orphan then sits in the chair and answers as though he is the parent. The dialogue takes place as the orphan sits in his own chair representing himself, and in the "empty chair" when representing the parent. In this way, the orphan can try to recreate the parent's feelings, attitudes, and underlying values.

If a child has not experienced a final goodbye with the parent, Halpern suggests the "empty chair" method as a second chance. In the privacy of one's own room, one can seat the "parent" in a chair opposite one's own. While sitting in one's own chair, one speaks for oneself, expressing whatever feelings come to mind. Then, the person sits in the parent's chair, and responds as the parent might be expected to respond. By going back and forth from chair to chair, the dialogue can help reopen the parent-child relationship and resolve unfinished business. "Your relationship with her (him) transcends death; it exists within you, and it is never too late to change that" (p. 232).

One may or not wish to follow the "empty chair" method of resolving problems with the deceased parent. There are other procedures that can prove helpful to the orphan in need of a posthumous last meeting. Visiting the grave of the parent and expressing one's feelings is a possible way of composing one's mind. There is a feeling of being in the presence of the parent and this itself may serve to assist the orphan in clarifying the relationship. Or, a person may evoke the presence of the parent by looking at a photograph; by visiting the place where the parent lived; by quiet contemplation. In the case of becoming a sudden orphan, some form of "communication" with the parent, even if only projected from the child's own mind, may be necessary or at least fairly important.

## Facing Reality

Whether one's final meeting with the parent was rewarding or unsatisfactory, or whether the parent died suddenly and unexpectedly, it is vital that the adult orphans face the situation realistically. The lifelong relationship between the parent and child is ultimately far more important than the short period preceding the parent's death.

For a number of adult orphans with whom I have discussed this point, the image of the final days of a parent's life long continues vividly in the memory. Some have told me that it took a year or more before they could even visualize the deceased parent as he or she was in health. The final image of the dying parent continued to dominate their memories of the parent. They found themselves often thinking over the parent's last words and gestures. They reviewed the last meeting with a hope of finding consolation. Every detail seemed to have its own mysterious significance.

It is only natural that children will mourn the death of their parents. And it is normal for the orphans to remember and reevaluate their relationship with the parent. The last meeting, the final farewell, plays an important role in the mourning process for many people. A parent has died; a child lives on, and remembers.

## CHAPTER 5

# GRIEF AND MOURNING

A Jewish poet of the last century, Solomon Frug, wrote a poignant poem, *The Daughter of the Sexton*. It tells the story of a dying rabbi, venerated by the community, whose members were distraught at the thought of losing him to the angel of death. A compromise was proposed. It was believed that God gave each person a specific span of time to live. Perhaps the members of the community could donate a part of their allotted years to the rabbi. If each person gave up just a few months of his own life, then the rabbi could gain added years.

This plan met with general favor. The sexton of the synagogue assumed the responsibility for collecting the "donations" for the rabbi's life. Some contributed a few months, some a few weeks. When the sexton came to his own home, his daughter answered the door. She was so moved that she told her father that she would donate her entire life to the rabbi. The sexton was alarmed, but it was too late. The contribution had been offered and had to be paid.

And so it was. The daughter of the sexton died, and the rabbi recovered from his illness. He continued to live "her" years. One day, many years later, the rabbi heard a voice within his head—the voice of the sexton's daughter at the wedding she never celebrated, her cries while giving birth to the babies she never bore, and finally her death groans. Her aborted life played itself out in the rabbi's mind. And then he, too, died.

This story, suggests a great truth of human experience. Our lives are intertwined with the lives of others. Our personalities, aside from their individual cores, are an amalgam of the relationships we have with others. People are constantly "donating" their time to us, and we are constantly reciprocating. The closer the relationship between people, the more their lives are interconnected, the more borrowing and lending of time, of life. In a symbolic sense, every person's life is composed of donations from the lives of others; and each person donates part of his time allotment to the people with whom he lives.

When the dying rabbi in the poem heard the voices of the unlived life of the sexton's daughter, he realized how much she had really given to him. In a less dramatic, but equally poignant way, each person hears the voices of those people who have contributed to his own life, and recognizes the debt owed them.

When our lives seem to flow into the lives of others, and their lives flow into us, we have a close relationship. When such a relationship is positive, we experience love. The people we love, and who love us, are parts of our lives.

When a loved one dies, the survivor is stricken. He has lost a human being who donated so much life to him. The survivor is grieved to be deprived of a loved one, and actually feels as though part of his own life was taken away; as it was.

David Peretz (1971), who has studied the bereavement

process, suggests that bereavement may be viewed as an illness. It is associated with physical and emotional symptoms. "As with any illness, recovery may be total or partial. The bereaved's reaction to loss may be likened to a wound or infection. For some, the wound or infection is minor, while for others it is major. For some, healing proceeds in a smooth, predictable way, without complications, while for others healing leaves serious scars which later interfere with function or produce weakness in a system which is then predisposed to later failures in function" (p. 20).

Sigmund Freud (1917), in *Mourning and Melancholia,* has examined the dynamics of the mourning process. When a person loses a loved one, what goes on in his psyche? What emotional conflicts are struggling within? How does the mourning process overcome the initial pain?

"Now in what consists the work which mourning performs? . . . The testing of reality, having shown that the love object no longer exists, requires forthwith that all the libido shall be withdrawn from its attachment from this object. Against this demand a struggle of course arises—it may be universally observed that man never willingly abandons a libido-position, not even when a substitute is already beckoning to him. This struggle can be so intense that a turning away from reality ensues, the object being clung to through the medium of a halucinatory wish-psychosis. The normal outcome is that deference for reality gains the day. Nevertheless its behest cannot be at once obeyed. . . . Why this process of carrying out the behest of reality bit by bit, which is in the nature of a compromise, should be extraordinarily painful is not at all easy to explain in terms of mental economics. It is worth noting that this pain seems natural to us. The fact is, however, that when the work of mourning is completed the ego becomes free and uninhibited again."

Freud believed, therefore, that the pain of mourning stems from an inner conflict. On the one hand, one knows that the loved one has died and is gone. On the other hand, one does not want to admit this reality. It takes time for one to accept the new situation, and it is "the work of mourning" which ultimately frees a person from the emotional struggle.

In the words of Martha Wolfenstein (1977), "when a beloved person dies, the problem arises of dissolving the emotional attachment which is bound to his image. Mourning, in Freud's sense, means this process of detachment from a lost love object. This process is a protracted and painful one. It consists of bringing up one by one the memories of the lost beloved, and slowly, reluctantly separating memory from hope, realizing that this will not come again" (p. 151).

Grief and mourning thus can be understood as a process with various stages. First, the survivor must deal with shock or disbelief that the death has actually occurred, that the loved one is gone forever. Then, he must undergo "the work of mourning," the coming to grips with the reality that the dead person has actually died. If the process goes normally, then at the end of a period of mourning a person can continue to function fully and be healed of the "illness" of bereavement. If the survivor cannot reach this final stage, he may need special help in dealing with the bereavement.

The grief process is painful and disorienting. Carol Ren Kneisl (1976), describes the grieving process as having five classes of symptoms. First, there is somatic distress—the loss of appetite, shortness of breath. Second, there is a preoccupation with the image of the deceased. Third, there are feelings of guilt. Fourth, the grieving person may manifest hostile reactions—irritability, anger, loss of warmth towards others. Finally, there may be a loss of patterns of conduct—restlessness, loss of zest. These are the symptoms of normal grieving (pp. 32–33).

C. S. Lewis (1961) has observed of his own experience with grief: "No one ever told me that grief felt so like fear. I am not afraid, but the sensation is like being afraid. The same fluttering in the stomach, the same restlessness, the yawning. I keep on swallowing" (p. 7).

The death of a loved one is an assault on the emotional and physical well-being of the survivors. Recent studies by various psychologists have found that the mortality rate among recently bereaved relatives was seven times greater than normal within 6 months of bereavement. To quote one expert in the field, Fulton (1977): "It is becoming increasingly evident in the literature, in the clinical reports, as well as in the more extensive empirical studies, that the loss of a loved person through death . . . can set in motion a train of emotional or social difficulties for the affected person" (pp. 5–6).

Even when the grief and mourning process is normal, the survivors undergo distress, disorientation, and physical and emotional problems. The extent and intensity of the reactions will, of course, be correlated to the type of relationship that existed between the dead person and the individual mourner.

## Children Mourning their Parents

When young children lose their parents to death, they face a particularly acute problem. Their lives have been almost totally dependent on the parent for their physical and emotional care and development. The absence of that parent creates a serious void in the children's lives. Wolfenstein (1977) has stated that "children are not developmentally ready to perform the work of mourning. Their emotions remain tenaciously attached to the image of the lost parent, whom they are unable to give up" (p. 156). There is ample evidence that being bereaved of a parent in childhood can have long-term emotional consequences (Slater, 1977, p. 149; Silverman, 1977, p. 165).

Since the parent-child relationship is so strong when the child is young and dependent on the parent, it is understandable that the death of a parent will cause serious problems for the orphans. As children grow older and become more independent, the death of a parent becomes more bearable. At least such children have some maturity; they can understand the reality of death; they have some experience with independence.

But once the child has become adult—has left the parent's home, earns his own living—the parent has already ceased to be the central figure in the child's life. The child may have a family of his own. He has found new loving relationships that supercede the relationship with the parent. When a parent dies, leaving adult orphans, what is the nature of their grief and mourning? They are obviously not in the same situation as young children who are orphaned. Yet they too have lost a parent, and they too face a crisis in their lives.

In the study of adults' reactions to the death of a parent conducted by Malinak, Hoyt, and Patterson (1979), quoted earlier, it is reported that the initial response to news of the death was a kind of denial. One woman had received notice of her mother's death by a telephone call from her brother. "At first she did not want to believe it, then she cried and received some comfort from her son. Then she lay in bed and cried for another 10 minutes, feeling sad and lonely, 'like part of me had gone.' Another woman said about the death of her father, 'it's hard to realize that it's actually happened. I haven't really because I'm not right there with it all the time. It just doesn't register—it's weird. I feel I haven't dealt with it, that something is hanging over me' " (pp. 1153–1154).

During the first days, even weeks, following the death of a parent, the adult orphan must come to a realization that the parent is truly dead. For many, the first impressions are that this death has not really happened, it is only a bad dream from which one will soon awaken.

During the summer following my own mother's death, I interviewed 40 members of my community to learn how they had reacted to the death of their parent(s). There was a consistent pattern of response, similar to the findings of Malinak, Hoyt and Patterson. One twenty-six year-old man, whose father had died recently, told me: "During the immediate day of death, a feeling of confusion abounded. I felt a numbness, a sense of not being myself." A fifty-two year-old man, who had lost his father some years ago, verbalized his first reaction to the death like this: "There was a numbness, knowing that you had sustained a loss but not really grasping the reality of the situation. Then there was a setting in of the real total and nonrevokable loss which left a raw tear in the fabric of one's life. Then there was the realization that you had lost a friend and mentor who would always give you the best of his knowledge and ability with no ulterior motive." A middle-aged woman, who lost her parents nearly 30 years earlier in an automobile accident, wrote to me: "In general there was a sense of it all not happening to me, of not being real. The actual grief came much later as the loss became real." Another woman, now in her seventies, told me, "I still don't realize sometimes that my mother is gone."

This pattern underscores Freud's insight that grief entails a struggle between a deep attachment to the deceased loved one and the acceptance that the death has occurred and is final. The first reaction to death is shock, denial, numbness. The survivor feels that he is dreaming, that this is not really happening.

The mourner does not easily move from the initial response of shock to the final acceptance of reality. The "work of mourning" is gradual. There are advances and regressions. In a certain sense, the mourner overcomes his sense of shock and achieves a resolution to the problem—with the passage of time. But in another sense, the mourner will continue to miss the dead loved one for all the rest of his life.

## Pining

Colin Murray Parkes (1972), in his book *Bereavement: Studies of Grief in Adult Life,* has correctly indicated that the main characteristic of grief "is not prolonged depression but acute and episodic 'pangs'. A pang of grief is an episode of severe anxiety and psychological pain. At such a time the lost person is strongly missed and the survivor sobs or cries aloud for him" (p. 39). These pangs reflect the emotional ties which still bind the survivor to the deceased person. I do not believe an orphan ever reaches the point where these pangs do not occur. Even many years after the death of a parent, the adult orphan will sometimes feel an emotional spasm remembering the parent. This is especially true when observing family celebrations or religious holidays which the parents had enjoyed during their lifetimes. It is also true when visiting a parent's grave, when seeing his former home, or other places that were significant to him.

Parkes goes further in suggesting that not only does a mourner feel these pangs of grief, but that he actually pines for the deceased loved one. "Pining is the subjective and emotional component of the urge to search for a lost object. I maintain that an adult human being has the same impulse to search that is shown by many species of social animal" (p. 40).

Parkes continues: "The bereaved adult human is likely to be well aware that there is no point in searching for a dead person but I maintain that this does not prevent him from experiencing a strong impulse to search. Because he recognizes that searching is irrational, he tends to resist the suggestion that this is what he wants to do" (p. 44).

In my own experience, and in my discussions with adult orphans over the past 16 years, I have come across many who have pined for their deceased parents; but none who felt the need to search for the parent, except in the sense of wanting to find out more about the parent's real self. Some orphans have wanted to learn more about the parent's childhood, the things that were especially important to him. But Parkes' suggestion that adult humans have the impulse to search for their dead may be true for some individuals.

## Identification with the Deceased

In their study of adults' reactions to the death of a parent, Malinak, Hoyt and Patterson (1979) reported: "The majority of our subjects reported noticing some change, usually transient, in their self-image or behavior, or becoming more aware of some aspect of themselves that made them seem more like the dead parent. These identifications sometimes had favorable aspects and sometimes were associated with more troubled features of the deceased, including the symptoms of the fatal illness. . . . One woman reported that her walking stride had become more like that of her father since his death. A young man said of his father, 'I find in myself . . . a lot of the characteristics that he had' " (p. 1154).

C. M. Parkes (1972) also includes the identification phenomenon as one of the major aspects of bereavement. This involves "the adoption of traits, mannerisms, or symptoms of the lost person, with or without a sense of his presence within the self" (p. 183).

Identification with the dead parent may take on different

forms. It might reflect itself in simple physical characteristics—feeling that one's way of walking resembles the way
the dead parent had walked. Or one may feel that his laugh
sounds just like that of the deceased parent. Identification
may occur with almost any mannerism. Likewise, the adult
orphan may identify his temperament with that of the parent—the same temper, the same calmness, the same patience. The identification phenomenon may be relatively
short-lived—for the first months following the parent's
death. Or it might go on for many years, even throughout
the child's lifetime. In speaking with many adult orphans
over the years, I have found that it is very common for
them to feel that their behavior or temperament patterns
mirror those of their deceased parents. It is almost as if the
children can actually feel the presence of their parents within
them.

The identification phenomenon reflects the continuing
attachment of the child to the parent. It underscores the
transcendent influence of the parent on the life of the child.
It is a way for the child to feel closer to the deceased parent,
to sense the continuity between the generations—a continuity that is not broken by death.

## Idealization of the Parent

During the mourning process, and possibly for the rest
of the orphan's life, there is a tendency to idealize the dead
parent. The parent is remembered as having been "perfect"
or at least nearly perfect. Conversely, in some cases, parents
are idealized negatively, as having been far worse than they
really were.

Since the physical presence of the parent has been removed by death, the survivors must rely on their memories.
The emotional stress of losing a parent leads one to idealization; the mourner believes what he wants or needs to

believe. Generally, with the passage of time, one gains a fairer perspective of the parent, recognizing the admirable qualities as well as some of the less praiseworthy. But it takes time for the sense of realism to take hold. And in many cases, it never quite does.

## Anger and Guilt

If a parent died unexpectedly, or too young, or as the result of an illness that might have been cured if detected earlier, it is normal for the surviving children to feel anger. They may vent their anger against the medical staff who cared for the parent. Why didn't they save Mom's life? Why didn't the doctor give Dad the right diagnosis? They could have saved the parent—and did not do so. Sometimes, these angry feelings have basis and lead to lawsuits against the doctors. Sometimes they are not justified at all. Yet, the orphan is so distraught, he uses the anger as an emotional outlet. It is always easier to blame others than to accept an unhappy situation with resignation.

The anger may also be turned against God. Why did God allow this to happen? How could God be so unfair? Again, it is much easier emotionally to find fault with an outside force, rather than to accept death with calmness. Although it should be obvious that God created both life and death, and that everyone who has ever lived has also died or will die—yet when one is jolted by the actual experience of this truth, he may express anger towards God. But God never promised anyone freedom from death.

It is not uncommon for an orphan to turn the feelings of anger against himself. This manifests itself as guilt. Malinak, Hoyt and Patterson (1979) found that many of their subjects acknowledged having feelings of responsibility and guilt (p. 1154). In my experience as a rabbi over the past 16 years, I have dealt with many individuals who have struggled with guilt feelings following the death of a parent.

The self-recrimination takes two forms. First, the orphan may feel guilty for not having done the right things during the dying phase of the parent's life. Perhaps he was too late in getting medical attention for the parent, or did not get appropriate medical advice; or did not visit the dying parent often enough to give him some comfort. Some children, who had kept long vigils at the bedside of dying parents, have reluctantly admitted that they had secretly wished their parents to die. The burden of caring for them had become too great. Now that the parent has died, these orphans feel guilty for having wished for the death.

A second form of guilt relates to the child-parent relationship before the parent was dying. Some adult orphans have reported being troubled by bad dreams or by memories of quarrels with the dead parent. Others feel guilty for not having visited the parent when he had been living in a home for the aged; or for not calling the parent regularly. Now that the parent is dead, such behavior seems more culpable. And there is another hidden fear within the guilt: Perhaps the same thing will happen to me. My children may not be any more attentive to me in my old age than I was to my parents.

We have seen, then, that anger over the death can be directed against others—doctors, God, or against oneself. In some cases (abnormal for adult orphans), the anger may be directed against the parent who died. When an adult orphan has been overly attached to the parent, he may respond to the death in ways similar to those of a young child. Monroe G. Gottsegen (1977), discusses several cases of depression following the death of a parent. In analyzing the phenomenon, he writes: "The parent's death precipitates letting-loose of the patient's developmentally formed memories. These loosened memories emerge in regressive grieving, spilling out of the repressed unconscious, one after another, as if set free, with no place to float but to the surface of the mind. The patient seems to cry out that the parent has abandoned him, and this is felt as a cruelty for which there can be no pardon'' (p. 37).

It is fairly common for the adult orphan to experience anger and guilt. When these are short-lived, there is no cause for much concern. However, if one carries these feelings of anger and guilt beyond a normal period of mourning—about a year—then one should seek professional counselling in order to work through these emotions.

## Mourning Customs

The event of death is followed by specific actions by the survivors. They must arrange for the funeral. In traditional communities, they must arrange for religious services and for an appropriate period of mourning; they must ready themselves for visits by friends.

Traditional Jews, for example, observe 7 days of mourning from the day of the funeral. On these days, the mourners remain home, while members of the community come to visit and express their condolences. Meals are prepared by community members for the mourners. Mourners sit on low benches or on the floor; they do not shave for the week; they wear a garment which they had torn on the day of the funeral. There are many other details in the Jewish laws of mourning. The mourners are thus immediately thrust into a situation where they are almost always surrounded by people, where they are preoccupied with a great many details of Jewish law and custom.

These observances keep the mourner from falling into a deep depression. They reassure him of the love and concern of the community. The 7-day period of mourning gives the mourner the opportunity gradually to accept the reality of the death which has occurred. Although the intense mourning period concludes on the seventh day, there is a lesser mourning period for 30 days, and a still lesser mourning period of 1 year. Jewish tradition teaches that after 1 year, the work of mourning should have been completed. Thereafter, the deceased is memorialized annually at a service on the anniversary of the death.

The mourning customs and observances of the different religions have the common goal of trying to help the mourner recover from the trauma of the loss. When a person has passed from the initial shock and grief, and has moved on to an acceptance of reality, then he can conduct life more satisfactorily.

Peter Marris (1974) has suggested: "Mourning customs can help to articulate grief—expressing its impulses in symbolic acts, containing them within a recognized period of social withdrawal, and setting a term for their resolution. These rites and gestures of remembrance continue a relationship with the dead into a world he or she no longer inhabits. They attenuate the loss and help to incorporate the meaning of the relationship in the continuing stream of life" (p. 29).

The mourning customs allow the mourners to vent their feelings, to come to grips with their pain and disorientation. As has been well stated by Roy and Jane Nichols (1975): "Emotional acceptance takes time and work and pain and hurt. Care-givers, be they professional or laymen, often allow themselves to be trapped into trying to shield and protect the grieved from pain, only to extend and delay the pain to a later date. We cannot take the pain away" (p. 91).

In our society, it generally is not fashionable to show deep signs of mourning. People try not to cry at funerals. Gatherings before and after funerals tend to be respectful, but not somber. People chat about one thing or another without making too much of the death that has just taken place. I have been in the car with mourners on the way to the cemetery many times over the years; and have noted that after a few comments about the deceased, most discussions continue without any reference to the death—until the car actually approaches the cemetery. Then the family members strengthen each other so they will not "break down" at the burial. Our society has trained us to shield others from our inner thoughts and feelings. As it is observed by Philippe Aries (1974): "A single person is missing for you, and the whole world is empty. But one no longer has the right to say so aloud" (p. 92).

But unless one can say this, one cannot deal completely with one's mourning. Customs and observances passed down through the generations provide an important symbolic framework to enable the mourner to confront death, and to proceed with the work of mourning.

## Pomp, Ceremony, and Monuments

Hans Christian Anderson told the story of a boy who had a pet bird. The boy was very negligent with his pet, letting it go hungry. The bird sang sad songs, vainly trying to catch the boy's attention and pity. Finally, the bird died. The boy then realized his callousness. To atone, he called his friends and buried his pet bird with great pomp and ceremony.

The story reminds us of some adult orphans, who after long neglect of a parent, hold an elaborate funeral, commission an expensive monument. Calm wisdom recognizes these actions as stemming from guilt or desire for social display. There can be no worthy reason for families to want more than a simple, unostentatious funeral and monument.

If the adult orphans truly wish to show respect for their departed parent, it is far better for them to spend their money on living memorials. By establishing a scholarship fund for needy children, supporting a religious or cultural institution dear to the parent, contributing to medical research, or participating in any other act of charity, the family shows real respect for the parent. The past errors cannot be undone. But perhaps the memory of the parent can inspire the children to help others live better lives. This is a way of showing true respect, even when there are no guilt feelings involved.

## Visiting a Parent's Grave

The Jerusalem Talmud (Shekalim 2:5) teaches: "One sets up no monuments for the righteous; their deeds are their memories." While this statement has profound meaning, it has long been customary to erect monuments on the graves of loved ones. The Bible itself offers ample precedent for this custom.

The monuments themselves are symbols. They are an attempt to project the memory of the deceased into the future. They are made with the idea of giving "permanence" to his resting place. His name, etched in stone or marble, is preserved for a long time to come. Although death has taken the person from us, the tombstone records his or her name; it is a touch of immortality on this earth.

Visiting the grave of a parent can be a very emotional experience. In the silence of the cemetery, the child reminisces about the parent's life. Although one can realize intellectually that a parent has died, standing at the gravesite makes a strong impression. Reading the parent's name on a monument engraves the reality of death on the orphan's mind.

The parent was so much a part of the life of the orphan, the orphan remembers so many details inextricably linked to the life of the parent. The orphan carries the genes of the parent, some of the parent's mannerisms, attitudes, ideals. An adult orphan who had a good relationship with the parent will often think of the parent, and will miss him. And now, standing at the grave, one is aware of how final and permanent is the loss.

Philippe Aries (1974) has suggested that people these days are not visiting the graves of parents as frequently as used to be the case. Death is somehow shameful (p. 91). This may be seen as a sign of weakness in modern Western society. People have disengaged themselves emotionally from each other. Families have lost much of their traditional cohesiveness. Sentimentality is frowned upon. People are reluctant to face the reality of death that appears so starkly and so convincingly in a cemetery.

Yet a visit to the parent's grave can be helpful to the orphan's emotional life, and intellectual life. It is part of the process of reconciling oneself to the actuality of the death of the parent. It is also a way of feeling that one is coming closer to the spirit of the parent—even though one knows intellectually that the parent's body is decomposed, and that the parent's spirit need not be confined to the grave.

The Talmud (Taanit 16b) discusses the custom of Jews in ancient times to visit the cemetery at times of crisis and to pray there for God's mercy. This custom has woven itself through the centuries in various forms. For many Jews today, it has become customary to visit the graves of parents during the period before Rosh Hashanah, the Jewish New Year.

The Talmud presents two opinions to explain the custom. Rabbi Levi bar Hama suggested that by praying in the cemetery, we remind God (and ourselves) that we are dust and will return to dust. We are humbled before God. We tell Him that we are considered in His eyes on the same level as the dead who populate the cemetery. Recognizing how small and helpless we are, we pray that God will be merciful with us.

The second opinion is presented by Rabbi Haninah. He

suggests that we pray in the cemetery so that we might gain merit before God for the sake of the good deeds of our ancestors. In some way, our parents and the others buried in the cemetery, may intercede with the Almighty on our behalf. This opinion presupposes that the merit of the ancestors can help us. Even if we are not worthy of God's mercy for our own sake, then perhaps we are worthy for the sake of the righteous people who have already lived out their lives.

The point is: There is a mysterious connection between the world of the dead and the world of the living. It is almost as if there is a shared community. When we stand at the grave of the parent we are certainly aware of the unbridgeable gulf between us. But, in some profound sense, we are also aware of the closeness between us. The generations are not cut off absolutely from each other.

Barbara Myerhoff (1978), in a study of a senior citizen community in California, interviewed one resident, Shmuel, who had the qualities of a philosopher. He described the feelings of his father when the family left their village in Poland to migrate to the United States. It was not an easy decision for his father to make. Before leaving the village, Shmuel's father took his family to the cemetery to visit the graves of his father, mother, sisters, and brothers. Standing before the grave of his father, "he started up a conversation there, telling his father why he was leaving, asking him for forgiveness and a blessing. All the while his tears are running through his beard until his shirtfront is altogether drenched." Shmuel continued: "You understand, it had never occurred to him that he would leave that place. His father lived there and his father before him, and so all the way back. My father had the custom of going often to his father's grave. Not just to keep it up, but to talk to him. When he had a trouble he couldn't solve, a fight with his brothers, or when there was a celebration. It was frequent among Jews to go to the graves in this way and invite the dead person to come to weddings and celebrations. So to leave all this behind meant something of the highest seriousness to him'' (p. 72).

The cultural world of Shmuel's father is far removed from that of most people in the present-day Western world. Indeed, Shmuel's father may appear to some to be a victim of superstition and lack of enlightenment. Yet the emotional richness of the relationship with his dead father was a strength in his life. He knew that his father was dead; yet he continued to experience his father's presence by a visit to his grave.

Visiting the graves of parents reminds us vividly of the fleeting nature of life, of the passing of the generations, of the values which are eternal. We are humbled. We sense the distance between us. But at the same time we sense the continuity, the closeness.

This chapter began with the story of the sexton's daughter who donated all the years of her life to the dying rabbi. In a real sense, our parents have donated many years of their lives to us. They have not only provided for our physical well-being, but for our intellectual, spiritual, and emotional development.

When we stand at the grave of parents, we may "hear" their voices within us. We may feel the "years" they donated to us. We recognize that we are the next generation; and that, at the same time, we are bound eternally to them.

## CHAPTER 6

# CONFRONTING MORTALITY

The Bhagavad-Gita (1962), the classic text of Hinduism, records the following dialogue:

"Of all the world's wonders, which is the most wonderful?

"That no man, though he sees others dying all around him, believes that he himself will die." (p. 26).

This seems to be a fundamental truth of human psychology. Although people recognize theoretically that they will die, they live their lives with a feeling of immortality. This illusion makes life bearable. If we were constantly to dwell on the fact of our mortality, we would lived frightened, depressed lives.

Actuarial charts appear to be impersonal abstractions. They reflect death data about *others*. Somehow, individuals can separate themselves intellectually and emotionally from the charts and the data they report. Death is a concept which applies to others, not to us.

In our mind of minds, each of us thinks he is special.

Even if others are dying, an inner voice assures us that we will not die. We feel that we are strong enough to ward off any danger; that God will save us.

The illusion of immortality persists until we are abruptly confronted with a crisis which reminds us that it *is* an illusion. Such crises challenge the comfortable peace of mind which our illusion has maintained for us.

Tolstoy (1960), in his *Death of Ivan Ilych,* tells of Peter Ivanovich who contemplated the death of his long-time friend. " 'Three days of frightful suffering and then death! Why, that might suddenly, at any time, happen to me,' he thought, and for a moment felt terrified. But—he himself did not know how—the customary reflection at once occurs to him, that this *had* happened to Ivan Ilych and not to him, and that it should not and could not happen to him and to think that it could would be yielding to depression which he ought not to do . . ." (p. 101–2).

This passage well describes an evasionary technique which people use to differentiate themselves from the one who has died. Somehow, we feel that the person's death may have been his own fault: he was a heavy smoker, she did not take care of herself. Since we do not indulge in those bad practices, we will go on living. Even if we cannot blame the person's death on his own behavior patterns, as in a death by a natural disaster, we still mysteriously feel that that kind of death would not take *us*.

In *Death, Society and Human Experience,* Robert Kastenbaum (1977) has described how individuals, especially when young, tend to dissociate themselves from the phenomenon of death. Commenting on youth's attitude, he writes: "Somebody else who happens to have my name may grow old someday, and may even die. But that's not really *me*. I am here right now, and I'm as full of life as can be. It's the only way I know to be. I have always been young, never old, always alive, never dead. Sure, I have a good imagination: but to see myself, *really* see myself as old or dead—say that's asking too much" (p. 141). Kastenbaum adds that it is difficult even for a middle-aged adult to realize personal mortality as an authentic fact.

I have often noticed in speaking with elderly people that they, too, separate themselves from the idea of their mortality. A human being is really composed of two different elements. The inner mind of a person may never get the sense that it is "old" or that it will die. A person's "self," the personality viewed from within the person's own mind, seems ageless. It is always contemporary. But the second element of a human being is the body. And the body very obviously is subject to a process of aging and deterioration. When we describe someone as being old, we are often referring to the external conditions of the body—gray hair, wrinkled skin, physical weakness.

Many people may experience the aging of their body, and yet still not feel old in their inner mind. I have spoken to elderly people who were dying, and who knew they were dying. Time and again they would say: "But I don't feel old." Or: "But inside me I feel that I am the same as I always have been." It is a puzzle to them that the deterioration of their body does not at all correspond to the continued vitality of their mind, their sense of self.

Because there is a strong tendency to feel the agelessness and immortality of our inner selves, we try to shut ourselves off from the reality of the aging and decline of our bodies. Our minds and bodies do not experience the sense of aging in the same way. Our minds prefer not to read the signals of the body too carefully, or too frequently. The illusion of immortality is too important to our emotional well-being.

While it is usually possible for us to glide along with our sustaining illusion, there are times when this illusion is threatened. Peter Ivanovich felt threatened by the death of his friend, and spontaneously recognized that his feeling of immortality was unrealistic. But before he let himself digest this bad news, he quickly separated himself from Ivan Ilych, taking some pride in the fact that it was his friend who died, not he. He let himself return to his illusion of immortality rather than suffer depression.

But some deaths are so emotionally jarring that the survivor cannot easily return to the peaceful illusion. On the contrary, he becomes perfectly aware of personal mortality, that death is not just for others but also for himself. It has been pointed out by Edna Furman (1974) that "before we can begin the task of mourning, we have to come to terms with the impact of death upon ourselves. Young children usually do not know yet that all living beings have to die. Older children and adults do know it but maintain more or less appropriate defenses in their daily lives to deal with the inevitability of death. When we are confronted with death our equilibrium is likely to be shaken. The closer we feel to the one who died, the more likely it seems that what happened to him could happen to us, the greater is our fear for ourselves. . . . The occurrence of death always entails a specific personal threat to the survivor. It sets the difficult task for him of finding the midway position between excessive identification and lack of empathy" (pp. 96–97).

The author, Ben Hecht (1954), noted: "I can recall the hour in which I lost my immortality, in which I tried on my shroud for the first time and saw how it became me. . . . The knowledge of my dying came to me when my mother died" (p. 114).

Indeed, the death of a parent is often the first direct assault on the child's illusion of immortality. The realization is, if it could happen to mother and to father, it could happen to me. Death is not just an abstraction or a poetic metaphor. It is real; it is personal; it has taken my parent; it will take me. There is no way to stop the process.

The death of any relative or loved one can drive the same message home. Yet, the death of a parent has a particularly strong impact. For one thing, a child usually loses a parent before any other very close loved one with whom he has lived on a daily basis. Moreover, a child realizes that 50 percent of his genes came from each parent, that he is a physical extension of the person who has died.

In the conscious or subconscious mind of children, their parents are buffers between them and eternity. As long as the parents are alive, the children can feel safely distant from death. It is as though the parents are standing guard for them. But once the parents die, the orphans are confronted with the fact that *they* are now the next generation, the only generation in the family separating the younger members from eternity. This is a subtle role change that affects the children's awareness of death as a reality. The illusion of immortality is more difficult to maintain when one knows that he is the next generation in line for death.

In officiating at a considerable number of funerals over the years, and in speaking with the bereaved families, I have noticed a general distinction in the way adult orphans relate to the death of their parents. When they have lost their first parent, they have tended to be more emotional, even traumatized, than when they have lost their second parent. With the first death, they have to confront the main issues of grieving and mourning, of orphanhood, of becoming aware of their own mortality—all for the first time. The experience of losing a parent is new and unique, without parallel.

When the second parent also dies, the adult orphans now go through the processes again. Emotions this time are generally less inflamed. The mourning and grieving are not as obviously painful. The first experience has already taken away the "innocence" of the adult orphans.

But with the death of the second parent, I have also found that there is a deeper, quieter kind of mourning. It is not only related to the loss of the particular parent; it is also introspective. The adult orphans are now without any living parents. They become more aware of their own growing proximity to death. They feel a void, an emptiness within them. They want to talk to a parent, to feel the reassurance of a parent's presence. But now they are totally cut off from the parents forever. A number of adult orphans have expressed this feeling to me quite candidly over the years— not with tears of grief in their eyes, but with a thoughtful introspectiveness.

## Parents as Symbols of Eternity

The death of a parent creates a vivid symbol of human mortality. The child who has lost a parent necessarily must confront death as a reality of life in general, and of his life in particular.

But, strikingly, parents also serve as a symbol of immortality. It was a familiar Stoic idea that parents stood midway between the human and the divine. G. Blidstein (1976), in his discussion of the role of parents, quotes the Hellenistic Jewish thinker, Philo, who wrote that "parents by their nature stand on the borderline between the mortal and immortal sides of existence; the mortal because of their kinship with men and other animals through the perishableness of the body; the immortal because the act of generation assimilates them to God, the generator of the All." He further quotes Philo: "Some bolder spirits, glorying the name of parenthood, say that a father and a mother are in fact gods revealed to sight who copy the Uncreated in His work as the framer of life. . . . Parents, in my opinion, are to their children what God is to the world, since just as He achieved existence for the non-existent, so they in immitation of His power, so far as they are capable, immortalize the race" (p. 7).

The above quotation indicates that parents may be exalted as Godlike. But beyond this, human beings tend to identify eternal things with parents. We speak of God our Father; of Mother Earth; of Mother Nature. The religious and literary traditions of many peoples make use of parent symbolism in connection with immortality, power, fecundity, compassion. This is true not only in Jewish and Christian traditions, but almost ubiquitously.

Primitive Australian tribes refer to their god as "allfather." In the *Teaching of Buddha* (1966), Buddha is described as "father to all the world; all human beings are the children of Buddha" (p. 68). We are further told that "Buddha is both father and mother to the people of the world" (p. 64). Li Kang (1085–1140), a statesman of the Sung Dynasty, said: "Heaven is to the sovereign as father and mother to a son, loving him with an extreme love" (Hastings, p. 273).

Sigmund Freud, dry rationalist that he was, deplored the depiction of immortal God as a parent. In *Civilization and Its Discontents* Freud (1930) lamented: "The common man cannot imagine this Providence otherwise than in the figure of an enormously exalted father. Only such a being can understand the needs of the children of men and be softened by their prayers and placated by the signs of their remorse. The whole thing is so patently infantile, so foreign to reality, that to anyone with a friendly attitude to humanity it is painful to think that the great majority of mortals will never be able to rise above this view of life" (p. 21).

But Freud missed the power of parent-symbolism. He reduced it to a childlike fatuity, as if people took the symbolism literally. But, of course, the use of the terms father and mother to denote eternal powers and to refer to the Divine is symbolic—not literal—language. Freud did not give *enough* credit to people's intelligence, in regretting its lack.

When people salute a flag, for instance, do they think the actual flag has any sanctity or meaning? Do the fabric and color command allegiance? It is obvious that it is not the material flag that people salute, but the idea of the nation which the flag represents. To condemn people who salute a piece of cloth is to miss their real intent, to be oblivious to the powerful symbols involved.

Or, we may draw an example from symbolic language. When one declares that he loves another with all his heart, is he referring to a muscle in the chest that pumps blood throughout the body? To think so, one must lack a basic sense of the symbolism of language. The heart, traditionally believed to be the seat of emotion, is the sustainer of life. Its pulsation is an obvious sign of life. When one says he loves another with all his heart, it is as though he is saying that he loves the other completely, with all his life, for all that he is.

When religious imagery refers to God as Father or Parent, it does not do so on the literal level. Only someone insensitive or hostile to religious teaching could argue otherwise.

Parents, after all, are the "creators" of their children. Parents nurture their children. Parents love and guide and chastise their offspring. In human experience, the parent occupies a very special role—approximating in religious consciousness the role of the Divine. The Talmud teaches that there are three partners in the creation of every person: mother, father, and God. It is not surprising, then, that parent imagery should be related to God. No other human role is so dramatically linked with God, the Creator and Sustainer of life.

Through our relationships with our specific parents, we move to the idea of Parent in the abstract. And that abstraction is then used as symbolic language in referring to eternal powers—God, nature, fecundity. This symbolism was able to develop only because people recognized the symbol of eternity in their own parents.

The need for parents transcends biology and genetics. Parents serve as the sustainers, comforters, and guides of their children. A parent's love can be as pure and selfless as any human love can be. When adult orphans have described to me what they miss since their parent has died, most have used words such as "unqualified love," "guidance," "complete compassion." Even in cases where the children clearly did not get along too well with their parent, most related to me that—as inadequate as their parents were—they felt that they missed simply knowing that the parent was a presence in their lives. There is a deep, even mysterious, bond between parents and their children.

Likewise, religious imagery recognizes the human need for a parent. While the actual physical parent is mortal, the Divine Parent is immortal and eternal. When a human being can truly perceive of God as a Parent, he has reached a high spiritual level. It is a level of intimacy with God attained by mystics and saintly people.

## Cultural Responses to Mortality

The death of a parent leads the orphans to confront their own mortality. But since the orphans do not live in a vacuum, their personal reactions will be conditioned by the social patterns of the society in which they live. The lesson of mortality may be more powerful or less powerful, depending on prevailing attitudes.

Borkenau (1966) has delineated three different types of cultures: death-denying; death-defying; death-accepting (pp. 44f). These categories are useful in evaluating peoples' responses to mortality.

A death-denying culture is one in which people prefer not to admit the reality of death. In fact, the word "died" is studiously avoided and is substituted by euphemisms—passed on, went to his eternal reward, expired. Since death is essentially a shameful and bad thing, it should be camouflaged as much as possible. Some behavior typical of a death-denying culture would be: dressing and making up a dead body to make it appear more "as in life" and "as if sleeping"; absenting oneself when the body is being buried; avoiding discussion of the reality of death or one's feelings about death with others; not showing signs of grief at a funeral.

Philippe Aries (1981) has argued that modern Western society tends generally to be death-denying. There is a certain underlying assumption that modern medicine can cure—or will soon be able to cure—every disease. As life expectancy has continually increased, the reality of death gets pushed further and further away. Might not the time come when death can be defeated altogether? Society is subject, writes Aries (1981) to "irresistible movements that put it in a state of crisis and impose a transitory unity of aggression or denial. One of these movements has unified mass society against death. More precisely, it has led society to be ashamed of death, more ashamed than afraid, to behave as if death did not exist" (p. 613).

We can sense the denial syndrome of our society when we see how carefully many dying people try to hide the gravity of their illness. It is as if they somehow feel ashamed of themselves, that it is their own fault that they are sick. Many families do not tell others, even close friends or relatives, the true nature of the condition afflicting a family member. Dying is shameful, something to be concealed as long as possible.

A death-denying culture does not approve of emotional mourning. Tears and crying can break the barrier of denial; so they ought to be repressed. Aries (1981) offers the following analysis: "How has the community come to reverse its role and to forbid the mourning which it was responsible for imposing until the twentieth century? The answer is that the community feels less and less involved in the death of one of its members. First, because it no longer thinks it necessary to defend itself against a nature which has been domesticated once and for all by the advance of technology, especially medical technology. Next, because it no longer has a sufficient sense of solidarity; it has actually abandoned responsibility for the organization of collective life. The community in the traditional sense of the word no longer exists. It has been replaced by an enormous mass of atomized individuals'' (pp. 612–613).

An adult orphan living in a death-denying culture may attempt to follow the social conventions and avoid a personal involvement in the dying and death of his parent. He may prefer to think of the parent's death as some kind of mistake, rather than as the inevitable end of all human beings. The orphan may restrain overt signs of mourning, out of respect to the norms of society.

Since our society has a strong death-denial bias, adult orphans need to overcome this bias in order to deal realistically with their parents' deaths. Dying is not shameful or unnatural; it is a normal feature of human life—and has always been the natural end of all living beings. To deny or suppress full awareness of human mortality is to create an artificial and superficial mind-set. The death of a parent should be occasion to reevaluate and reject the death-denial elements of our culture; and to face squarely the reality of death. Coming to grips with human mortality—with our own mortality—is an important component of our spiritual, intellectual, and emotional lives. This confrontation is too vital to our well-being to be denied or camouflaged.

A death-defying culture recognizes that death is inevitable; but teaches that death is not *final*. There is a life after death. The dead will one day be resurrected. At some point, the order of the world will change so that death will no longer exist. Death-defying elements are certainly evident in Judaism and Christianity; indeed, such teachings are significant in these religions' understanding of the immortality of the soul and in their eschatologies.

Death defiance, tempered with realism, can provide meaning and comfort for the faithful. But if taken to an extreme, death-defying tendencies can be problematic. Fanatical religious terrorists commit acts of murder in suicide missions—stimulated by their belief that they will be amply rewarded by God in the world to come. They defy earthly death, since they expect to live in eternal bliss in heaven. Excessive death defiance leads to a disrespect for life, to the willingness to threaten the lives of others as well as one's own.

By stressing the "impermanence" of death, death-defying cultures soften the blow of losing a loved one. Mortality on this earth is accepted; but so is spiritual immortality.

Death-accepting cultures teach that death is inevitable, and should not be denied or defied. Eastern religions are often characterized as being death-accepting. When taken to an extreme, death acceptance leads to a pessimism about this life, or to a negation of the significance of earthly life.

One scholar of Buddhism has observed that Buddhist monks use a form of meditation, "the recollection of death." They sit in a cemetery or crematorium and contemplate the ashes of cremated bodies, or the corpses that still lie there in various states of decay. By contemplating these substances, the monk becomes profoundly aware of the brevity, uncertainty, and impermanence of life as well as the inevitability of death. The monk is instructed to consider his own body, though still full of life, to be a potential corpse. When he realizes that his own life and that of everyone else is constituted and supported by a compound of birth and death in each and every moment, that life ends in death, he will obtain a perfect freedom *(vimukti)* from the illusion that he and the objects of his pleasure are enduring entities. From this insight, one recognizes the vanity of desiring to wield the world according to his own will. "And," (in the words of J. Bruce Long) "with the passing of this habit of living a life of willfulness (and its offspring, anxiety and fear) will come automatically a piece of mind and tranquility which will abide unaltered in all conditions of life and all states of mind" (pp. 68–69).

To quote from Buddha's (1966) own teachings: "Do not vainly lament, but realize that nothing is permanent and learn from it the emptiness of human life" (p. 24). Death acceptance thus may lead to an extreme passivity and to a belief that life is ultimately not important.

Most of us live in a culture composed of all three elements: denial, defiance, and acceptance of death. The issue for us is to be aware of these tendencies and to balance them—avoiding extreme denial, defiance, or acceptance.

In confronting the death of one's parent, the adult orphan has the opportunity to reevaluate his own attitudes toward mortality. He also must try to understand the different cultural responses to death, and their implications.

We live our day-to-day lives under the illusion that we will not die. Death is a remote, vague abstraction; or a poetic flourish. It happens to others, but not to us. This illusion helps us to maintain a comfortable feeling about our lives.

The death of a parent is often the first major challenge to the illusion of immortality. Our progenitor has died; so must we eventually die. The adult orphan, meditating on his loss—meditating on the passing of the generations—grows older and wiser.

## CHAPTER 7

# THE PARENTS WITHIN

A member of my congregation, then a man well into his seventies, was the guest of honor at a dinner sponsored by a national humanitarian organization some years ago. He was a distinguished philanthropist, a successful businessman, a popular man with a lovely family. When he was given an award that evening, he had tears in his eyes. In his acceptance speech, he commented with deep emotion on how he wished his father could have been alive to see this moment.

The remark struck me as out of character. Here was a man already well advanced in years, who had led an active and successful life—and yet he wished his father could have witnessed that special moment. His father had been dead for 40 years. Why did the recipient of the award feel the absence of his father so much that he felt compelled to mention it?

I later told this congregant that I was interested in the fact that he referred to his father on the evening of the dinner. He indicated that he and his father had had a very close relationship and that he continues to feel the presence of his father in all that he does. "I constantly think many times a day about my father and wonder if I am living up to his expectations, which is now my goal." The father was physically dead, yet his influence lived on in the life of the son.

A similar thought was expressed to me by a woman in her sixties, when we happened to be sitting at the same table at a wedding reception. The waitress for our table was a middle-aged woman, whose graying black hair was tied in a bun on the back of her head. The lady with whom I was sitting looked wistfully at the waitress. "My mother wore her hair just like that," she told me. "So many years have passed since my mother's death, and yet it seems like she is still right here with me." Certain events, sights, fragrances can evoke memories of deceased parents. These memories are more than the recall of objective facts from the past; they bring with them a whole mood, a set of emotions—a real feeling that the parent is actually present in some way.

Barbara Myerhoff (1978) describes a ceremony at the senior citizen center in her book *Number Our Days*. One of the men read a poem he had recently written about his mother. He described her as "a poor woman who could always find a little water to put in the samovar so that a guest was never sent away without at least a glass of tea. If it was weak, still it was hot and the mother's hospitality gave it taste enough for anyone" (p. 89). Another elderly man described the synagogue in his native village in Poland. "The first time I went there was with my beloved father, who up to the present moment I feel is with me, so that when I think of the synagogue, I can still feel his hand in mine as he introduced me to the world it held" (p. 52).

The above examples illustrate the pervasive influence of parents, even long after they have died. Adult orphans may try to live up to the standards set by their deceased parents. They may remember the physical, emotional, and spiritual qualities of their parents regularly, or at least when their memories are stimulated. Every adult orphan feels the continued influence of the dead parent(s). This recollection of parents is a more profound phenomenon than simply remembering some external facts or some casual acquaintances. Rather, the parents are in a real way still *part* of the orphan. Each person has a parent within, a parental presence which continues to be felt and responded to from within the person's mind.

## The Inner Parent

Dr. Wilder Penfield, of the Department of Neurology and Neurosurgery of McGill University, delivered a paper at the annual meeting of the American Neurological Association in June 1951, entitled *Memory Mechanisms*. This presentation captured the imagination of many, and influenced the development of a method of psychological therapy known as Transactional Analysis to be popularized by such individuals as Dr. Thomas Harris in his book, *"I'm OK— You're OK."*

Penfield suggested, on the basis of neurosurgical tests he performed on a number of patients, that the brain records everything that happens to a person and stores the records as memories (or potential memories). "The records of an individual's thinking lie dormant in the patterns of his temporal cortex until he activates them in some normal process of recall or until they come into spontaneous, and perhaps distorted, existence in his dreams. Whenever a normal person is paying conscious attention to something, he is simultaneously recording it in the temporal cortex of each hemisphere. Every conscious aspect of the experience seems to be included in these cortical records" (pp. 185–186).

According to Penfield, there are three major categories involved in the processes of memory: recording the event; recalling it; and reliving it. The last category goes beyond an intellectual recalling of an event; it actually involves *feeling* as though one is virtually reliving the event. Thomas Harris (1969) has commented on Penfield's analysis that "perhaps the most significant discovery was that not only past events are recorded in detail but also the feelings that were associated with those events. An event and the feeling which was produced by the event are inextricably locked together in the brain so that one cannot be evoked without the other" (p. 27).

We can sense the general truth of Penfield's observations without needing to evaluate the clinical evidence. Who has not experienced the actual reliving of a past event? The fragrance of baking bread can transport one back to his mother's kitchen of years gone by. We not only remember the scene objectively; we actually feel that we are part of it—we can smell the bread, we can taste it, we can talk to mother and hear her responses. And so it is with other such memories. We sometimes experience the past not just intellectually; but emotionally, and with our sensory abilities.

Much of our store of memories, especially in the early years of our lives, includes memories of parents. Indeed, parents are the dominant characters in our childhood. They leave us not only a host of memories, but also a pattern of behavior and thought.

Transactional Analysis views each person as composed of three distinct elements: the Parent; the Child; and the Adult. Harris describes the Parent as "a huge collection of recordings in the brain of unquestioned or imposed external events perceived by a person in his early years, a period which we have designated roughly as the first five years of life. This is the period before the social birth of the individual, before he leaves home in response to the demands of society and enters school. The name Parent is most descriptive of this data inasmuch as the most significant 'tapes' are those provided by the example and pronouncements of his own real parents or parent substitutes. Everything the child saw his parents do and everything he heard them say is recorded in the Parent. Everyone has a Parent in that everyone experienced external stimuli in the first five years of life. Parent is specific for every person, being the recording of that set of early experiences unique to him'' (p. 40).

For the purposes of Transactional Analysis, the Parent is seen primarily as judgmental, giving orders, being authoritative without self-doubt or self-reflection. The child perceives the parent as the one who makes the rules and who knows everything. The Child, in the terms of Transactional Analysis, is dependent on the judgments and instructions of others. The Adult is able to evaluate data and to make reasonable decisions independently.

It is clear that the Parent, so described, is a basic feature in human personalities. Each person can think about his own situation and find this to be true. Parents were the ones who established the early patterns of our lives; to a great extent, those patterns stay with us in one form or another throughout our lives. An old Judeo-Spanish proverb teaches *"fin la ocho a la ochenta"*—"from eight to eighty." In other words, the character traits you can see in a child of eight will also be evident in that same person when he is eighty years old.

Yet, our present discussion must go far beyond the limited terminology of Transactional Analysis. The "parent" in us is far more than a series of do's and don'ts, of uncritical instructions and beliefs. Even as we grow into adolescence and adulthood, the role of the parent continues to grow within us.

Parents have a complicated set of responsibilities toward their children. Certainly, they must provide for the children's physical well-being—food, shelter, clothing. They must also preside over the children's educational, cultural, and spiritual development. Parents need to strike a fine balance between protecting and guiding their children, on the one hand, and letting the children become independent and self-sufficient, on the other. Many parents struggle with this tension, and some never resolve it adequately.

In the best of cases, parents love and protect their small children; love and guide their growing children; love and encourage their older children; love and let go of their now adult children. Good parents want their children to grow into independence, even if they know that the children will then be out of the parents' control. There is a subtle pathos in child rearing. Yet, good parents know that their relationship with their children must necessarily change with time—and the change can be positive and friendly.

Even when children are out of the parents' home, they may continue to have a loving and respectful relationship with them. In fact, parents and their adult children can have a very deep and meaningful relationship—based on mutual love and respect. Such a relationship, to use the term of Martin Buber, is an I-Thou relationship. Both parties recognize the worth of each other; they are as equals; they understand each other and are sensitive to each other. This type of relationship is possible when both parties are mature and independent. When the child is still young, his relationship with the parents is unequal and dependent. A full I-Thou relationship is not likely.

When children have this kind of relationship with their parents, the influence of the parents continues to be felt in their lives in a positive sense. The adult child continues to learn from and share with his parents. The adult child's inner "parent" continues to grow and flourish. This process goes on until the relationship ceases to be positive; or until the parent dies.

But all parent-child relationships are not as excellent as the type just described. Some parents are overdemanding; they want their children always to be dependent on them. They stifle the children's emotional growth. Everyone knows someone whose development was suppressed by an overdemanding parent—so that the child never left the parent's home to marry and live an independent life.

Howard M. Halpern (1976) has well described this phenomenon: "Often our parents' inner child is not pleased by our being strong and independent. The child within them may be apprehensive and angry at the separateness and the loss of control over us implied by our autonomy. . . . When we behave in ways that mark us as individuals separate from our parents, individuals with our own ideas, feelings and lives, the child within our parents feels an overwhelming threat of losing us and may react with disapproval, upset, hurt or anger" (p. 17).

The adult child who has this type of relationship with his parent also carries an inner "parent" through life. But this inner parent is actually a problem, a weight on his emotional freedom. A child may spend a lifetime trying to battle against the parents' domination. Or, he may well give in to the parents, constantly seeking to placate them by following their injunctions.

Regardless of the specific nature of the parent-child relationship, it is fair to state that adult children do carry their inner "parent." The parents continue to form part of the child's personality, even when the child is an adult. Indeed, a person cannot fully understand himself without understanding the role of the parents within.

## When Dead Parents Seem So Near Us

Rabbi Joseph B. Soloveichik (1983), one of the leading contemporary religious philosophers, delivered a lecture on the anniversary of the death of his father. He said: ". . . it seems to me as if my father were yet alive, although four years have come and gone since his death. It is in a qualitative sense that I experience his nearness and spirit tonight. I cannot explain the . . . spiritual picture of father that hovers near me tonight, as in yester-year of physical existence" (p. 29).

Rabbi Soloveichik continued: "Our sages have said . . . 'the righteous are exalted in death more than in life.' If time be measured qualitatively, we may understand how their influence lingers on after their death and why the past is eternally bound with the present. Yet, how do their mortal lives acquire a new significance in death?" (p. 29).

Rabbi Soloveichik postulates that we have a "qualitative time-awareness" which allows us to intersperse the chronological time of the life of a deceased loved one with his values and creativity. Stated more simply, we do not just remember the day-to-day details of their lives, but we evaluate their lives more meditatively, taking into consideration their ideas, aspirations, achievements. A person who has died and has "disappeared from the stage of the present, takes on a new and profound significance in contrast with the changed scene" (p. 29). From our present vantage point, we look back at the past and at the lives of those who have died. We see them and understand them differently now than we did when they were alive.

A number of adult orphans have told me that with the passage of time they have in some way come to a fuller or deeper appreciation of their deceased parents. One woman described her feelings in these words: "The passage of time has affected my sense of loss as a scar tissue that never heals. It has healed sufficiently so that it does not impair my living as I once thought it would; but not enough to cover up moments of deep sadness. My father's goodness and his many wise words plus the fun times spent with him come back to me more and more. Now, I am better able to appreciate them and integrate them in my life." Another woman reported: "I do think of my father very often and do find that he was even smarter than I knew (and believe me I knew he was smart then). I also knew he was very honest and good, and as time passes, it has been proven over and over again." A thirty-eight year-old man told me that following his mother's death he came to a much deeper understanding of her. He had had an excellent relationship with her throughout her life; yet, he never seemed to have enough time or motivation to think really seriously about the meaning of her life until she had died.

This "qualitative time-awareness" creates a closeness between the adult orphan and the deceased parent. Indeed, the orphan may sense the continued nearness of the parent regularly, or at least on certain occasions.

A fifty-two-year-old lawyer, discussing the death of his father 6 years earlier, noted: "I think of my father often. He had certain wonderful expressions which I often use (or misuse) and I find myself repeating other of his remarks. I feel he is still with me, although not in a 'life hereafter' sense."

An insurance dealer, in his early sixties, lost his father about 11 years before. When I asked him if he felt as though he were an orphan, he responded in the negative. "I don't believe I have really lost someone, in the sense of being an 'orphan,' since my father still lives in my mind and deeds. His example and guidance still mold my life."

A twenty-eight-year-old man also told me that he did not consider himself orphaned due to the death of his father. "I have not been deprived of a parent. My father continues to live inside me. I think about him and how he would act in various situations. He is still a guiding force. I feel as if I have been deprived of a peer."

In chapter 5, we briefly discussed the phenomenon of

"identification" which is part of the mourning process for many people. Mourners identify with the deceased, believing that their mannerisms or spiritual qualities resemble those of the person who has died. In discussing with many people their reactions to the death of their parents, I have found a large number of adult orphans who continue to identify with their deceased parents. Many have told me that they laugh like their parent, or have the same style of walking, or support the same causes, or have the same stubborn streak. There is a strong, often unspoken, sense that the parent continues to live in them in some way. Almost everyone I spoke to on this subject told me that there are times when they feel their parents are very close to them, are actually present, or are somehow still within them. There can be little doubt that parents, even after their deaths, continue to wield significant influence over the lives of their children.

## Understanding the Parent Within

Just as relationships with living parents can be good or bad, so relationships with deceased parents can vary in quality. Very often, the same kind of relationship that existed during the parent's lifetime will continue after the parent's death.

In fortunate cases, the adult orphans had had respectful and loving relationships with their parents. The memory of their parents is a source of strength and happiness for them. Since they had functioned as independent adults during the parents' lifetime, and with the parents' blessings, they deal with their orphanhood in a mature fashion. In the words of Peter Marris (1974), they master their grief "not by ceasing to care for the dead, but by abstracting what was fundamentally important in the relationship and rehabilitating it" (p. 24).

For such adult orphans, the memory of parents is a positive feature of life. The sense of nearness to the parent's values and traits generates a feeling of warmth and inner happiness. Although the parents' physical presence is missed, the orphan still has a sense of continuity with the parents and a feeling of being part of a shared community.

The "parent within" can often be more than a pleasant set of memories; it can also be an active guide in the orphans' lives. The parent may continue to exert considerable pressure on the children and shape their decisions. When the parent is a good model, this kind of guidance can have positive ramifications. This chapter began with the story of a successful businessman who, even in advanced age, still tries to live up to the example of his father. This goal has led the man to be a noteworthy philanthropist and communal leader. Many orphans have told me that they try to live up to the standards of their parents; that they imagine what their parents would want them to do in certain situations.

Yet, the "parent within" may exert too much influence on the orphans' lives, which may become onerous. This is true especially in those situations where parents, during their lifetimes, attempted to dominate their children and stifle their independence.

It is useful for adult orphans to reevaluate the relationship they had had with their parents and to determine what role the deceased parent(s) continues to play in their lives. Such a process helps the orphan to understand himself better, to recognize patterns of thought and behavior that parents have imposed on him.

There is a tendency to idealize parents after they have died. Idealization can be positive: Father always made the right decisions, mother was always so understanding and compassionate. Idealization can also be negative: Father was always picking on me, mother was always whining and complaining. Neither form of idealization is true to reality.

Orphans who harbor illusions about parents can damage their own lives and the lives of those people with whom they live.

They may maintain the fantasy that their parents were perfect, and that they must devote their lives to living up to the parents' standards. Such an attitude can lead the orphan to feel inadequate—it is difficult to be as perfect as idealized parents. It can lead the orphan to be compulsive, and quite obnoxious to be with. Idealization hinders the orphan's ability to make decisions on his own, since the parents' wishes are still dominant in the child's mentality.

Negative idealization can also be a source of feelings of inadequacy for the adult orphan. If the child believes the parent was never satisfied with him, this obviously is damaging to the self-esteem. Or if a child believes he had unfit parents, he may feel shame or regret about them, which can affect other relationships.

Halpern (1976) discusses the power of parental injunctions and the problems they may cause for their adult orphans. Parental injunctions are always powerful, but once the parent has died these admonitions can seem chiseled in granite. Halpern notes some common expressions: "Poppa would have wanted it that way"; "My mother would turn over in her grave if she knew"; "My father would be so proud of me today." These expressions assume that the child knows the demands of the dead parent. They also assume that the child is still seeking the approval of the parent who is dead (pp. 218–219).

Halpern correctly suggests that the adult orphan must reopen his relationship with the deceased parents in order to become free from their domination. Otherwise, the orphan might spend his life trying to win the approval of dead parents, or at least to avoid their disapproval. The fallacy in this scenario is that of course no living dialogue with the parent is possible. The child imagines what the parent would want, would say, would do, would expect. And then, he tries to adjust life to fit into those imagined parental injunctions.

To quote Halpern further: "Your image of him (the dead parent)—of what he thought, of how he felt about you and others, of what he expected of you and what his injunctions for living were—became frozen when he died." Death has robbed the parent of the opportunity for further growth and development. Although changes have occurred in the child, one's images of the parent have probably remained static. These frozen images replay as prerecorded voices in the child's mind. Thus interaction with the parent is really interaction with one's fixed images of that parent (pp. 215–216).

Each child has a specific, personal view of the parent who has died. Adult siblings, though they have been raised by the same parents, had different relationships with the parents and different experiences with them. A firstborn child views the parents differently from a middle child or the youngest child. An only daughter or an only son will have different experiences from those of other children. A child born when the parents were young has a different childhood from the child born when the parents were older. In fact, no two children in the same family have identical relationships with the parents.

It is obvious, therefore, that adult orphans remember their parents based on their own specific relationship with them, as well as their age when the parent died. When adult orphans honestly discuss their feelings towards their deceased parent(s), they are often surprised at how differently they each perceive the parent(s).

Halpern has noted that the most subjective aspect of the image of one's deceased parent is how that parent felt about you. Many adults have expressed the wish that their parent had lived longer so they could have obtained a clearer picture of what the parent's real feelings about them were (pp. 217–218).

When adult orphans find that their lives are still dominated by their parents, even after the parents have died, they are deprived of living independently, as mature adults. It is one thing to respect, love, and admire the memory of parents; it is another to be controlled by those memories.

Halpern recommends that adult orphans do their best to come to a realistic appraisal of who their parents really were. He suggests talking to people who knew the parent in many different facets of the parent's life. What did they like or dislike about the parent? Moreover, the orphan can look at photographs of the deceased parent and search for clues to the actual personality. "Note his posture—is he rigid or relaxed, assertive or passive, firmly grounded or weak and unstable? And how about his facial expression—is it friendly? Forbidding? Warm? Seductive? Phony? Open? Happy? Anxious? Depressed? Masklike? . . . If you have photos of your parent as a child study them closely. What kind of child was he (or she)? One can also study letters or other writings of a parent, review anything about the parent's past that one can come up with. These lead to getting a truer picture of the parent" (p. 225).

By coming to a realistic, non-idealized picture of the deceased parent, the orphan can come to appreciate father or mother for what they really were. The orphan can treat the parents more objectively, and create enough emotional distance to be able to conduct life as an independent adult.

It is necessary for an adult orphan to recognize that life is a process in which people are constantly undergoing changes. Every living organism changes. None of us is the same person we were 10 years ago, or even 1 year ago. We change physically, emotionally, spiritually. Our attitudes on many things are altered with time and maturity.

Just as we change, so our parents—during their lifetimes—were also undergoing changes. But in death they no longer change. Our image of them freezes at that point in time when they have ceased to be part of the living world. Therefore, in trying to live according to the injunctions of deceased parents, it is only too easy to ignore the fact that those injunctions may have been different had the parent continued to live. The parents' attitudes may have changed; the parents' opinion of the children may have altered. It is essential for the adult orphan to be realistic about his parents. The "parents within" can be a very positive and gratifying part of the adult orphan's life; or a source of anguish, guilt, and feelings of inadequacy. A sense of realism can help deal with the "parents within," and help the adult orphan understand his own life much better.

There is a permanent bond between parents and their children. This bond transcends death. The parents form part of the personality of the children. Understanding the parents helps the children to understand themselves. As adult orphans contemplate the lives of their deceased parents, they may come to a fuller awareness of their relationship with the parents; of the quality of that relationship; of the continued influences of the parents on their lives.

The parents within are permanent elements in the lives of their children. Honesty and realism about the inner parents is necessary for self-understanding and emotional independence.

## CHAPTER 8

# PARENTS AND OUR PAST

There is a short but significant episode in the latter part of Herman Melville's *Moby Dick*. Captain Ahab is consumed with the desire to kill his nemesis, the great white whale. He drives the crew of his ship with irrational devotion to this one cause: to spot, pursue, and destroy that whale.

At last the hated whale is sighted. Captain Ahab mobilizes his men with furious zeal so that the ship can hunt it down. In the commotion, a young black boy—Pip—falls overboard. If the ship is held back in order to save Pip, the whale will get away. The captain decides not to lose any time. He orders the crew to move the ship after the whale as quickly as possible. Since Pip can swim, he reasoned, the crew could pursue the whale and then return to pick up Pip later on.

Pip flounders about in the ocean and watches as the ship moves away from him, finally dropping out of his line of vision. He is now all alone in the universe. Above him is the infinite sky; beneath him is the deep of the ocean; in all directions, he can see only the eternal sway of the sea. There is no place for him to anchor his thoughts. There is no context for his life except the vastness of the sky and the sea.

The ship does not succeed in catching the whale on this venture. It returns to pick up Pip. Pip is discovered, still swimming in the water, and is lifted to safety onto the ship. But the crew quickly discovers that Pip has lost his mind.

This short episode makes the point that a human being needs a clear context in order to maintain stability in life. Pip was temporarily robbed of this context—and went mad. The strain was too great for him.

The crisis of Pip was a vivid crisis of identity. He was faced with the existential questions: Who am I? What is the meaning of my life? Where do I belong? Why do I exist? Although few people are left alone in the ocean to ponder these questions as was Pip, everyone does confront them at one time or another during the course of life. At times, a person shares the spiritual crisis—the identity crisis— symbolized by Pip's dilemma. Hopefully, though, the crisis can be met without one going mad.

A person may face serious crises of identity throughout the course of life; but at some times be more prone to them than at others. During adolescence, the growing child is in the predicament of being tied to the parents while longing to be independent. Typical of adolescent behavior are fluc-tuations between being very childlike and very rebellious. The adolescent struggles to find his own place in the world. He tries to resolve the desire to be independent with the desire to remain dependent on the parents. The identity cri-sis of adolescence is related to the role of the parents in the life of the adolescent.

Another usual occasion for crisis occurs in the early twenties when the person must plan to take on the respon-sibilities of independent adulthood—full-time employment, marriage. A person may or may not be ready to move from the relative irresponsibility of youth to the serious responsibilities of adulthood. As the time approaches when life-affecting decisions must be made, everyone becomes introspective. Am I making the right choices? Am I able to succeed in what I want? Do I know what I want? What and who am I, really? During this crisis, parents may be helpful or may exacerbate the conflict. But the parents are not at the center of this spiritual struggle, as they were in the struggle of adolescence.

Life is punctuated by other crises—at around age thirty, age forty, and at other "landmark" birthdays as one grows older. It is natural for an individual to reevaluate the direction and meaning of his life. Midlife crises reflect the inner conflict: the knowledge that youth is past, that old age is approaching—and that the person is not ready to accept this reality. It is also common for people to suffer the death of a parent somewhere during midlife. This may further contribute to one's feeling of vulnerability, and may intensify one's feelings of depression and anxiety. Although midlife crises are not directly related to one's relationship with his parents, the death of a parent during these crises often does occur and then does play a role.

Parents can serve their children as healing and helping agents in the identity crises that confront them throughout life, especially those occurring during adulthood. Parents are symbols of family roots, of the past, of stability in an unstable world. (Even where the parents were themselves unstable, or had an unstable marriage, they still can at least serve symbolically as connections with one's past. They may still be viewed as links to earlier generations when life was—at least theoretically—stable.)

Everyone finds himself floundering in a spiritual sea of turmoil at some points in the course of life. Everyone feels isolated, stranded, deracinated at times. They may be involved in breaking away from their parents' control; or they may not find their parents to be particularly understanding or helpful in their predicament. Yet, the existence of parents—and what they represent—can provide a context for one's life and can assuage the desperate feelings of isolation and meaninglessness. Parents need to be considered for what they are—people with strengths and limitations: but also for what they symbolize. Parents are the links between their children and the past, the bridges that bring the generations together.

## Parents and Tradition

To a great extent, parents are symbols of tradition and continuity. When children want to express their own freedom, the first targets are their own parents. In order to establish themselves as free agents, they need to assert their independence from the authority of the parents. Violating the strictures and values of parents is part of the process of growing up, of testing the authority of tradition.

Yet, as the children grow into adulthood, their need to establish their independence from their parents wanes. They may feel confident to lead their lives without engaging in emotional competition with parents. On the contrary, parents can become friends on a mature, adult-to-adult level.

As a person matures, he can come to realize the significance of parents as links with the past. Norman Linzer (1984) has observed: "Parents themselves symbolically represent history, for their origins appear to be in the distant past in the time-consciousness of the child. . . . They represent this history in their person, and when they perform rituals with historical significance, the child sees the history come alive through their actions" (p. 72). Linzer, in discussing the specific situation of Jewish parents, refers to the opinion of the medieval Rabbi Levi ben Gershom who argued that parents themselves represent Jewish history even as they are duty bound to transmit Jewish history. In other words, the history and tradition of the Jews is passed down by parents not merely by their telling things to their children; but by their very being. The parents are symbols of the history and are embodiments of the tradition.

The famous nineteenth century Rabbi Samson Raphael Hirsch (1982), in his commentary on Exodus 20:12, noted: "The knowledge and acknowledgement of historical facts depends solely on tradition, and tradition depends solely on the faithful transmission by parent to children, and on the willing acceptance by children from the hands of their parents" (p. 274).

Of course, these observations are true not only of Jewish tradition, but of human civilization in general. Parents are the repositories of the cultural traditions and they convey them to their children. As the children assimilate or reject these traditions, society reflects stability, dynamism, or instability. By fostering a strong relationship between parents and children and by insisting that children honor and respect their parents, a strong culture establishes the basis of its own stability and viability.

## Reminiscing

People enjoy reminiscing about their youth. Even children like to hear stories about themselves when they were younger. And children also enjoy hearing about the childhood experiences of their own parents.

The fascination with the past does not stem from a scholarly interest in historic details. Rather, there is a deep emotional bond which each person has with his own past as well as with the past of his parents and ancestors. In recounting old family stories, family members gain a deeper sense of their own being, a greater awareness of their own roots. A strong family tradition imbues a person with good feelings about himself. It affords a sense of belonging, a sense of connection with the family and its history.

Parents play a vital role in giving their children a feeling of being part of a tradition, of having roots. Indeed, as the children grow older, much of their own reminiscing involves memories of their parents.

When adults reminisce about their deceased parents, they often come to a new appreciation of the significance of their parents' lives. Sometimes, a person does not realize quite how much impact the parent had on him until the parent has died. Then the adult orphan begins to remember and reevaluate his relationship with the parent. And new insights emerge.

Amnon Shamosh (1983), a leading Israeli author, wrote a moving poem which he called *The Great Confession*. Shamosh had migrated to Israel from Syria as a young child. He lived on a kibbutz, separated from his family. Each summer, his mother would come to visit him. Being a young boy who was anxious to succeed in his new life in the kibbutz, Shamosh did not pay close attention to his mother's words on these annual visits. Or at least he did not seem to pay attention.

One summer
she
did not
come
and in the winter
she was released from
this world
and the burdens which are
part and parcel
of life
Spring passed
summer ended

and in the autumn
my hand
began
jotting down stories
I read them
and discovered
my mother's
world
a culture
departed

Shamosh goes on to say that his mother's words, which he thought he had not heard, had filtered through to him. Now he was telling stories which he had heard from her, which were inspired by her.

I wanted
to tell
my stories
to my mother
I wanted to hear
her tell
more and more
but my mother
who came
to me
each summer
(across the barrier)
had been—
and gone (p. 49)

Shamosh's haunting poem articulates how a child absorbs the words and culture of the parent—even when not realizing that he is doing so. Once the parent has died, the child's mind and memory open to the things he experienced with the parent. The child wants to tell the parent what he has discovered, and wants to hear the parent tell more: but it is too late. Memory, nostalgia, reminiscence take the place of the living relationship.

Similarly, Marcel Proust was deeply moved by the death of his beloved mother. After she died, he set himself seriously to work for the first time in his life. He wrote *Remembrance of Things Past* in which he demonstrated his wish to retrieve the past, to establish an emotional connection with the past and with the people who had now passed on. The fact that Proust's work won him such wide acclaim is an indication of the fact that many people share his sensitivity and his need to remember times past.

When one feels deracinated, the memories of parents can serve as connections with the past, with rootedness. The memory of parents can provide a source of stability and continuity.

## Searching for Roots

It is commonplace for adults to do research into their family history. They draw up family trees, attempt to establish contact with people who may be relatives, collect family photographs. Some diligent individuals conduct serious research in libraries and archives, all in the hope of shedding some new light on the family's background.

Such a process seems to become especially important to adults when aged parents are approaching death, or have already died. Since the parents are the connecting links with the past, they are the best living repositories of the information the adult children seek. When a parent is dying, the children become vividly aware of the fact that this link with their past will soon be gone. They may attempt to learn as much as they can from the parent before death actually comes.

Moreover, when parents realize that they are approaching death, they often feel the need and desire to tell

their children as much as they can about their past. In doing
so, they emotionally relive their lives and try to convey its
meaning to their offspring. The transmission of the past is
a precious legacy. I recall that during my mother's final illness she reminisced a great deal about her own childhood,
about important events in her adult life, about her experiences with the family. It was clear that she enjoyed telling
us these stories and remembering so many details. In recounting these reminiscences from the past, she also drew
some philosophical lessons which she imparted to us.
Through the experiences of the past, she tried to understand
the general meaning of her life. And she shared with us the
insights she had gained. It is natural for parents to want to
transmit to their children a sense of security, pride, and
happiness in their family traditions.

But once the parents have died, the adult orphans are
forced to seek other sources of family history. They may
consult elderly relatives, or study family photographs and
documents. Yet they still will rely heavily on their memories
of what their parents told them. They will often find themselves calling to mind stories and bits of information their
parents had conveyed to them. To some extent, they will
internalize the family traditions inherited from the parents
and will sense their own obligation to pass them on to their
children.

These reminiscences can give balance and stability to
life. They can greatly deepen one's understanding of who
he is and what he represents.

In some cases, the adult orphans tend to become more
conservative and traditional in the style of their lives. They
adopt the role of family elder. Since their parents have died,
they now have become the link with the past. If they take
this responsibility seriously, they may become more involved in religious life and in communal life. They will want
their own children to understand what the family tradition

is and what it stands for. To do this, they will be more conscious of their own role as symbols, as agents of tradition and continuity.

In speaking with a number of congregants and friends who have experienced the death of a parent, I have found that there is a difference in reaction among adult orphans depending on whether they have lost one parent, or both. Generally, those who have lost both have spoken in more "traditional" terms about their own roles in life. One man, a noted scholar at a major university, told me that when his father died—some years after his mother—he felt as though he had somehow crossed over to a new phase in life. "I now have become the elder generation. There is no one between me and eternity. Losing one's last parent has a profound effect on the way one deals with life." A medical doctor, who had lost his mother several years after the death of his father, indicated that with the loss of both parents he felt a greater need to be a "model" to his children. He became more active in communal activities and in religious concerns. With the absence of parents as symbols of tradition and continuity, the adult orphan often accepts the fact that he has now become the ultimate symbol in the family.

Although I have encountered this pattern in many of the interviews I have conducted over the years, an opposite tendency has also been expressed from time to time. Some adult orphans, rather than becoming more traditional, have become more distant from tradition and have asserted their own independence.

## Tradition and Rebellion

While the adult orphan may gain a sense of stability and tradition by recalling the lives of the parents, he may also become cut loose from tradition by the death of the parents. In some cases, the children may be reluctant or hesitant keepers of the family traditions. During their parents' lifetimes, they may have felt compelled to adhere to the rules and regulations set forth by their parents. This was done out of fear or respect, but not necessarily from a real commitment to those values. Now that the parents have died, the adult orphans may feel free to break away from the heritage they had followed only to please their parents.

A number of adult orphans have told me frankly that once their parents had died, they gained a new feeling of freedom. They could now live according to their own values, without needing to worry about offending their parents. One businessman said: "In a very peculiar way I feel less restrained by the need to meet standards my parents might have set. If I want to alter my religious, ethical, moral, or other codes, I feel no compulsion to avoid this because of my parents. Nor do I feel a requirement to meet their ideas on family, social status, etc. It may sound contradictory, but all of my life, up until my parents were gone, I was under some sort of restraint to match their concepts of what I was to do under various situations, and now that they are gone, I am free of the restraints."

One woman told me that as long as her parents were alive, she felt constrained not to marry a certain man whom the parents had disapproved of. Now that they had died, she married him without worrying about her parents' approval. A number of individuals have told me that their parents were overly domineering and had caused them considerable unhappiness. Now that the parents were gone, these individuals experienced a feeling of relief and newfound freedom.

Yet, if one cuts himself off as completely as possible from the memories of parents, one may become like Pip, stranded and isolated in the middle of the eternal sea. One may expand in a new freedom upon the death of the parents;

but this may be dangerous if taken to an extreme. Children need to understand who their parents really were and what they represented. This means recognizing the parents as human beings with virtues as well as faults. A sympathetic and thoughtful consideration of parents can help one maintain a balanced relationship with them—even after they have died.

Since parents are an integral part of their children's personalities, and since they play such a significant role in their children's memories, a good parent-child relationship can give the children a strong basis for a healthy emotional life. Reminiscing can be a beautiful and powerful experience for the adult orphan—it can give a sense of security, continuity, and rootedness. On the other hand, a poor parent-child relationship can continue to have a detrimental effect on the children even after the parents have died.

Jewish tradition teaches that the commandment to honor parents is applicable even after the parents have died. By respecting their deceased parents, adult orphans maintain a positive relationship with their own past, with their own family traditions.

# CHAPTER 9

# THE SURVIVORS

Most families who have experienced the death of a parent feel that the circle is broken, never to be restored. A parent dies and everything suddenly becomes different. Family relationships change. Responsibilities change. Life for the survivors is now different in a variety of ways. The previous family organism is shattered beyond repair, and no one can put things back the way they were.

I was thirteen years old when my grandmother died. She had been the central figure in her extended family of seven children and 20 grandchildren. Her five daughters, all of whom were married and had families of their own, lived within walking distance of my grandmother's home. Her two sons, one of whom was married, though not living as close by, still maintained a very devoted relationship with her. When she died, the close family organism was shaken and ultimately became something quite different from what it had been. I remember making the analogy of removing the pit of a peach and then trying to put the peach back together. It might look almost the same; but the center was gone.

After her death, her children became the heads of new family organizations. They were the parents and were now beginning to be the grandparents of the next generations. Instead of having one family unit with my grandmother (and grandfather) at the head, there were now six family units with her daughters and her married son at the head. These families remained friendly with each other—but they developed along their own lines. Everyone knew that the family had reached a turning point with the death of my grandmother.

This is not an isolated example. Many people have told me the same thing. When the matriarch or patriarch of the family has died, the family begins a process of reorganization. The former sense of unity dissolves. Each child moves away in his own direction; the unifying force of the parent is gone.

Peter Marris (1974) has observed: "Whenever we lose someone who occupied a central position in our lives, all the activities which related to that person lose their accustomed meaning. Ambitions, plans, skills, everyday routines which used to occupy us become pointless. Any severe loss tends to undermine the meaning of other relationships, too, because they are interrelated. The crisis of meaning tends to become pervasive, so that the whole organization of reality, from which the sense of life derived, is cast in doubt" (p. 23).

When people become nostalgic about the "good old days," they are often dreaming about a time when their lives were more closely united with those of their family and community. They idealize a warm, loving quality to life— a quality that was infused by the family matriarch or patriarch. Life seemed simpler then—and better in important ways. The "good old days" were generally not so good from a material point of view. People were poorer, less educated; they lacked many of the conveniences that modern science and industry have been able to produce for our generation. But, at least in an idealized way, they had a better idea of who they were and why they were. They lacked many material advantages; but they had spiritual, communal, and emotional assets.

Parents, as central figures in the family members' lives, were responsible for maintaining the unity and harmony of the family. They were the ones who created the context for the children's lives. Their attitudes and actions influenced the way the children would develop and the way they would relate to the other members of the family and community.

The death of a parent causes the extended family to reconsider their relationships. The family now becomes a new organism, facing new challenges.

## The Surviving Parent

A man and a woman have shared most of their adult lives together. They have had children, grandchildren. They have worked together in good times and bad. Their relationship was based on love and responsibility for one another.

They grew old together. They helped each other in times of illness and emotional distress. They celebrated the joys of their family. They were two people—yet they have experienced their most important experiences together, as though they were one unit.

One of them dies. Perhaps death comes suddenly, or perhaps it comes after a long illness. The one who survives feels stranded.

The life of the surviving spouse has suffered a profound rupture. Since life had been oriented in partnership with the now deceased spouse, the survivor loses his sense of stability. There is a profound emptiness, silence, loneliness. There is a void which no one can quite fill.

Adult children have lives of their own. They sympathize with the surviving parent. They may even ask the parent to move in with them. Yet the surviving parent feels out of place somehow; feels incomplete. In some cases, the surviving parent will find it possible, with the passage of time, to remarry. In other cases, the parent will live alone in the same domicile in which he had been living prior to the spouse's death. Or, the parent will move to new, generally smaller living quarters. He also may move to a senior citizens community or a home for the aged. The trial of reorienting one's life in old age following the death of a spouse is one of the greatest challenges a person can face.

Ruth Gale Elder (1976), in the article *Dying and Society,* notes that most deaths do occur among the elderly and most elderly people are no longer members of a nuclear family. "The burden of emotional suffering most frequently falls on the elderly themselves, when they lose their partners and friends" (p. 10). Adult children, even when sympathetic and loving, cannot fully cope with the surviving parent's dilemma and sense of loss.

The adult children find themselves in a new relationship with their surviving parent. Until now, they had been relatively free of physical and emotional responsibility for their parents. Actually, the parents had taken care of each other. The children related to their parents together, in a unified context. With the death of one parent, the children must enter a new phase in their relationship with the survivor. He necessarily requires more care, more time, more concern. Since the crisis of widowhood is so acute, especially in old age, the children recognize that there is a dramatically increased demand on them to help the surviving parent cope with life.

The sad fact is that the children can never fully solve

the surviving parent's problem. They cannot replace or restore the loss completely. If the surviving parent has a strong personality and is self-sufficient and independent, then the children have an easier time in adjusting to the changed situation. But even the strongest person may go through periods of intense depression and seeming helplessness. It is quite common for newly widowed elderly people to lose confidence in their ability to make decisions. They may turn to their children for advice and guidance. The parent-child roles become somewhat reversed. It is now the parent who is dependent on the children.

Howard Halpern (1976) has pointed out a serious problem: "Just at a time when you are in mourning for the one [parent] who died, the surviving parent may be plunged into an abyss of loneliness, despair, and confusion that severely impairs his independent functioning. . . . For you it is like losing both parents at once even though only one has died. Psychologically, you are orphaned. Practically, to some extent, you have just become the parent of another child" (p. 204).

Basically, children would like to have their surviving parent cared for properly. Ideally, they would like the parent to be able to care for himself with a minimum of extra responsibility placed on the children. After all, they are in the middle years of their own lives and are busy with their families, occupations, and social lives. An elderly parent, especially if he needs considerable time and attention, will disrupt the normal life patterns of the children.

Halpern has correctly observed that taking care of elderly parents, even in a limited way, places new restrictions on one's freedom. It may involve heavy financial burdens, as well as an enormous drain on one's time and energy. These things may contribute to a quiet rage. "And it is not uncommon, when these kinds of burdens are present, for there to be wishes on the part of the children that their parents would die" (pp. 206–207).

Of course, if children harbor such wishes concerning their surviving parent, they may well feel guilt and they also may unknowingly convey their rage to the parent.

In a traditional post-figurative culture, where parents were considered to be the authority figures, children would willingly sacrifice their own comforts for the sake of a surviving parent. This was a normal and approved mode of behavior. No child would want to do otherwise. In spite of any hardships entailed in devoted care to the parent's needs, the adult children would personally assume whatever responsibilities were necessary.

Although this pattern still is evident in our modern society, it is not the norm. Rather than the children adapting their lives to the needs of the parent, the usual pattern is to have the parent adapt to the needs of the children. If they can care for him directly, that is fine. If not, they may arrange for others to care for the parent. In many cases, children do not even live in the vicinity of the parent. They may rely on relatives who live near the parent to provide help; or they may hire someone; or they may convince the parent to enter a facility where he can be cared for.

Increasingly, elder parents wish to maintain their own independence. As long as they are in reasonably good health, they can continue to lead active and productive lives with minimal dependence on their children. Yet even in these cases, thoughtful children constantly have their parent in mind; just as the parents had continued to feel concern for their children when they had gone off on their own.

Where possible, it is advisable for adult orphans to encourage their surviving parent to remain active and independent. If the parent ultimately wishes to remarry, this is a positive development. The parent should not be thought of as a helpless child. Although the initial blow of widowhood drastically shakes the parent's sense of security and well-being, the children should provide constructive guidance and love in assisting the parent to regain self-confidence and meaning in life. When elderly people are treated as though they are helpless and incompetent, they may tend to internalize these feelings about themselves. On the other hand, when they are encouraged and respected, they may tend to regain their self-esteem and personal pride.

Adult orphans should not feel inhibited from speaking about their deceased parent to the surviving one. Actually, such conversations and joint reminiscences are helpful both to the children and the surviving parent. Dealing with reality in a natural way is the best way to help along the mourning process.

I have talked with a number of elderly individuals who have been widowed. Many confided in me, as their rabbi, that they are looking forward to death, when they believe they will be eternally reunited with their departed spouse. They feel as though their lives are not really important anymore. They make the best of things, but do not have a strong will to live.

It is difficult for adult children to deal with parents who have this attitude toward life. To offer logical arguments about the value of life, the good things yet to be experienced, does not alter the parent's inner perception. Moreover, adult children may share the parent's point of view, whether they admit it or not. The children may also think that the parent's life is without real meaning, and they may consciously or subconsciously pass the days and years awaiting the parent's desired death.

On the other hand, other elderly widows and widowers have expressed to me their deep desire to live as vibrantly as possible. They have become active in volunteer work, in sports, in travel, in a variety of hobbies. They express the belief that as long as they have their health, they want to lead constructive and meaningful lives. Certainly, they always feel the absence of their deceased spouse. But they have not given up on their own lives.

Adult children need to pay close attention to the attitudes of their surviving parent. They need to help that parent establish and maintain a sense of value in life. They should not let the parent give up on life, nor should they give up on the parent's life. Many elderly people have done great things for themselves and for society. Losing a spouse is an awesome personal tragedy; but tragedy can be transcended through love, realism, encouragement.

## Siblings

Throughout life, sibling relationships are complex. They are characterized by family affection, love, rivalry, jealousy. Selflessness and selfishness often go hand in hand. While growing up in the parents' household, the siblings develop their relationships—for better or worse; and these relationships continue during adulthood.

With the death of one parent, the siblings find themselves in a new setting. They now must share, in some way, the responsibility of caring for and worrying about the surviving parent. The division of responsibilities is seldom "fair." One brother lives out of town and can't be of much assistance on a day-to-day basis. One sister has an occupation that consumes much of her time and energy. She can't be of much help. One brother is glad to do his utmost— but he has a wife and children and cannot be available to the parent all the time. He will be glad to see the parent once a week, or have him to dinner now and then. One sister, unmarried, feels that all the burden is placed on her. One brother, who constantly makes personal sacrifices for the parent while his siblings do next to nothing, is filled with resentment. Though every family situation will vary, these or similar elements will emerge. They exacerbate tensions among siblings. These feelings have been known to cause permanent breaks in family relationships.

Sometimes, siblings rally together at this time of crisis and demonstrate a true sense of family loyalty. They distribute financial, emotional, and practical responsibilities equitably and all are satisfied. But such harmony, in my experience, is rare, even in the closest and strongest of families.

The deceased parent was often the one who was able to keep the family together, to smooth over the tensions among siblings. With that parent's death, the siblings are "let loose"; ancient antagonisms and jealousies may resurface. The extended family shows signs of crumbling apart.

Problems are even more acute with the death of the second parent. Then there are questions of dividing the parents' estate. Often, siblings have difficulties with each other when dividing the inheritance. Even when the estate is distributed evenly, it is difficult to avoid disagreements about the division of family heirlooms. Many quarrels have raged over items of strong sentimental value that are irreplaceable. Each child wants exactly that article, not a substitute.

Quarrels over the division of the estate can leave permanent scars in sibling relationships. Even if individuals do not verbalize resentment, they may harbor it within their hearts and may behave more coldly to their siblings. It has happened to me that a person on his or her deathbed asked me to obtain something for them from one of their siblings. They lived for years without ever mentioning that they wanted that item from their own parents' home. But, confronting their own death, they finally gained the courage to ask for what they thought all along was rightfully theirs. The resentment had been lingering within them for years.

No material object is worth destroying a family relationship. Siblings should do their best to divide things as evenly and fairly as they can, leaving the least possible chance of resentment among themselves. No one should arrogate for himself the right to do the dividing; rather, everything should be divided in the presence of all involved. If there are any differences, they should be aired right then. As long as everyone feels that the division was made with the consent and good will of all the siblings, it is less likely that one will carry a grudge against the brothers and sisters. Most problems that have come to my attention have stemmed from the fact that one of the siblings simply took a number of valued heirlooms before the others had a chance to discuss the matter. Or, one of the siblings assumed that he was entitled to a greater portion of the estate since he did more for the parents. Instead of acting on one's own, it is preferable to involve all the siblings in the decision making.

It is an excellent idea for the siblings to take part of the estate and dedicate it to a charitable cause in memory of their parents. Sometimes, parents leave such specifications in their wills. But even where no such bequest is made, the children should devote a generous portion of the parents' assets to causes that were important to the parents during their lifetimes.

Such a procedure serves several important purposes. It provides needed funds for worthy causes. It identifies the memory of the parents with causes they supported while living. Moreover, it serves as a reminder to the heirs that the estate after all was created by the parents by their own labor. The children did not earn that estate, and should feel no proprietary right to it. If they are inheriting something from the parents, it should be seen as a gift from the parents, not as an entitlement. By making this mental adjustment, siblings can avoid haggling over the estate.

Once both parents are dead, it becomes somewhat more difficult for the siblings and their families to get together. Very often, the parents were the unifying forces in the family structure. Unless the siblings really like each other, their contacts may subside with the passing of years. They become the matriarchs and patriarchs of their own families and their family life tends to be vertical—towards their children and grandchildren—rather than horizontal, toward their siblings. Unmarried children will find themselves more and more on their own, without strong family connections.

## The Orphan's Spouse

The orphan's spouse is deeply affected by the death of the orphan's parents. The father-in-law and mother-in-law were important characters in the cast of the spouse's life. The spouse shares in the suffering, worrying, financial burdens, personal sacrifices. Moreover, the spouse must cope with the emotional condition of the orphan by offering needed comfort and support.

When the relationship between parents-in-law and children-in-law were close, the death of the parents-in-law may be experienced almost as deeply as the death of one's own parents. The mourning process may be equally applicable to the orphan and the spouse.

An adult who has just lost a parent may sometimes become so involved in his personal crisis that the needs and feelings of the spouse are not adequately considered. Yet it should be understood that the spouse, too, undergoes a personal crisis and has to resolve his own feelings in response to the death of a parent-in-law.

## The Grandchildren

For the grandchildren of the deceased, this may be their first serious experience with losing someone to death. Depending on the age of the children, they will react in different ways. Younger children generally have difficulty understanding the finality of death. They may simply believe that the grandparent has left temporarily, but may return at some future date. Or they may have exaggerated fears about death as well as feelings of anger, frustration, even guilt.

Older children who already have a clearer concept of the meaning of death will have to undergo a period of their own personal mourning. Especially where the grandparent-grandchild relationship was close and loving, there is a keen sense of loss.

In some families, an effort is made to shield the children from the reality of death. They are left out of the funeral discussions, and are not allowed to attend the funeral or go to the cemetery. Where the children are too young to know what is going on, this approach may be acceptable. But older children should not be prevented from attending the funeral and the cemetery. On the contrary, they too have to deal with grief and mourning; their needs as members of the family and as sharers in the loss should be fully recognized.

Memories of grandparents last a lifetime. If parents represent the family traditions and are symbols of the past, grandparents fill these roles even more dramatically. As a child grows into adulthood, good memories of grandparents can provide a deep sense of happiness and well-being.

Adult orphans and their spouses should be sensitive to the feelings of their children and try to understand their own special crisis in losing a grandparent. The young people are engaged in a complicated process of reconciling themselves to the death of a loved one; of learning the lesson of human mortality; of wondering if anyone is concerned about their situation.

It is wise to discuss the death of the parent-grandparent openly and honestly. Deception, even if well-intentioned, seldom serves family members well. When families can openly articulate their feelings, when they can cry together, they can also come closer together and work together in the healing process. In the weeks and months following the death, parents should speak openly about the deceased to the grandchildren, and encourage them to say what is on their minds. This is part of their maturing process and will help shape the way they deal with death in the future.

Ultimately, the survivors will need to readjust their lives due to the death of the parent(s). Relationships among family members are tested. Honesty, generosity of spirit, and sensitivity will enable the survivors to maintain an optimum family structure. Deception, selfishness, jealousy, and self-centeredness can only create or deepen rifts among family members.

Death is an integral part of the human life rhythm. In the normal course of events, individuals will encounter the deaths of grandparents and parents. These encounters will influence one's philosophy of life. Ultimately, everyone will encounter his own death as well and will be drawing on the previous encounters with death of the grandparents and parents. These events are too important to be wrapped in silence, to be denied or camouflaged.

Sometimes, as has been noted, the death of a parent causes a family to become unravelled. Family members move away from each other emotionally. The uniting force, the parent, is no longer present to keep the house in order, so to speak.

Yet sometimes, the death of a parent causes a family to come closer together. The survivors realize the transience of life; the importance of strong family ties; the need to live up to the parent's expectations.

With the death of the parent(s), the survivors have serious decisions to make.

## CHAPTER 10

# A SOCIETY OF ORPHANS

The Bible tells the story of the origin of humanity in the opening chapters of Genesis. God created Adam and Eve and placed them in the Garden of Eden, a comfortable and lush setting, where all their needs could be met easily. They were given only one restriction: not to eat from the tree of knowledge of good and evil. God warned that on the day they ate from that tree, they would die.

Temptation proved too great for our first ancestors. The snake convinced Eve to eat the forbidden fruit, and she gave some to her husband as well. Having thus transgressed God's commandment, they were confronted by God—and were chastised. God told Eve that henceforth she would give birth only with great pain and travail. He told Adam that from then on he would have to toil to raise his own food; by the sweat of his brow would he have his bread.

The story requires interpretation. The details, at first glance, do not seem to fit. First: God said that they would die on the day they ate from the tree of knowledge of good and evil—but they did not die. Second: What was the great knowledge that Adam and Eve attained upon eating from the tree? They are not described in the Bible as having had any exceptional wisdom; they did not leave posterity words of genius. If all they learned from eating the fruit was that they were naked, this hardly strikes us as amazing knowledge. Third: What was the relationship between the punishments God meted out to them and their sin? If Eve sinned by eating, why was she told she would suffer in childbirth? Wouldn't it have been more appropriate to punish her with difficulty in swallowing, or with constant indigestion? And what does Adam's necessity of working to raise food have to do with his having eaten from the tree of knowledge?

The story's meaning becomes clear once we realize what knowledge Adam and Eve attained upon eating the fruit of the tree of knowledge of good and evil. It was the knowledge of death. When God told them that on the day they ate from the tree they would surely die, this meant they would surely understand the real meaning of death in their lives.

Prior to attaining this knowledge, Adam and Eve were much like other animals grazing in paradise. They were not conscious of their own mortality, just as grazing animals do not seem to be preoccupied with contemplation of death. But once they ate from the tree, their consciousness of death emerged. Life was no longer a simple matter. They now felt fear, anxiety, frailty. God's "punishments" were not really punishments at all. They were revelations to Adam and Eve of the consequences of their having eaten from the tree of knowledge. Eve would now realize the pain and danger of childbirth. Unlike an animal who gives birth and who groans with dull animal pain, Eve's pain would be far greater. Not only would she have the physical suffering; but also the emotional and intellectual travail. Childbirth is dangerous: Will I die? And Adam would now learn that he could not simply graze in the Garden of Eden and find the food he needed. Rather, being aware of the responsibility of insuring life against the possibility of death, he would have to cultivate the fields. He now had to plan ahead to provide a food supply to keep himself and his family alive.

In short, this was the turning point when human beings emerged from a kind of calm animal existence to the uniquely human, death-conscious existence. By creating the tree of knowledge of good and evil, God knew full well that Adam and Eve would eat from it. God certainly planned for them to reach the level of full human consciousness. However, He wanted humans to undergo the transition. The "sin" of Adam and Eve was that they ate from the tree too soon.

Indeed, the awareness of death is the distinguishing feature of humanity. All of life is lived in the valley of the shadow of death. The transience of life gives it its intensity, its melancholy, its meaning, its meaninglessness. The rose that flowers today, tomorrow fades—and therefore its beauty while in bloom is more deeply to be appreciated.

Human beings, thus, are paradoxical creatures. We participate in the animal world by the functioning of our bodies; and we also participate in a uniquely human world of consciousness colored by death-awareness. Ernest Becker (1973), in *The Denial of Death*, has written: "Man has a symbolic identity that brings him sharply out of nature. He is a symbolic self, a creature with a name, a life history. He is a creator with a mind that soars out to speculate about atoms and infinity, who can place himself imaginatively at a point in space and contemplate bemusedly his own planet. . . . Yet, at the same time . . . man is a worm and food for worms. This is the paradox: he is out of nature and hopelessly in it. . . . Man is literally split in two: he has an awareness of his own splendid uniqueness in that he sticks out of nature with a towering majesty, and yet he goes back into the ground a few feet in order blindly and dumbly to rot and disappear forever'' (p. 26). Becker goes on to observe: "The knowledge of death is reflective and conceptual, and animals are spared it. They live and they disappear with the same thoughtlessness: a few minutes of fear, a few seconds of anguish, and it is over. But to live a whole lifetime with the fate of death haunting one's dreams and even the most sun-filled days—that's something else" (p. 27).

Consciousness of death, therefore, is the distinguishing feature of humanity. In one way or another, awareness of the possibility and reality of death dominates our entire thinking lives.

## The Eternal Rhythm of History

Ecclesiastes wrote: "A generation comes and a generation goes and there is nothing new under the sun." The rhythm of history seems mechanical and uncontrollable. The individual person's life is only a speck in the eternity of time.

In meditative moods, everyone has pondered the ultimate question of the meaning of life. One of the outstanding sages of the Talmud, Rabbi Yohanan, after completing his study of the book of Job, reflected: "The end of a human is to die and the end of an animal is to be slaughtered and all are fated to die. Happy is the one who was raised in the Torah and whose involvement was in the Torah: he brings pleasure to his Creator. He was raised with a good name and he departed this world with a good name. About such a one, Solomon said: 'A good name is better than precious oil, and the day of death than the day of birth' '' (Berakhot 17a). The rabbi believed that death is natural and inevitable and therefore one should live with dedication to Torah, to ultimate values. A person should earn a good name for himself. If life has been lived in this spirit, then the day of death is better than the day of birth—the struggle though life has been completed, and completed well.

Religious people can find meaning in their lives since they recognize their finiteness and their relationship with an infinite God. This life is ephemeral. It is not the beginning or end of our existence, but only a stage in our existence. The rhythms of life, the birth and death of generations, can be accepted as part of God's design.

It is also possible to attempt to rise above one's own life, to unite oneself spiritually with a greater reality. Religious mystics refer to this phenomenon as union with God. Albert Einstein, though not a spokesman for religion, was intrigued by the mysteries of the universe. He was quoted in the *New York Post,* November 28, 1972: "A human being is a part of the whole, called by us the 'universe,' a part limited in time and space. He experiences himself, his thoughts and feelings as something separated from the rest— a kind of optical delusion of his consciousness. This delusion is a kind of prison for us, restricting us to our personal desires and to affection for a few persons nearest to us. Our task would be to free ourselves from this prison by widening our circle of compassion to enhance all living creatures and the whole of nature in its beauty. Nobody is able to achieve this completely, but the striving for such achievement is in itself a part of the liberation and a foundation for inner security."

In other words, as a person humbly recognizes his limitations and transcends them to feel a strong relationship with the universe, he attains a foundation for inner security. One is no longer frightened by the eternal rhythms of nature, the rhythms of life and death. Rather, one identifies with the rhythms, is part of them, flows with them.

Whether one is religious or not, philosophic or not, the

reality of death is a central concern of one's life. Generally, we can put it out of mind in our normal everyday lives; but we know it's there all the same. Becker has suggested that "reality and fear go together naturally" (p. 17). When Adam and Eve learned that they would die, they also learned the meaning of fear.

Every person is part of the eternal rhythm of history, whether one likes it or not. One can make peace with this truth as best as one can. One may ignore it as much as possible. One may try to defy it in one way or another. But the rhythm is there just the same. It is normal for a generation to be born, to grow, to give birth to a new generation, and then to die. Each generation finds itself orphaned from its parent generation; and each will die, leaving an orphan generation behind. What does this process mean?

## Feeling Lost

Soren Kierkegaard, in *The Concept of Dread* (Lowrie trans., 1957), has proposed that one cannot understand the meaning of life unless one faces the reality of death honestly and directly. "He who is educated by dread [anxiety] is educated by possibility. . . . When such a person . . . knows . . . that he demands of life absolutely nothing, and that terror, perdition, annihilation, dwell next door to every man, and has learned the profitable lesson that every dread which alarms may the next instant become a fact, he will then interpret reality differently" (p. 41).

This idea has been expressed by a variety of thinkers. Becker quotes the words of William James on the subject of salvation through self-despair in Lutheran theology. The individual reaches a deep abyss of despair, a feeling of being nothing. Once one has been able to break down the protective layers of self-deceit and arrive at this "passage into *nothing*," he can go on to find real truth.

Jewish mysticism also contains the idea that wisdom begins when one first attains the state of "nothing." To achieve this state requires serious meditation. Or a dramatic crisis.

Ortega y Gasset (1957) has taught: "And this is the simple truth—that to live is to feel oneself lost—he who accepts it has already begun to find himself, to be on firm ground. Instinctively, as do the shipwrecked, he will look round for something to which to cling, and that tragic, ruthless glance, absolutely sincere, because it is a question of his salvation, will cause him to bring order into the chaos of his life. These are the only genuine ideas; the ideas of the shipwrecked. All the rest is rhetoric, posturing, farce. He who does not really feel himself lost, is without remission; that is to say, he never finds himself, never comes up against his own reality" (p. 157).

If this is so—that we cannot understand the meaning of our lives without first feeling lost and shipwrecked—then the rhythm of the generations plays its role in forcing us into self-analysis. It is built into nature that the parent generation will die, leaving the next generation to feel a sense of being lost, deprived of sure guides. The death of the parent is a crisis which compels the child to the state of the "shipwrecked"—the state which is essential to reach in order to evaluate one's life. This process of self-evaluation, of the search for meaning in life, is incumbent upon each generation of people. One does not inherit the necessary wisdom; one does not learn it in school. "A generation comes and a generation goes, and there is nothing new under the sun": perhaps viewed objectively from outer space, everything still looks the same. But from within the hearts and minds of the generation of orphans, it seems that indeed there is something new. At least, it is new for each of them.

## Survivors

Elias Canetti (1978), in his *Crowds and Power,* discusses at length the psychology of being a survivor. Overtly, one mourns the death of the loved one. Yet, Canetti believes there is also a feeling of triumph in the survivor, the satisfaction that he is still alive. This ambivalence in the survivor is reflected in mourning customs. Canetti notes: "No one who studies the original documents of any religion can fail to be amazed at the power of the dead. There are peoples whose existence is almost wholly dominated by rites connected with them." He goes on: "For the same people who have cause to lament are also survivors. They lament their loss, but they feel a kind of satisfaction in their own survival. They will not normally admit this, even to themselves, for they regard it as improper, but they are always perfectly aware of what the dead man's feelings must be. He is bound to hate them, for they still have what he has lost, which is life. Therefore they call his soul to return in order to convince him that they did not want his death. They remind him how good they were to him while he was amongst them. They count up the practical proofs of their having done everything he would have wanted done. His last wishes are conscientiously carried out; in many places they have the force of law. And behind all they do lies the unshakable conviction that the dead man must hate them for having survived him" (pp. 262–263).

Canetti's case may strike us as being overstated. His notion that the survivors imagine that the dead hate them may have been truer for primitive societies than it is for us today. Yet, he touches on a feeling that deserves attention. Even when the survivors mourn their dead sincerely, they still have the recognition that they themselves are yet alive. This recognition might cause them guilt, secret satisfaction, or a mixture of emotions.

Implicit in Canetti's analysis is the notion that a survivor gains some kind of personal strength when confronted with someone else's death. He realizes that, after all, it was the other person who has died. The survivor has been spared. As we noted earlier, in the story of *The Death of Ivan Ilych,* the surviving friend took consolation in the fact that the death occurred to Ivan, not to him.

When children confront the death of their parents, their sense of themselves as survivors is less than when they experience the loss of a contemporary friend or relative. It is the unspoken expectation that parents will predecease their children. When this happens, the children cannot honestly say that they did not expect this to occur. It is in the nature of things that the children will be survivors of their parents deaths. What kind of "satisfaction in their own survival" will adult orphans have?

Lily Pincus, in her study *Death and the Family,* observed that individuals who were mourning the death of a spouse tended to regress in their behavior. They became more childlike, less independent. But sons and daughters who were mourning the death of a parent did not demonstrate the need for regression. ". . . Rather the opposite: there was a need for self-assertion, for taking the dead parent's place both in relation to the surviving parent in the family and in the relation to the lost parent's position, his work, his creativity. . . . The loss of a parent rouses the need to progress, to mature, to be potent" (p. 210).

Pincus states that an adult son who had never been able to stand up for himself during his father's lifetime "may feel supported in his masculinity by his internalized dead father." An adult orphan may also feel that he is now free of the constraints set upon him by the deceased parent. There is more freedom for self-assertion without fear of parental disapproval. Likewise, there may be a desire to be independent and successful as a way of demonstrating to the deceased parent that the orphan is really a worthy and capable person.

In their study of adults who have experienced the loss of a parent, Malinak, Hoyt, and Patterson (1979) found that about half of their subjects reported having realized some benefit or felt some personal growth. "These gains included an increased sense of strength and self-reliance, a greater caring for friends and loved ones, and a more general quickening to life and deepening of their appreciation of existence." They quote the statement of a professionally oriented woman who reacted to the death of her mother, and at the same time considered the needs of her own two-and-a-half-year-old daughter. "It wasn't until she died that I realized how important it is to be a mother, that time with my daughter is as important to me as work." One graduate student had told them that before his mother's death he felt that he had plenty of time ahead of him to do what he liked with his life. Having experienced the loss of his mother, he came to believe that he would not have enough time to do everything he wanted to do. He moved his doctoral graduation date ahead one year and for the first time allowed himself to feel "truly in love." (p. 1155).

Adult orphans, as survivors, may develop new attitudes upon experiencing the death of a parent. They lament their loss; but they also may find satisfaction in being able to direct their lives in different ways.

But the influence of parents on their children transcends the parents' death. The survivors, even if they feel a new power and independence, still have feelings of inadequacy. They are adults—but still sometimes want to be treated as children. In moments of despair, even mature adults may call out for their mother or father. The parent is in fact or in symbol a source of security and love. S. Ferenczi (1916) wrote: "In our innermost soul we are still children, and we remain so throughout life" (p. 6). Being a survivor, then, is a bittersweet experience.

## The Mystery of the Generations: Continuity and Discontinuity

Human history is the story of generations coming forth, procreating, and then passing on. This rhythm provides the dynamic of human civilization: a blend of continuity and discontinuity.

Continuity in culture is dependent on the transferral of knowledge, values, and technology from one generation to the next. Each generation is not called upon to reinvent the wheel, create world literature, art, music, religion. Each generation is not obliged to build new cities, social struc-tures, commercial patterns. On the contrary, each genera-tion learns from the accumulated wisdom and experience of humanity going back thousands of years.

One of my literature professors told his students that we were the "oldest" people in the history of the world. We stand on the shoulders of ancestors who go back many generations. They have provided us with the basis of our lives. We are "older" in the sense that we are later. With each new generation, humanity becomes older. The mem-bers of the new generation draw on everything that has come before them.

Yet, if the new generation were entirely constrained by the traditions and patterns of the previous generations, there could be no change in human civilization, no development. Old ideas and institutions would be maintained simply be-cause they were the legacy of the earlier generations.

The Bible tells the famous story of the tower of Babel. In that ancient time, shortly after the flood from which

Noah, his family, and the animals on the ark were saved, everyone spoke the same language. They lived in close proximity. The idea emerged to build a tall tower, the top of which would reach to heaven "in order to make for ourselves a name." The people began working on this project; but God ruined their plans. He confused their languages so that they could not understand one another. The project failed. The old unity of society had ended.

I think that this story may be understood as an example of the tension between continuity and discontinuity. The people of the story realized that their society was growing. The children were starting to move away. The control of the parents and all they represented would necessarily diminish if society expanded too much, if the next generation moved away. So they decided to build a tower that could be seen for miles, a tower so tall that it would reach the heavens. In this way, they would make for themselves a name—that is, a clear declaration of their identity and role. Even if people moved away from the town, they would always be within sight of the tower, and they would therefore remember where the seat of authority was located and who the authorities were. The tower was a means of maintaining unity and cohesiveness among all the people, even as society expanded and changed. But this goal was not to be achieved. God confused their languages, as if to say that humanity is not meant to be restricted to one place and one set of human authorities. As society expanded, people needed to be inventive and imaginative. They could draw from tradition; but need not be completely restricted by it.

The rhythm of the generations provides the elements of continuity and discontinuity that make civilization dynamic. Tradition gives us a solid base from which to derive strength and security. But discontinuity allows us to make personal contributions to society. We may respect tradition; we may also evaluate its meaning to us; we may question ideas and institutions and patterns which strike us as problematic.

And this dynamism is linked to the process of the generations. The dominance of one generation over the next is necessarily of limited duration. The parents will die, often when their children are somewhere in the middle of their own lives. These adult orphans have learned the traditions from the parents; now, while they are at the peak of their own lives, their parents die. The remainder of their lives is lived without direct parental control. The mechanism for discontinuity, for breaking with tradition is in place.

Obviously, human life cannot be fitted into such neat categories. Continuity and discontinuity are elements present throughout life. Yet, as a general natural pattern of human existence, this description offers insight. The first part of one's life, one lives under the control and strong influence of parents—the sources of tradition. As one grows older, elements of discontinuity assert themselves more. The child becomes more independent, braver. As the child grows to midlife, the parents die. The child reacts to their death; and with the passage of time recognizes his own authority and creativity. Then comes the recognition that the child has become the older generation, a blend of traditional authority and independent creativity.

The rhythm of the generations is a rhythm of stability and change, tradition and dynamism, respect for the past and dreams for the future. We are a society of orphans.

# REFERENCES

Angel, M.D. *Aging and dying as aspects of living*. United Jewish Appeal Young Leadership Cabinet Judaica Series, May, 1984.

Aries, P. *The hour of our death*. H. Weaver, trans. New York: Knopf, 1981.

———. *Western attitudes towards death*. P.M. Ranum, trans. Baltimore and London: Johns Hopkins University Press, 1974.

Becker, E. *The denial of death*. New York and London: The Free Press, 1973.

Berne, E. *Games people play*. New York: Grove Press, 1964.

*Bhagavad-Gita*. S. Prabhavananda, trans. New York: Mentor Books, 1962.

Blidstein, G. *Honor thy father and mother*. New York: Ktav, 1976.

Borkenau, F. The concept of death. In R. Fulton, Ed. *Death and identity*. New York: Charles Press, 1966.

Butler, R. The life review: An interruption of reminiscence in the aged. *Psychiatry*, 1963, *119*, 721–728.

Canetti, E. *Crowds and power*. New York: Viking, 1978.

DeVries, P. *Let me count the ways*. Boston and Toronto: Little, Brown and Company, 1965.

Elder, R. Dying and society. In R. Caughill, Ed. *The dying patient: a supportive approach.* Boston: Little, Brown and Co., 1976.

Ferenczi, S. *Sex in psycho-analysis.* New York: Dover Publications, 1956.

Freud, S. *Civilization and its discontents.* J. Strachey, trans. and Ed. New York: Norton, 1961. (originally published, 1930)

———. *Mourning and melancholia.* J. Strachey, trans. and Ed. Standard edition, *14,* 237–260, London: Hogarth Press, 1917.

Fulton, R. Comments. In N. Linzer, ed. *Understanding bereavement and grief.* New York: Yeshiva University Press, 1977.

Furman, E. *A child's parent dies.* New Haven and London: Yale University Press, 1974.

Gottsegen, M. G. Management of mourning of a dead or dying parent. *American Journal of Psychotherapy, 1977, 31,* 36–42.

Halpern, H.M. *Cutting loose.* New York: Simon and Schuster, 1976.

Harris, T. *I'm O.K. you're O.K.* New York: Harper and Row, 1969.

Hastings, J. Ed. *Encyclopaedia of religion and ethics.* Volume 6. New York: Charles Scribner's Sons, 1928, 243–306.

Hecht, B. *A child of the century.* New York: Simon and Schuster, 1954.

Hirsch, S.R. *The Pentateuch, Exodus.* I. Levy, trans. Gateshead: Judaica Press, 1982.

Kalish, R. The effects of death upon the family. In L. Pearson, Ed. *Death and dying: Current issues in the treatment of a dying person.* Cleveland: The University Press, 1969.

Kastenbaum, R. *Death, society and human experience.* St. Louis: Mosby, 1977.

Kierkegaard, S. *The concept of dread.* W. Lowrie, trans. Princeton: Princeton University Press, 1957.

Kneisl, C.R. Grieving: A response to loss. In R. Caughill, Ed. *The dying patient: a supportive approach.* Boston: Little, Brown and Co., 1976.

Kubler-Ross, E. *On death and dying.* New York and London: Macmillan, 1975.

———. *Questions and answers on death and dying.* New York and London: Macmillan, 1974.

Lamm, M. *The Jewish way in death and mourning*. Middle Village: Jonathan David, 1972.

Lerner, M. My father "moved". In J. Riemer, Ed. *Jewish reflections on death*. New York: Schocken Books and The Jewish Publication Society of America, 1974.

Lewis, C. S. *A grief observed*. London: Faber and Faber, 1961.

Linzer, N. *The Jewish family*. New York: Human Sciences Press, 1984.

———. Ed. *Understanding bereavement and grief*. New York: Yeshiva University Press, 1977.

Long, J.B. The death that ends death in Hinduism and Buddhism. In E. Kubler-Ross, Ed. *Death, the final stage of growth*. Englewood Cliffs: Prentice-Hall, 1975.

Malinak, D., Hoyt, M. & Patterson, V. Adults' reactions to the death of a parent: A preliminary study. *American Journal of Psychiatry*, September 1979, 1152–1156.

Marris, P. Comments. In N. Linzer, Ed. *Understanding bereavement and grief*. New York: Yeshiva University Press, 1977.

———. *Loss and change*. New York: Pantheon Books, 1974.

Mead, M. *Culture and commitment: A study of the generation gap*. Garden City: Natural History Press and Doubleday and Company, 1970.

Miller, J. Children's reactions to the death of a parent: A review of the psychoanalytic literature. *The Journal of the American Psychological Association*, 1971, *19*, 679–719.

Mitford, J. *The American way of death*. New York: Simon and Schuster, 1962.

Myerhoff, B. *Number our days*. New York: Touchstone, 1978.

Nichols, R. & J. Funerals: A time for grief and growth. In E. Kubler-Ross, Ed. *Death, the final stage of growth*. Englewood Cliffs: Prentice-Hall, 1975.

Ortega y Gasset, J. *The revolt of the masses*. New York: Norton, 1957.

Parkes, C.M. *Bereavement: Studies of grief in adult life*. New York: International Universities Press, 1972.

Penfield, W. Memory mechanisms. *A.M.A. Archives of Neurology and Psychiatry*, 1952, *67*, 178–198.

Peretz, D. Reaction to loss. In B. Schoenberg, A. Carr, D. Peretz, and A. Kutscher, Eds. *Loss and grief: Psychological management in medical practice.* New York: Columbia University Press, 1971.

Pincus, L. *Death and the family.* New York: Pantheon Books, 1974.

Riemer, J. Ed. *Jewish reflections on death.* New York: Schocken Books and Jewish Publication Society of America, 1974.

Shamosh, A. The great confession. J. Levy, trans. *Moment,* January 1983, 49.

Silverman, P. Comments. In N. Linzer, Ed. *Understanding bereavement and grief.* New York: Yeshiva University Press, 1977.

Slater, R. Comments. In N. Linzer, Ed. *Understanding bereavement and grief.* New York: Yeshiva University Press, 1977.

Soloveichik, J. *Halakhic man.* L. Kaplan, trans. Philadelphia: Jewish Publication Society of America, 1983a.

———. Kodesh and Chol. In a *Reader for students of Yeshiva University,* New York, 1983b.

*The teaching of buddha.* Tokyo: Bukkyo Dendo Kyokai, 1966.

Tolstoy, L. *Death of Ivan Ilych.* New York: Basil Blackwell, 1960.

Wolfenstein, M. Comments. In N. Linzer, Ed. *Understanding bereavement and grief.* New York: Yeshiva University Press, 1977.

# INDEX

159

# DEATH AT
# THE CROSSROADS

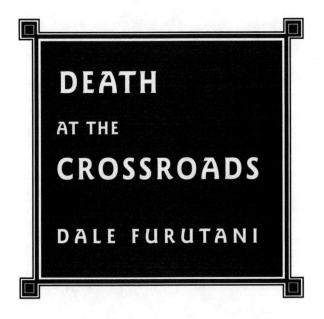

# DEATH
## AT THE
# CROSSROADS

## DALE FURUTANI

*A SAMURAI MYSTERY*

**WILLIAM MORROW AND COMPANY, INC.**

**NEW YORK**

It is the policy of William Morrow and Company, and its imprints and affiliates,
recognizing the importance of preserving what has been written, to print the books we
publish on acid-free paper, and we exert our best efforts to that end.

Library of Congress Cataloging-in-Publication Data

Furutani, Dale.
    Death at the crossroads  :  a samurai mystery  /  Dale Furutani.—
1st ed.
        p.      cm.
    ISBN 0-688-15817-X
    I.  Title.
PS3556.U778D38    1998
813'.54—dc21                                                                98-10007
                                                                                CIP

Printed in the United States of America

First Edition

1   2   3   4   5   6   7   8   9   10

BOOK DESIGN BY ANN GOLD

www.williammorrow.com

## To Steve

His life was marked by an abiding faith, a loving heart, a generous
spirit, and a wonderful sense of adventure.
But it was extinguished much too soon.
We miss him.

# AUTHOR'S NOTE

The idea for this trilogy was conceived while I was sitting in a seventeenth-century Japanese farmhouse in the Sankei-en garden in Yokohama. I was sipping a steaming cup of green tea and marveling at floorboards worn glass smooth by centuries of bare feet crossing them. It occurred to me that in fiction about ancient Japan, the people who lived in that farmhouse were often just stage props to some greater pageantry, such as the fight to become the Shogun. Yet they also had stories to tell, and I decided to tell at least some of them through the vehicle of a mystery trilogy.

Having chosen the actors, my next decision was to select the time of the action. To most Japanese, the year 1603 has the same familiarity to it as the year 1776 has to Americans; 1603 is the year Tokugawa Ieyasu declared himself to be Shogun of Japan, and it marked a turning point in Japanese history. For the next 250 years, Japanese culture, politics, and the social order were regulated by the oppressive hand of the Tokugawa Shogunate. This period has been covered by many works of fiction and nonfiction, but I was interested in the hinge of history—that brief period when an entire nation was in the midst of a pervasive and profound change, before the Tokugawa Shogunate had extended its tentacles into every aspect of Japanese life.

My intent is to write this trilogy as entertainment. To the best of my ability, I've tried to be accurate in my rendition of Japanese life in 1603, but I've obviously had to take some liberties in the interest of creating a work of fiction.

For instance, seventeenth-century Japanese, like seventeenth-century English, would sound stilted and strange to modern ears if translated faithfully. In addition, Japanese court language, with its stentorian cadence, would soon grow tiresome to read if carried throughout a book. For these reasons, I've tried to give a bit of the flavor of the speech patterns while using modern dialogue.

I hope these concessions to telling my story won't introduce anachronisms or offend scholars whose knowledge of this period far exceeds mine.

—DALE FURUTANI

# MAJOR CHARACTERS

In this book, names follow the Japanese convention, in which the family name is listed first, then the given name. Therefore, in "Matsuyama Kaze," Matsuyama is the family name and Kaze the given name.

**Aoi,** the village prostitute
**Boss Kuemon,** the bandit chief
**Hachiro,** a young man who is part of Boss Kuemon's gang
**Ichiro,** the headman for Suzaka village
**Jiro,** the charcoal seller
**Manase,** Lord of the District
**Matsuyama Kaze,** a ronin samurai
**Nagahara Munehisa,** a Sensei (teacher) who studies Heian Japan
**Nagato Takamasu,** the District Magistrate
**Okubo,** a boyhood acquaintance of Kaze's
**The Sensei,** Kaze's mentor

# SUZAKA VILLAGE
# AND SURROUNDING AREA

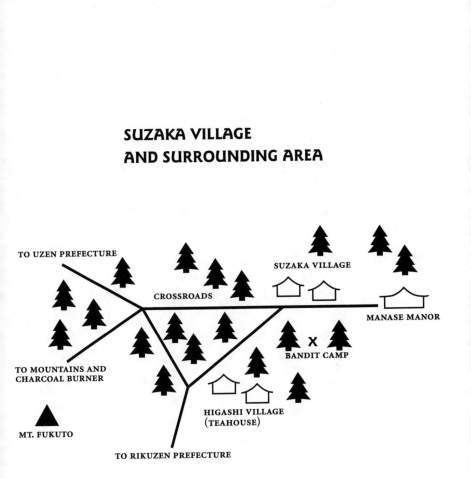

# DEATH AT
# THE CROSSROADS

**CHAPTER 1**

*Deep mist hides in the
mountains. A rabbit crouches
under the dampness.*

## Japan, the Sixteenth Year of Emperor Go-Yozei (1603)

"**A**re you ready to die?"

The young *samurai*'s face was a mask of anger, and spittle flew from his mouth as he issued his challenge. Three of the other four passengers in the tiny boat hugged the gunwales, bent back by the young swordsman's words. The fourth, the object of the samurai's fury, sat calmly at the back of the boat, near the oarsman, who had stopped rowing as the confrontation started to escalate.

"Well? Why won't you answer? I am a student of the Yagyu school of swordsmanship, and I have challenged you!"

The muscular man in the back of the boat took the time to wipe a bit of spit that had landed on the back of his hand with the sleeve of his *kimono* before answering. His other hand held a single *katana*, a samurai's sword, in a plain black scabbard. He was clearly a samurai, but his head wasn't shaved in samurai fashion, and he had the appearance of a *ronin*, a masterless samurai who wandered about looking for employment.

A few moments before, a group of five had gathered by the riverbank to be ferried across the stream: two samurai, two peasants, and a merchant, all thrown together by their common need to cross the river. Instead of politely introducing himself to the older samurai, the youth had immediately started talking about his training in the Yagyu style of fencing and his prowess with the sword. At first the peasants and merchant had found the talk entertaining, because skill with a sword was valued above all else in a warrior culture. But soon after embarking on the voyage across the river, the youth had become increasingly boastful of his swordsmanship, asking the other samurai to confirm that the Yagyu school of fencing was the greatest in the land. When the middle-aged samurai remained silent, the youth had become agitated, taking the older man's silence as a judgment on both his school and his own skill as a swordsman. Standing in the bow of the flat-bottomed boat, the young samurai faced the older man, his hand on the hilt of one of the two swords stuck in his sash.

"Why don't you answer? Are you ready to die?" the young man screamed.

The other warrior looked at the aggressive samurai thoughtfully, his thick black eyebrows furrowing together into a V. He said, "A true samurai is always ready to die. But I am from a quite different school of fencing. Like Tsukahara Bokuden, I am from the 'No Sword' school of fencing, and I am quite certain a man of your character can be defeated by it."

"No Sword?" the young man repeated. "That's ridiculous! How can a samurai fight with no sword? Now you have pushed me beyond tolerance! I demand that this impudent insult be cleansed with blood. I challenge you to a duel."

"All right," said the older man. He pointed to a small island in the middle of the stream. "Boatman, stop there. It's a good place for a duel."

Nodding, but with fear on his face, the boatman sculled the boat toward the island. He stood at the end of the boat, both propelling and steering it with a single, two-piece oar that trailed the boat like the tail on a fish. When the boat hit the shore, the young man leaped out of the boat and landed on the sandy shore of the island. He immediately drew his katana, ran a few feet onto the island, and took an aggressive stance, with both hands on the hilt and the blade in the "aimed at the eye" position.

"Come on!" he shouted to the samurai in the boat. "Let's see if this ridiculous No Sword school of fencing can defeat one who has studied with the Yagyu!"

The other man calmly stood up and handed his sword to the boatman. "Here, hold this," he said. "For this duel I truly need no sword."

The boatman clumsily reached out for the sword, releasing his grip on the oar as he did so. Before the oar could clatter to the bottom of the boat, the samurai caught it, lifted it out of the guides in the back of the boat that held it in place when it was used for steering and propulsion, and used it to push the boat away from the island.

"What are you doing!" the youth screamed.

"I am defeating you with the No Sword school of fencing. If you had truly studied with the Yagyu, you would know that fencing is more than just killing people; it is developing all your faculties, including your mind. Now, because of your stupidity and without using my sword, I can continue my journey and also eliminate the impediment of a troublesome character."

The boat was away from the island and moving with the current before the young samurai could get back to the shore. "I think a cold swim will be excellent training for you," the older man shouted as the youth started running along the shore. "Just as a bucket of cold water will dampen the ardor of amorous dogs, a dose of cold water will also be good for a young man too full of himself for his own good and the good of others."

The swiftly flowing stream drew the boat away from the island at an increasing pace and, before the young man reached the final spit of land on the tiny island, the boat was much too far away to catch. Too angry to speak, the young man jumped about in rage in ankle-deep water, waving his sword and watching the boat draw away from him. He heard the sound that all samurai, caught up in their importance and honor, dreaded: The occupants of the boat were laughing at him.

Jiro the charcoal seller had many things on his mind, but death was not one of them. He was late, and his regular customers would scold him if they had to use branches and twigs in their *hibachi* instead of charcoal to heat water for their morning tea. Worse yet, if the Lord's household needed charcoal, Jiro would be beaten if he wasn't there to provide it. The Lord was neither patient nor understanding. Several villagers had felt the cudgels of the Lord's men, and Jiro was not anxious to join their number.

Around him, mist clung tenaciously to the jagged folds that formed the ravines and valleys of the mountains. Through the low-lying white haze, the ragged black pines and reddish cryptomeria poked through the white curtain, looking like some enigmatic calligraphy of the gods, a message written with the slashing brush strokes of trunks and branches on a shifting silver paper.

The sun had been in the sky for half an hour, but its beams had not yet penetrated to the bottom of the steep-sided valley. In the blue gloom of this extended dawn, Jiro padded along a narrow trail, finding his way by habit and instinct as much as by sight.

Hung on his back was an enormous woven basket filled with charcoal. The basket was draped from his shoulders by twisted ropes made of summer grass and padded with torn-up rags. A line reached from the basket to a headband to help stabilize the load and to bear some of the weight. Jiro was naked except for a homespun loincloth, but despite the chill of the mountains and the morning, he was sweating from his steady run with a heavy load.

Pad, pad, pad . . . His naked feet, encrusted with an armor of horny calluses built over a fifty-year life span, slapped against the dirt of the trail, forming a gentle rhythm that complemented Jiro's rolling gait. He used the oscillation of the weighty basket to help him down the path, shifting the weight first to one side, then the other, calling on his long years of experience to work with the pendulum forces of momentum instead of fighting them. This was a metaphor for how Jiro dealt with life. Every Japanese child was given the example of how the flexible bamboo could survive a storm that would snap a rigid tree, and they were admonished to follow this example.

He was making good time. Perhaps he wouldn't be too late after all.

In his mind he started practicing a speech. By nature he was a taciturn man, but his part-time profession of selling charcoal in the small village of Suzaka forced him to communicate with his customers. That was sometimes the hardest part of having his small charcoal business, because words did not come easily to Jiro's mind or tongue. When he wasn't selling charcoal, he was farming, and he much preferred the life of the soil to the life of commerce.

With farming he could go for days without making a sound, save for the occasional grunt as he dug his hoe into an especially stubborn piece of earth. The tender green shoots only required a gentle touch, sunlight, and water to respond with their bounty, and oily words were not necessary for their growth. The birds and rabbits were startled by raucous human speech, and Jiro's habitual silence allowed him to glide in and out of their world with little or no interruption. When a man talked, he couldn't listen to the subtle rustle of tall grass bending in the quickening breeze or the frothing music of a nearby stream. With so much to listen to, Jiro had no problems being silent. It was communicating with humans that always challenged him.

Because he was such a quiet man, Jiro always marveled that he had managed to marry Yuko. In fact, however, his marriage had been arranged with almost no words spoken, at least on Jiro's part.

Jiro's mother died less than a year after his father, when Jiro was still a teenager, so the elder women of the village took it into their hands to arrange a wife for the young man. In an agrarian village, the men and women worked as a unit, and it was simply taken for granted that Jiro would need a wife, even if he was taking no action to get one. In a cultured family, the marriage would have been arranged through intermediaries, complete with subtle hints, a "chance" meeting, and formal matchmakers, but in the rough life of the village, it was handled more directly, while the elder women sat around weaving straw sandals.

A bundle of straw was taken and twisted into a skein. Then the skein was plaited with others, forming a rough base for a sandal. Then cord or strips of rag were used to form ties for the sandal. Despite its rough appearance, the resulting footwear was surprisingly durable and comfortable. This was done as a community project by the older women of the village. It had a utilitarian product as its output in the form of the sandals, but a more important function was the chance for an informal council among the women who wielded considerable influence in the village.

"Who shall we get for Jiro?" one of the elder women of the village asked bluntly, grabbing a fist full of straw.

"There aren't too many choices," said another, repeating what they all knew anyway.

"What about the daughter of the barrel maker?" another mused, throwing out a trial candidate.

"She is a tart," Elder Grandma, the oldest matriarch in the village, said bluntly. "Jiro will have a hard enough time without his mother there. Any wife who doesn't have a strong mother-in-law can be trouble, and that girl will be a handful even with a strong woman to guide her."

"How about my daughter?" Yuko's mother said quietly. As a suggestion for a match, it was explosive. The other women were flabbergasted. Gnarled hands stopped the plaiting of straw into sandals. Faces creased and weathered brown from years of working in the sun took on expressions of surprise and even shock.

Jiro was not handsome, and his family's plot of land was far from the biggest, so it was astounding that Yuko's mother had let it be known that her daughter was available. Yuko was one of the prettiest girls in the small village, although at age fifteen she was a bit past the average age when girls got married. The natural assumption was that

Yuko's mother was waiting for an exceptional match for her daughter, perhaps even hoping that the pretty girl would catch the eye of a lord or samurai so she could become a rich man's concubine.

The other village women considered Yuko far too clever and far too pretty for Jiro, and said so. But Yuko's mother had seen kindness and a good heart and a hard worker in the young man, and she knew it would be a match where Yuko would not be abused and, most likely, would be in charge. She wanted that, because of all of her eight children, Yuko was the favorite.

Jiro was presented with the proposition of Yuko as a wife by a small delegation of village women showing up at his hut one morning before he went to his rice paddy to work. The bewildered teen, still smarting from the death of his parents, simply accepted the collective wisdom of the elder women of the village and nodded his agreement. Within a few days, there was a small wedding feast, where the people of the village were fed *sake, tofu,* and some fish. Yuko served the feast and made sure each of the guests went home with a bit of food wrapped in a broad leaf. After cleaning up, Yuko moved into Jiro's hut, and they were tentatively considered married, pending the birth of their first child.

Although smart, Yuko wasn't talkative herself, and she and Jiro made an excellent match. Through the shared communion of their silence, they went through the stages of awkward adjustment, awakening sexual enthusiasm, then love and friendship. The elder women of the village soon looked upon the bond developed by the couple with proprietary pride, a symbol of their matchmaking abilities, forgetting their initial skepticism over the union of the pretty girl and the awkward farmer.

Starting the charcoal-selling business as a sideline to farming was Yuko's idea. Yuko was always a thinker, and prior to Jiro's going into business, the people of Suzaka village would have to make the long journey into the mountains to seek out charcoal sellers themselves. It was a constant source of complaint among the women, and in this complaint Yuko saw opportunity. She decided that by charging a small amount, a neat profit could be made without the others in the village feeling that she and Jiro had become like greedy merchants.

At first, Jiro thought he was incapable of operating this small sideline. He was strong enough and hardy enough to go into the mountains to get the charcoal, but selling it was something else. Charcoal selling, like all village selling, involved a whole symphony of speech. First was the shouting: walking through the village with the basket and singing out, "Charcoal! Fine charcoal!" Jiro actually didn't mind this part because it wasn't directed to anyone in particular. But next he was expected to make real conversation. When a woman heard his call and emerged from a hut with a basket or pot for the charcoal, she expected entertainment, not just goods.

A housewife expected a polite ritual of greetings and small talk from any village vendor. It was often the high point of her day, and a purchase usually involved a chance to catch up with news and gossip. In this, Jiro felt hopeless and awkward, even though his customers were lifelong neighbors. With Yuko's patient support and tutoring in the fine art of gossip, Jiro was able to make a modest success of their small business, and Jiro's periodic trips into the mountains became a natural adjunct to the rhythm of life, like the spring rains and the planting and the harvest and the winter snows.

Yuko died in childbirth, trying to give life to their first son, who also died. By village custom, Yuko wasn't really considered Jiro's wife until she had borne him a child, but this didn't make his grief any less. Uncharacteristically, Jiro rebelled against all efforts of the village women to get him a second wife. He would not bend like the bamboo to the collective wisdom of the village. He could never articulate the reason for rebuffing the matchmaking efforts of the elder women, even to himself, but in his heart he loved and cherished the memory of Yuko and couldn't conceive of replacing her.

So for over thirty years he had remained alone. And although he was never as articulate as when he was under the tutelage of Yuko, he kept the charcoal-selling business in addition to his modest farm.

The extra income, usually in the form of rice instead of money, was useful because it allowed him to buy things which would otherwise require the help of a wife and family to make. If it weren't for the fact that he remained the only charcoal seller in the village, Jiro knew his business would surely suffer because of his lack of conversational skills, but no one else seemed inclined to take on the hard and sometimes dangerous task.

On this morning he was fretting because to every customer he had to make a speech and they would shower him with abuse and anger. He was raising prices.

The day before he had gone into the mountains to buy charcoal from one of the solitary charcoal burners. For once, Jiro wished he had the gift of conversation when he was told that the price of charcoal was being doubled because of the danger from Boss Kuemon's bandits.

Instead of coherent protest, all Jiro could do was scowl and stare at the charcoal maker in mute rebuke. Finally, he was able to splutter, "That's too much. I'll buy from someone else."

"There is no one else," the charcoal burner said blandly. "Kintaro was killed last week, and I'm the only one burning charcoal in these parts."

Jiro took this news with surprise. "Killed?"

"The bandits wanted salt and *miso*, and I guess Kintaro put up a fuss. He said he was running low on salt the last time I saw him, and I guess he thought if he gave the bandits all he had, he wouldn't be able to make the offerings of salt and sake to the Stove God when he made the charcoal. *Baka!* Fool! When they come and tell me to give them things, I just give them. You can always get more salt or miso or sake. There is only one life." The burner held out his hands in the universal gesture of helplessness. "It's stupid to fight them."

"This place is going to the dogs."

"Yes, and we know why," the burner said, leaving a long pause as an invitation to Jiro to amplify.

Jiro ignored it. He wouldn't make idle small talk unless required to by a customer, and he also knew better than to criticize the administration of the District by the new Lord. After thinking of alternate courses of action and finding none, he thrust out a container of homemade sake and said, "Here."

The burner was not surprised by the lack of transition between business talk and a gift. In the complicated ballet of Japanese commerce, one usually accompanied the other, although Jiro was not the most skilled practitioner of the art of moving from one to the other.

"Thanks!" the burner said with a grin. "I know you probably didn't bring enough money for the new, higher price. I'll give you credit for it, and you can pay me the next time you come out for charcoal. Come! Warm yourself by the fire. You must be cold after your walk out from the village."

Jiro accepted the hospitality and spent the night drinking with the burner. The sake was rich and sweet, with plenty of grains of fermented rice still floating around in the liquid. The burner, after weeks alone in the mountains cutting down trees to make charcoal, was garrulous. Jiro responded with grunts and short phrases, but the burner didn't mind. The Japanese believe communication involves the whole being, not just words, and Jiro's grunts and gestures, after a few drinks, seemed as eloquent as the spoken remarks of any companion the burner could want.

Because of the drink, Jiro woke up later than planned. It was still before the dawn, but he was tardy returning to the village. The sky was still black, and familiar stars made their stately procession across the heavens. Peeking over the top of Mount Fukuto, Jiro could see the stars of the Two Lovers very close to each other. They had already come together for their annual kiss that marked the fall, yet the weather was still teetering on the last edge of summer.

In haste, Jiro gathered up his basket of charcoal and paid what money he had brought with him to the burner. Now, as he ran along the path back to the crossroads and the village, he racked his brain to figure out the best way to explain the higher prices to his customers in the village. As usual, his lack of skill in using words failed him, and he couldn't come up with a satisfactory speech that would soften the blow. As the sun rose in the sky, burning off some of the mist loitering at the bottom of the mountain valley and revealing the low-lying *hagi,* or bush clover, Jiro still wrestled with the problem.

Jiro was so involved in composing what he was going to say about the higher prices that when he got to the crossroads he almost didn't see the body exposed by the thinning silver mist until he ran into it.

The body was lying on its side in the center of the crossroads. The crossroads marked the meeting of four paths. One went east to the village of Suzaka, where Jiro lived. One led north out of the area and into the prefecture of Uzen and the rivers beyond. Another led south to the village of Higashi and the prefecture of Rikuzen, and the last path, the one that Jiro was on, went west, deeper into the mountains toward Mount Fukuto.

The body was that of a man, perhaps in his early thirties. He was dressed in a brown kimono with gray *hakama,* or pants. It was the dress of a man intent on traveling. The legs were splayed and one of the man's sandals was missing. The remaining sandal, precariously clinging to the other foot, was the coarse-rope sandal of a traveler or pilgrim.

His hair was bound up in the style favored by merchants. The expression on his face was one of pain, and his eyes were squeezed shut, as if he could avoid the darkness of death by eclipsing it with a darkness of his own making.

In his back was an arrow. A bloodstain spread from the point where the arrow penetrated, running parallel to the ground and up toward the man's head. The arrow was well made, with a straight shaft of clear, dark wood, and gray feathers, finely trimmed.

Jiro had seen death many times before. Some of the deaths were violent. It was hard not to see violent death when you lived in a land where over three hundred years of lethal clan warfare had left its legacy. Yet coming across the body so suddenly and unexpectedly unnerved him.

He skidded to an abrupt halt, the heavy basket of charcoal pushing against his back and shoulders. He dipped backward with a familiar move that simultaneously placed the charcoal basket on the ground and released the shoulder and head lines. He advanced toward the body tentatively, double-checking to make sure the man was not breathing. Jiro squatted next to the body, poked him, and said, "*Oi!* You!" No movement. He touched the face of the man. The man's cheek was cold and lifeless.

Jiro was annoyed. On a morning when mundane problems like being late or explaining a price increase loomed so large, the discovery of this body caused a new level of anxiety. With the increasing breakdown of safety in the District, it wouldn't surprise him to find bodies in the middle of the village next.

He had to decide what he would do about his discovery. He could avoid the most trouble if he just ignored the body and continued into the village, but the next people through the crossroads would report it, and Jiro might somehow be implicated in the murder.

Of course, when he did report it, he would have to deal with Magistrate Nagato, and that would involve more disruption and unpleasantness. It might even involve a beating if the bullying Magistrate took it into his head to administer one, just on general principle. Jiro sighed. What an annoyance!

Suddenly, behind him, Jiro heard a sound on the path leading to Uzen. He looked around and saw a man rounding a bend in the path, walking toward him. Like the dead man, he was also dressed in the kimono and hakama of a man traveling. Unlike the dead man, this new stranger was clearly a samurai. Over one shoulder, he negligently had a katana in its scabbard, one hand holding the hilt. The black lacquer of the plain scabbard caught the intense morning sun, and Jiro was mesmerized by the glint of the weapon's sheath.

As soon as the man saw Jiro, his thick eyebrows crashed together into a frowning V. "*Nani?* What?" the man asked, quickening his steps.

Jiro thought of grabbing his charcoal basket for a brief second, then abandoned the idea. He sprang to his feet and nimbly hopped over the body. Then he ran down the path to the village as fast as his legs could carry him, not once looking behind him.

The samurai approached the corpse and stopped next to it. He looked at the body for several minutes, then he thoughtfully looked down the path where Jiro had neatly disappeared.

## CHAPTER 2

*Monkeys marching all*
*in a row. Fierce martial stance.*
*What fine samurai!*

The parade was more like a comic scroll painting than a military procession.

In the lead was Ichiro, the village headman. He was a loose collection of lanky bones and oversize joints covered by yellowing skin. He carried a *naginata,* a type of spear with a broad sword blade for a point. He handled the weapon as if it were an alien device rather than something he had been drilled in. Ichiro was naked except for a loincloth and leather cuffs on his wrist, which were supposed to act as armor. Across his forehead he had a plate of metal strapped on by thin leather thongs. It would take a skilled swordsman, consciously trying to hit this headband, for it to provide any protection.

Behind Ichiro came Nagato Takamasu, the District Magistrate. His corpulent body strained at the cloth of his blue kimono, and the two swords that marked him as a samurai stuck out from his body like the spines of a blowfish. Nagato's enormous belly jiggled as he waddled along. In an age when food was precious, Nagato's fat marked him as someone of relative wealth and privilege.

Following Nagato were two guardsmen. Only one had a metal tipped spear; the other had a locally made spear of sharpened bamboo. One man wore a breastplate of chain mail as armor, but aside from this flimsy shield they both had only loincloths.

At the tail of the procession was Jiro. Jiro was supposed to lead the party, but he was put at the end as a matter of rank. As a result, every time Nagato wanted to ask how far it was to the body, the message had to be passed up and down the line by the two guardsmen. Jiro silently cursed the stupidity of the military as the conversation turned to farce.

"How far to the body?" Nagato asked.

"How far to the body?" the first guardsman repeated.

"How far to the what?" the second asked.

"The body, the body, baka!"

"Magistrate Nagato wants to know something," the second guardsman said to Jiro.

Jiro, who couldn't hear the telegraphed conversation, said, "*Hai!* Yes!"

"Where's the body?"

"The crossroads," Jiro answered, bewildered at why Nagato couldn't remember what Jiro had reported when he first came to the village.

"It's at the crossroads," the second guardsman said.

"What's at the crossroads?" the first asked.

"The body, the body, stupid," the second said, mimicking the first.

The first guardsman looked over his shoulder and glared at the second. Then he turned to Nagato and said, "It's at the crossroads, sir."

"Of course it's at the crossroads," Nagato snapped. "Ask him how far from here."

"How far from here?" the first relayed.

"How far is the body from the crossroads?" the second relayed.

Puzzled, Jiro answered, "It's right at the crossroads."

"To the right at the crossroads," the second said.

The first said to Nagato, "We go to the right at the crossroads, sir."

"To the right?" Nagato said, puzzled. "I thought he said the body was right at the crossroads. Ask him how far to the right."

"How far to the right of the crossroads is it?"

"How far to the right?"

"How far to the right?" Jiro said perplexed. "How far to the right is what?"

"The body, stupid!"

"The body isn't to the right of the crossroads."

"It isn't right."

"He says it isn't to the right, sir. Perhaps it's to the left. These stupid farmers can't tell right from left!"

"The body's to the left at the crossroads?" Nagato said. "I thought he said it was right at the crossroads."

The scrambled conversation would have continued for some time, except that Ichiro turned a bend and saw the body lying in the middle of the crossroads. Ichiro jerked to a halt, his naginata at the ready, as if the body would spring back to life and attack him.

Nagato almost walked into the butt of Ichiro's naginata and came to a sudden halt himself. This unexpected stop echoed down the line as the first guardsman stopped short to avoid running into Magistrate Nagato, and the second guardsmen hit the first, bumping the first into Nagato's back, despite the best efforts of the first guardsman not to hit the Magistrate.

At the bump of the first guardsman Nagato turned and roared in anger, "Baka! Fool! What do you think you're doing!"

The guardsman fell to his knees in a deep bow of apology. "Excuse me, sir! Excuse me! It's that stupid fool behind me. He pushed me! It was not my fault!"

Jiro, who had witnessed the entire sequence from his vantage point at the end of the procession, suppressed a laugh at the discomfort of the Magistrate and the guardsmen.

Nagato pointed at the body and yelled, "Don't just sit there banging your miserable head on the ground! Get up and investigate the body!"

"Yes, sir!" The guardsman got to his feet and ran to the body, with the second guardsman nipping at his heels. When the first guardsman tried to stop as he reached the body, the second guardsman ran into him again. That tumbled both men down on top of the body, knocking over Jiro's large basket of charcoal for good measure. The guards and body formed a wriggling bundle of hands, legs, and feet. The first guardsman, out of frustration and anger, started punching the second in the face.

As Nagato and Ichiro ran to sort out the squabbling guardsmen, a deep, ringing laugh came rolling down from the steep hillside by the crossroads. Jiro looked up the slope and was surprised to see the samurai who had startled him.

He was sitting on the supine trunk of a low-lying, windswept pine. The trunk was growing parallel to the ground, and the samurai was on it in the lotus position, his sword laying across his lap. In his hands he had a small knife and a piece of wood. His laughter was so hearty that he had to drop the wood into the lap of his kimono and place a hand down on the branch to steady himself, lest he fall off.

Nagato looked up the slope, scowling at the samurai. "What are you laughing at?" he bellowed.

The samurai's laughter continued. Nagato, expecting an answer, demanded "Well? Well?"

The samurai's laughter gradually died down. When it did, he grinned down at the outraged Magistrate and said, "Snow monkeys are always a source of amusement."

The Magistrate was puzzled. "Why do you . . ." The meaning became clear. "Who are you to call us monkeys!" he shouted.

"You're men who act like monkeys, so I'm just a man confused by what manner of creatures are before me: men or monkeys."

The Magistrate, his face red with anger, kicked at the two guardsmen who were still tangled on the ground with the body. "Get up and arrest that man!" he screamed.

It took several moments for the guards to get themselves back on their feet with their weapons at the ready. They looked up the slope, then at each other. Then, with Nagato's screams urging them on, they took a few tentative steps up the hillside toward the samurai.

As they scrambled up the hillside, all semblance of martial readiness disintegrated. Instead of holding their spears as weapons, they used them as hiking sticks. Neither guard seemed willing to lead the other, and both kept a wary eye on the samurai. When they were halfway to the samurai, he put the small piece of wood on the branch. Then he took the small knife, a *ko-gatana,* and slipped it into its niche in the side of his sword scabbard. He unfolded his legs and put them on the ground, standing up and shoving his sword into his sash. All this was done with an economy of movement and swiftness that mesmerized Jiro. The troops advancing up the hill were not entranced, however. This activity by the samurai was the signal for a pell-mell retreat by the guardsmen, who tumbled and slid down the slope back to the road.

Seeing his forces in disarray, Nagato's shouts ended, although his purple face looked like it was about to explode.

"If you ask me politely, I'll come down to talk to you," the samurai said.

Looking at the cowering Ichiro and the two disheveled guards, Nagato swallowed his anger and stood in the road looking up at the samurai. He bowed slightly and said, "Please come down so we can talk to you."

Showing an agility and balance that amazed Jiro, the samurai nimbly made his way down the hillside to the road. When he arrived at the crossroads, the two guards actually took a step back from him, as if to make sure they were out of his reach.

Seeing that the apoplectic Nagato was in no shape to talk, Ichiro presumed to address the samurai.

"I'm Ichiro, the village headman for Suzaka," he said. "This is Magistrate Nagato and two of his men. As you can see, we are here to investigate what happened to this murdered man."

The samurai gestured in Jiro's direction with his chin. "And who is he?"

Surprised, Jiro stammered his name. He was used to being treated as part of the background and not acknowledged or recognized by those who were clearly his betters. The samurai was obviously a ronin. But even a masterless samurai was still a samurai. If he cared to, he could cut down Jiro or any peasant with his sword with no fear of penalty by the law.

Introductions handled to the samurai's satisfaction, he asked, "Now, what do you want to know?"

"What's your name?" Nagato Takamasu inquired, finally regaining enough control to talk. At the tone of Nagato's voice, the samurai gave the Magistrate a hard stare. "I, ah, I need your name for my report to the District Lord," Nagato stammered, giving his head a quick bow to show there was no disrespect intended in the question. "I'm the Magistrate of this District."

The samurai stopped and looked up the hillside. Jiro followed his gaze but could see nothing except the wind rustling through the pine trees that covered the mountain's slope. "I am Matsuyama Kaze," the samurai said.

Jiro thought it unusual that the samurai's name should be "Pine Mountain Wind," when that was just what he was looking at. Jiro wondered if the Magistrate would notice the coincidence and decided that Nagato Takamasu was a man who didn't notice much, despite his two names. Anyone with two names was either from a samurai or noble family. If they became a District Lord, they became a "great name," or Daimyo. For the mass of peasants, merchants, and others who made up the rest of Japanese society, only one name was deemed sufficient. If this caused confusion, they were commonly given some kind of identifying tag, such as Jiro the charcoal seller.

"And what do you know of this?" the Magistrate said, pointing at the now-disturbed body lying at their feet.

"He's dead." Jiro thought the samurai had a hint of a smile when he replied, although his face remained serious.

"Yes, yes, of course he's dead," Nagato said, "but do you know how he died?"

"An arrow." Although Matsuyama Kaze kept a serious visage, Jiro was now sure there was a twinkle in his eye. He's playing with the Magistrate, Jiro thought. The Magistrate literally had the power of life or death, and the idea of manipulating him for sport seemed inconceivable.

"Of course, of course. I can see that. An arrow killed him. But do you know how he was killed?"

"Only what my eyes tell me. I didn't see the murder. When I came up the path, I saw Jiro squatting over the body, examining it. He saw me and got frightened, leaving his charcoal basket behind and running away. I decided to stop for awhile to see what would happen next. I thought it might be interesting. It was."

"Yes, yes, I understand all that. But do you know anything except what you saw?"

Kaze smiled. "Apparently some men can't even understand what they do see. It's foolish to ask me about things I did not see."

The Magistrate wasn't sure if he had been insulted or not, and paused for a few moments to see if he could figure it out. He couldn't, so he turned his attention back to the body. He circled it several times, mumbling, "Yes, yes," to himself as he looked things over. Finally, he stopped, put his hands on his hips, and announced, "Well, of course, it's obvious."

No one, including Kaze, encouraged the Magistrate to explain what was so obvious. He did so anyway. "This man is a stranger. Certainly not from our village. He was obviously walking along the path and bandits shot him in the back and robbed him. Yes, yes, it's all very clear."

Kaze started laughing. Irritated, the Magistrate turned to him and said, "I am the Magistrate."

"Yes, you are," Kaze said, "and one of your functions is to assure that justice is done. That won't happen if you can't even see where a man was killed."

"What are you talking about?"

"How many men walk around with only one sandal?"

"None! What a ridiculous question!"

"Then why does this man have only one sandal? Men wear two sandals or go barefoot, like Jiro."

Peering down at the body, the Magistrate said, "Yes, yes. I see what you mean." Looking at the guardsmen, he said, "Find the other sandal."

"Don't bother," Kaze said. "It isn't here. It was lost where the man was killed."

"He probably lost it running to this spot. Just because the sandal isn't here, that doesn't mean that he wasn't killed here."

"Your circling of the body erased any footprints, but before you came I looked at the path. There were prints from a horse and prints of bare feet and sandals from people who have walked through this crossroads. There are no prints of one bare foot and one sandaled foot. This man was not killed here."

"But it's ridiculous to think he was killed elsewhere. Why would a bandit kill a man and go to the trouble of moving him to this crossroads?" the Magistrate asked.

"Why would a bandit leave the man's money?"

"What? He still has his money?"

"Check his money pouch."

The Magistrate pointed to Ichiro to execute Kaze's command. The village headman bent down and found the dead man's money pouch, held to his kimono sash by a short cord ending in a wooden toggle, designed to prevent the cord from slipping out of the sash. Instead of the usual carved ivory *netsuke,* this toggle was just a plain square of wood with a hole drilled in it.

Ichiro hefted the pouch, then looked inside. "It's true, Magistrate-*sama,* there is money in here. Several copper pieces and even one silver piece."

"Yes, yes, very strange. How did you know that, samurai?"

"I looked," Kaze said.

"You seem to know a lot about this for a man who said he came upon the body after the charcoal seller here discovered it."

"You would also know a lot more if you looked. For instance, see the man's sash? How it's wound around him?"

The Magistrate stared at the body for several minutes. Jiro also looked. A long sash was wrapped several times around the body. Despite its length, it seemed to be a little loose. Jiro wasn't sure what the samurai was talking about. The Magistrate echoed Jiro's bafflement. "I don't see anything," he said.

The samurai sighed. "You can hold a lighted candle to a man's face, but even if he feels the heat, you can't make him open his eyes to look at the flame."

"Here, here," the Magistrate said. "I'm getting tired of these remarks of yours. They don't make sense, and I think they might be disrespectful."

The samurai gave a short bow. "I have the deepest respect for the position of Magistrate," he said. "It is an important function and vital to keeping order in a district. If any of my remarks have offended you, I am sorry. They are simply reflective of the caliber of the actions and words I've seen before me."

The Magistrate blinked a few times, not sure if he had been apologized to or insulted again. Finally he said, "Yes, yes, well, I'll have to report this to the District Lord to see what he thinks. His manor is next to Suzaka village. This is all very unusual, very unusual. Samurai, I'll require you to stay until our Lord decides what to do about this whole situation."

"Is there a teahouse in Suzaka?"

"No, but you can stay with the charcoal seller."

Jiro didn't want the Magistrate extending an invitation to this ronin. He didn't want a guest imposed on him, especially a strange ronin. "Excuse me, Magistrate-sama, but my house is too meager for a samurai."

"Nonsense," the Magistrate said. "He has to stay someplace. He certainly can't stay with me or at the Lord's manor. Your farmhouse is as good as any."

"But perhaps the samurai would object to staying at such a lowly dwelling?"

"Oh no," Kaze said with a smile. "Two nights ago I slept in the bottom of a boat I was in, and last night I slept in an open field. I'm sure your house will be quite adequate."

"But—"

Jiro's last try at an indirect protest was cut off by the Magistrate, who said, "Good, good. It's all settled then. Let's go into the village. I have to report this to the Lord. You two men stay here and bury the corpse," the Magistrate said to the guards.

"You're not going to take the body into Suzaka? Maybe someone in the village will know this man. Just because he's a stranger to you, that doesn't mean others won't know him," Kaze said.

"What for? It's a needless effort. Here we just bury dead strangers by the side of the road. That's our custom. Yes, yes, that's the proper thing to do." The Magistrate started waddling off toward the village.

The samurai didn't immediately follow, and both Jiro and Ichiro were torn between trailing after the Magistrate and making sure the samurai would go.

Almost to himself, the samurai said, "What kind of place is this, where the bodies of strange men are so common that you have a custom for how you bury them?"

He stuck his sword into his sash, adjusting it carefully, then started down the path toward the village with the headman Ichiro trailing. Curious, Jiro looked up the hillside, then down the path at the retreating figures of the Magistrate, the ronin, and the village headman. He decided to satisfy his curiosity and started scrambling up the hillside to the place where the samurai had been sitting.

When he got to the tree trunk, he picked up the piece of wood the samurai had been carving. It was a piece of a limb as tall as a hand and as big around as a spear butt. From this hunk of wood, the samurai had carved a statue of Kannon, the Goddess of Mercy. The statue wasn't finished. Only her face and shoulders were emerging from the rough bark, but Jiro marveled at the delicate beauty and serene expression staring up at him.

Kannon's eyes were lidded slits, and her smooth cheekbones framed a tiny mouth with perfectly formed lips. As always, she was patient and inviting, ready to extend her mercy to any supplicant sincere enough to ask for it. That the hands of a man could evoke a living representation of the Goddess from a common piece of wood was a source of wonder for Jiro, who was used to much cruder representations of the Gods and Goddesses that inhabit the Land of the Gods.

Jiro looked down the slope and saw the two soldiers scraping out a shallow grave by the side of the road. From his vantage point the crossroads and all that occurred there was spread before him like a scene framed by tree trunks and branches. Where the samurai had placed the Kannon, the Goddess could look down on the slain man and all who traveled this place, extending her mercy to weary travelers on dangerous roads. Jiro placed the half-formed statue back on the branch, just where the samurai had left her. He clapped his hands together and bowed, asking the Goddess to extend her benevolence to him, too.

The men digging the grave looked up at Jiro's clap, but didn't have enough curiosity to see what the charcoal seller was doing. Slipping and sliding, Jiro made his way down the slope that the samurai had so nimbly navigated just a few minutes before. After loading the spilled charcoal into his basket and hoisting the basket on his back, Jiro scurried down the path that led to Suzaka village.

## CHAPTER 3

*A spider sits and
waits in an iridescent
web. Poor little moth!*

"**S**ooooo?"

Nagato hated this. Lord Manase loved subtlety and indirectness. Nagato was just a rough country samurai, and he knew it. He was at a loss as to how to deal with this peculiar master, who kept such strange customs and who talked with such an odd accent. Now, after reporting the murder at the crossroads and the encounter with the samurai, the Lord was expecting Nagato to make some comment, but Nagato could get no hint of what kind of comment the Lord was expecting from his one-word question.

"It was probably the work of Boss Kuemon, Manase-sama," Nagato said.

"Sooooo?"

That response again. They were sitting in the Lord's study. For some reason, Lord Manase preferred a study with sturdy wooden shutters, instead of the usual paper *shoji* screens. The result was a dark and gloomy place, with deep shadows like a cave. Lord Manase sat in the center of the room, surrounded by books and trinkets. When the servants of the manor gossiped with village people, they talked of the Lord's scholarship, how he would sit in his study late into the night, as a single candle flickered in a large metal candlestick sitting on the floor, and peruse ancient texts. The Lord loved fine things and lived and dressed in opulence, but his habits were monk-ish and austere. Past lords of the small district had always been rough country samurai, interested in hunting, eating, and gathering con-cubines. A bookish lord was something outside the realm of expe-rience.

Nagato always found the effect of the dark study, crammed with books, unsettling. It was made all the more unsettling by the strong perfume the Lord wore. The servants said that Lord Manase seldom bathed. In this, he was just like the hairy barbarians from the far-off country of Europe, creatures that Nagato had heard of, but never seen. Lord Manase used a variety of perfumes, both purchased and invented by himself. The perfume combined with the memory of candle smoke and the grassy smell of old *tatami* mats made a suf-focating, heavy, and complex atmosphere that Nagato found quite unbearable.

Nagato knew enough not to mention this to his master, but when they were locked together in the small, closed study, the pungent scents assaulted his nose. Nagato was desperate to say the right things to his master for many reasons. First, he wanted leave to escape the claustrophobic study. Next, the Lord's strange speech behavior al-ways made him uncomfortable in any circumstances. And last, and most important, this murder was one he didn't want his Lord taking an interest in.

Lord Manase raised his closed fan to his lips, a sure sign he was losing patience with Nagato's silence. "Perhaps there's another ex-planation, Manase-sama," Nagato blurted out.

"Sooooo?" This time Nagato could tell the intonation of the single word indicated interest.

"Yes, yes. Perhaps that ronin killed him."

Manase gave a high, tittering laugh. "Whyyyy wooould you think that?"

Nagato knew he wasn't clever, but he was certainly cunning. "I noticed many things about the body that indicated it wasn't killed at the crossroads."

"Sooooo?" Now more interest.

"Yes, yes, Lord. The merchant had only one sandal. The other sandal was not at the crossroads, which meant it was lost where the merchant was really killed."

"Aaannd you observed that?"

Nagato squirmed a bit. Manase might ask that fool of a village headsman, Ichiro, so he didn't want to lie directly. "I got that information by questioning the ronin."

Lord Manase started absently tapping his closed fan into the palm of his hand, a sure sign he was thinking.

"Interesting," Lord Manase said.

"And there's more, Manase-sama."

"So?"

"I am almost certain it wasn't Boss Kuemon who killed this merchant."

"*Honto?* Truthfully?"

"Yes, Lord."

"How do you know this?"

Nagato almost smiled. He had gotten the Lord to communicate with him in full sentences, instead of the single words and subtle movements of a fan or eyebrow that the Lord normally used. "Because," Nagato said, "when I examined the dead merchant, he still had money in his pouch. Even if for some reason Boss Kuemon would move a body to get rid of it, he would never allow it to be dumped with money."

Nagato felt the Lord look at him with new respect.

"That's a very interesting point, Nagato," Lord Manase said. It was one of the few times he used Nagato's name, and the Magistrate sat up straighter. "But why do you think the ronin killed the merchant?"

"He just knows too much about it," Nagato said flatly. "He said the merchant wasn't killed at the crossroads, and he said he knew even more about the murder, but he wouldn't tell me what it was. The only way he could know so much was if he did it himself."

Once again the tapping of the fan in the open palm of the other hand. Finally, Lord Manase said, "But I thought the charcoal seller said he saw the ronin coming down the road from Uzen after he found the body."

Now Nagato played his trump card, one that had occurred to him only moments before. "The charcoal seller and the ronin did it together. Yes, yes. Maybe he was paid, but for some reason that peasant is lying about how he found the body and the time when the ronin appeared."

"That's a very interesting idea. Frankly, Nagato, I'm surprised you were able to think of it." Nagato didn't hear the rebuke, instead he only heard the surprise and pleasure in Lord Manase's voice. Nagato gave a solemn bow of thanks to his master.

"Sooo . . . are you going to arrest him?" Lord Manase said, putting his fan up to his mouth to indicate his boredom with these mundane details of administration.

Nagato started licking his lips. He gave another bow, this time one of apology. "That might be very difficult to do," he said. "The samurai seems very strong, and with my men . . . that is, it seems . . . ahh . . ."

Lord Manase looked at Nagato as if he were an especially interesting variety of cricket. "In other words, you're afraid to arrest him."

Nagato bobbed down again. "It's not a matter of . . . well . . ." He bowed yet another time.

"All right," Lord Manase said. "I'll think about this when I find the time. After all, what's the death of another merchant? This conversation has gotten very tedious." Manase flicked his closed fan as if he were knocking away a flea. "Leave now. When I think of something, I'll tell you."

Nagato gave a final bow and left the chamber of the District Lord. As soon as he was out of the room, he gave a sigh of relief. The Lord had not asked too many questions, and he had not been ordered to capture the samurai. Nagato's objectives for the interview had been met. He swaggered down the path from the Lord's manor to the village.

It was a fifteen-minute walk from the Lord's manor to the village. As he made his way on the path, Nagato congratulated himself for outsmarting the weird Lord. All too often, the Lord had made it clear that he considered Nagato a fool, openly laughing at some of Nagato's responses to the cryptic questions he asked. The snot.

The Lord affected the old-time courtly speech of nobles, but Nagato knew that the Lord's family was no more noble than his own. They were both samurai, and although Nagato had let his own martial skills decline over the years, he was still convinced that he could best the effete Lord in a duel, if only the iron-clad bindings of duty would allow such a thing. Instead, because of an accident of battle that everyone in the village knew, the small, pasty-faced man sitting in the darkened room was absolute master of the District, and Nagato was Magistrate, sworn to serve him until death. Nagato summoned up a viscous ball of phlegm from deep within his throat and spat it out on the side of the path.

The unfairness of the situation was something that Nagato ruminated on often, especially when he was in his cups and feeling unhappy with his circumstances in life. It was a dangerous feeling to have, but it was a dangerous time. If the Taiko had risen from peasant to ruler of Japan, why couldn't a samurai like Nagato Takamasu dream of ruling one miserable, 150-*koku* district like this one? (A koku was the amount of rice it took to keep one warrior fed for a year.) This was a common fantasy for the Magistrate, and it was a measure of his limited horizons that his fantasies never extended to ruling more than the tiny mountain district. Unfortunately, despite his fearsome attitude toward the farmers and peasants of the village, Nagato was not even the ruler of his own household.

Nagato's mother-in-law had reached the age of sixty-one, the traditional age when a Japanese could say and do what he or she pleased.

Of course, she had never inhibited herself too much from doing that anyway, at least in the confines of the Nagato house. But she was increasingly more blatant about her disappointment over the adoption of Nagato.

The Magistrate was not born a son of the Nagato household, and the old woman would lament that her now-deceased husband had made a terrible mistake in his haste to perpetuate the Nagato line. The Magistrate also thought a mistake was made, but for very different reasons.

The Magistrate was the firstborn son of Hotta Masahiro. By tradition, the firstborn son should inherit the rights and lands of his father, but the fact that the Magistrate had been offered for adoption meant that he was actually the product of a love affair that occurred before his mother married Hotta. Otherwise, a firstborn son would never be adopted out. Undoubtedly, this love affair had been with someone other than Hotta, although the Magistrate was never able to ascertain who his real father was.

An unexpected pregnancy would also explain why his mother, who was of a higher social status than Hotta, would marry beneath her. It was hard to arrange marriages on short notice with families of equal social status. Such marriages were complicated affairs done to solidify position or, by using the marriage to cement a military alliance, security. They took considerable time, and with a pregnant daughter growing larger by the day, a family did not have as much time as a normal marriage would require. It could arrange a marriage that was a step down the social ladder much faster than a union of peers. The groom who accepted such a bride ended up with a mate that enhanced his social status, even though the pregnancy was obviously an embarrassing inconvenience that would have to be ignored.

The Magistrate's mother had married beneath her, and sending her firstborn to be adopted by the Nagatos was a further step down for the child. Since the child was not really a Hotta, his reputed father could adopt him out with no social stigma attached to the transaction. Hotta was a doting father to his own children, but the Magistrate was never given the privileges that a firstborn son should receive in a Japanese family, and even at an early age he knew it. When the child became a teenager, Hotta saw an opportunity to get rid of a longtime embarrassment and had him married and adopted into the Nagato family.

The Nagatos had no male heir, and they were using their daughter as a way to continue the Nagato name. A husband would be found for their daughter, and then the new son-in-law would be adopted into the family, assuming the Nagato name. Then the next generation would be "real" Nagatos.

Since the adoption could be undone, the Nagato family had tremendous power over the Magistrate, forcing him to put up with a meddling mother-in-law and a disobedient wife. The wife took strength and pleasure from her mother's support and sharp tongue, and together they would regularly berate the man who was supposed to be the strong force in the District. It made Nagato feel small and impotent to be trapped in life by the indiscretion of his mother.

Still, Nagato thought, it was possible to better yourself even if you couldn't undo a bad birth, a worse marriage, or a position as the vassal of a strange District Lord. It only required money, and money was what Nagato was focused on currently because he had a goal. He wanted a concubine.

Nagato's wife had done her duty by bearing him a son; a small, nasty child that clung to, and acted like, his mother. Having done her duty, she was not expected to bring passion into his life. For that, a samurai was expected to find other women or boys. She, of course, was expected to remain faithful to him while he satisfied his appetites with others.

Nagato was a man of large appetites, but except for food, his appetites had been thwarted. Power, money, status, and women had eluded him. Now he was determined to change that. Money was the key, and once he had money, he could have the rest.

He idly thought about whom he would acquire as his concubine.

That fool of a village headman, Ichiro, had a tasty eleven-year-old daughter who would do for a start. She was artless, but the thought of her taut skin brought a familiar stirring to his groin.

Nagato was taught that grace and delicacy were the marks of femininity, but the child was gawky and awkward and ran around the village like a boy. He was taught that soft flesh and a lack of muscle was desirable in a woman, but the child had bony limbs and she had already been hardened by a short lifetime filled with work. He was taught that refinement in the arts was erotic, but the child was ignorant in the ways of the Court and culture and only familiar with the life of a farmer. He was taught that the nape of a long, swanlike neck was the apex of feminine beauty, but her neck was short and stubby. Finally, as Nagato could see for himself when the child walked around, she had large peasant's feet, not the tiny mincing feet he associated with a lovely woman.

Despite all this, the child still provoked Nagato's lust for a simple reason: She was vulnerable.

How such a succulent morsel could come from that bag of bones of a village headman was beyond Nagato's comprehension. He had often intimated that he would be willing to bestow his favors on the headman's nubile daughter, but the peasant always seemed oblivious to what Nagato was talking about. Nagato sighed. Peasants were always so stupid! No matter; when the money was there he could simply buy the girl from the fool.

"*Tadaima!* I'm home!" he gruffly shouted as he entered his house, which was bigger and grander than that of the peasants in the village. He sat at the entryway and untied his sandals. His wizened mother-in-law came to greet him, instead of his wife, as was proper. She curled up her nose as she approached him.

"You smell of that place again. You've been up to see the Lord. Wash your dirty body before you come into the house," the old woman ordered.

Nagato's lips twisted with frustration and hatred, but he stepped outside to comply.

## CHAPTER 4

*A warm fire with a*
*kettle bubbling over it.*
*It's good to have friends.*

"**F**ood?"

"Yes."

Jiro ladled out some porridge made from millet and brown rice into a bowl. He begrudged the use of rice in the meal, but he thought he should add it to the millet or the samurai might get angry with him.

Both men were in Jiro's farmhouse, sitting on a raised wooden platform that formed the main flooring for the hut. The farmhouse was perhaps eight paces long by six wide, with a high thatched roof, the underside of which was made black with soot. In the joists of the roof, crude platforms of bamboo were built to act as storage places. The walls of the hut were planks hand sawn but painstakingly fitted together so the biting winds of winter would not cut through the joints to freeze the inhabitants of the hut. The planks fitted between posts and beams, many of which were left in a seminatural shape: the bark and limbs trimmed off, but the natural shape of the trunk remaining. Like the underside of the thatch, all the wood had been smoked to a dark color by countless fires used to provide heat and to cook food. The entire house was put together with cunning joints that locked it together, along with a few pegs.

The fire was made in a gap in the center of the platform that Jiro and Kaze sat on. There, in an open square in the floorboards, a charcoal fire was glowing on the exposed ground below. Hanging over the fire, from a rope thrown over a beam in the roof, was an iron pot with the bubbling porridge. By raising or lowering the other end of the rope and tying it off, Jiro could control the cooking temperature.

A steady stream of gray wisps rose from the fire and curled past the pot, wafting up into the recesses of the thatched roof. It was supposed to escape through a hole in the eaves, but the truth was that a great deal of the smoke remained to permeate the entire farmhouse, causing watery eyes and drying the throat to a leathery consistency.

High in the rafters, on the ridgepole of the roof, was a black-painted arrow pointing northeast, the *kimon*, or devil's direction. The arrow was tied with hemp rope, a Shinto ceremonial article, and it was designed to keep away evil spirits. Jiro's grandfather and the carpenter who supervised the building of the house had tied the arrow there as part of the construction rites more than ninety years before. The entire village had participated in the construction of the house, just as Jiro, his father, and his father before him had participated in the construction of all the other houses in the village. If a house survived earthquakes, fires, and war, it might stay in a family for hundreds of years, little bits of it being constantly renewed and replaced as age and rot took their toll. In that way it was like a family or the village itself because the long-term survival of the whole was more important than the survival of any individual piece.

Jiro handed the bowl of porridge over to Kaze. As Kaze accepted the bowl, he did something astonishing. He gave a small nod of his head to acknowledge the food and thank Jiro. In his entire fifty years, Jiro had never had a samurai thank him for anything, much less give a bow to him, however small. He almost dropped the ladle.

Kaze acted as if he had done nothing unusual. He brought the bowl to his face and, using a pair of *hashi*, chopsticks, he shoveled some of the porridge into his mouth, sucking air in along with porridge to cool the hot mixture. "It's good," he said.

Jiro stared at this unusual man, not sure what to make of him. When they returned to the village of Suzaka, the Magistrate went off to report to the District Lord. Jiro had offered Kaze breakfast, but Kaze refused, saying he had eaten some toasted rice balls when he started on the road that morning.

Jiro spent the morning delivering charcoal to his regular customers. Kaze also roamed the village, looking as if he were searching for something. His presence made the villagers nervous, and in a way this was good for Jiro because it took attention away from his news about the increase in charcoal prices.

As Kaze looked around, he realized that Suzaka was more like a *buraku*, a hamlet, than a *mura*, a real village. The buraku was a relatively small grouping of farmhouses, and groups of buraku would form a mura. Here in the mountains, the land could not sustain a large number of buraku.

Now, with the sun down and the evening meal cooked, Jiro didn't know what to expect from this samurai. He worried about what might happen, because he had never had a samurai stay in his farmhouse before. In fact, since his wife died, he rarely had people in his house at all. He fretted over possible scenarios in which the samurai would be demanding or threatening. He even thought the samurai might beat him because the fare he was offering was so meager. He would never have predicted that the samurai would actually thank him.

"*Chotto matte, kudasai.* Wait a minute, please," Jiro said. He hesitated a moment, then moved over to a corner of the platform. He lifted up one of the floorboards. The use of a metal nail or wooden pegs to hold them down would have been an unthinkable luxury. The floorboards were simply laid on the floor joist.

Jiro reached under the board and lifted out a pottery jar with a piece of coarse cloth covering the mouth. Jiro removed the cloth and offered the jar to the samurai. "*Tsukemono?* Pickles?"

The samurai peered into the jar and quickly jerked his head back as the pungent odor assaulted his nostrils, overpowering even the smell of smoke and the loamy smell of earth. Inside the jar were small eggplants and cabbage leaves fermented in bran and salt. He gingerly picked some of the pickles out of the jar with his hashi and nibbled at one.

"Good, but powerful enough to kill flies."

Jiro laughed. "It's my own recipe. It's my secret to long life."

"How old are you?"

"Fifty years."

Fifty years was positively ancient. Boys could see their first battle at twelve, people were often married at fourteen, and a woman past thirty-five could expect to be addressed as *obaasan:* grandmother. A peasant living through his forties was unusual. Kaze was thirty-one. He had lived through the dangerous year of twenty-nine, but that year had indeed been a fateful one, just as the folk belief said it would be. So much of his life had been lost or changed since then; he had no wish to catalog the changes. He dipped his hashi back into the pungent jar and fished out some more pickles.

"The village looks run down," Kaze said as he continued to eat small bites of pickle with his porridge.

"It might as well be taken by devils," Jiro answered.

"Why?"

Jiro's wariness, temporarily dispelled by the samurai's politeness, quickly returned.

"Problems," he said vaguely.

"What kind of problems?"

"Our District Lord is a little . . . strange."

"In what way?"

"I'm sorry. I'm very ignorant. I shouldn't talk of my betters."

"Why are you suddenly acting stupid when I can tell you're an intelligent man?"

Jiro bowed. "Please forgive me, but . . ." He let the sentence trail off. A clear sign he didn't want to continue. Kaze turned his attention back to his porridge and didn't press the charcoal seller.

Jiro surreptitiously examined the man eating his food. Kaze was of normal height for a man of his time, which would make him five foot one or five foot two. From the swell of his forearms and the bulge of his shoulders under his kimono, Jiro could see that Kaze was very muscular, but he was also exceptionally agile, as Jiro had witnessed when Kaze came down the mountain to the crossroads. The samurai's face was square-cut and had high cheekbones, with dark brows that almost met above the bridge of his nose. His face was burnt brown from the sun, the result of a long time on the road. Kaze didn't shave the front part of his head as other samurai did. Instead he drew his glossy black hair back into a ponytail. Jiro decided this strange samurai was handsome.

Despite an outwardly casual manner, one aspect of the samurai did bother Jiro. Kaze seemed to keep his sword close at hand at all times, as if he expected an attack at any moment. Jiro knew that samurai considered their swords to be extensions of their souls, but he found it strange that Kaze never had his sword farther away than a short stretch of his arm. He also found it strange that Kaze only carried one sword, the long katana. Samurai usually carried two swords, the long katana and the shorter *wakizashi*. The short waki-zashi was used as an auxiliary weapon and for other tasks, such as ritual suicide. Samurai called the wakizashi the "guardian of honor." Jiro wondered why Kaze didn't carry one.

After closing off any conversation about the Lord, Jiro tried to make amends through small talk. It was an effort for him, but he decided civility was the right tack to take with this particular samurai.

"Have you been on the road long?"

"Too long."

"Where is your home?"

"I no longer have a home. I'm a ronin, a 'wave man.' Like the waves of the ocean, I call no land home. Like water on rocks, I can't mix in and settle. I am always pulled back to flow to the next shore."

Jiro, who was not an articulate man, found this rush of words both peculiar and pleasing. The play off the meaning of "ronin" was something he could easily understand but which would have been beyond his power to invent. It gave him a feeling of both awe and sadness.

"That's good. I wish I could think like that."

"It's true. I wish I had no reason to think like that."

Jiro had no response. He sucked air through his teeth, cocked his head to one side, and smiled. The samurai smiled back.

"Tell me something," Kaze said.

"What?"

"Are there many farmhouses outside the village?"

"A few. No one lives in most of them. Too many bandits."

"Do you know the families that do live there?'

"Yes."

"Have any bought a girl recently? She'd be around nine years old now. She would probably be sold as a servant. She might have a kimono with a *mon*, a family crest, of three plum blossoms."

"No one has money here but the bandits. They take what they want, not buy. No one here has servants, except the Magistrate and the Lord."

"How long has the bandit problem been so severe here?"

"There've always been a few, but the last two years have been terrible."

"Why has it gotten so terrible in the last two years?"

"No reason," Jiro said warily.

"No reason at all?"

"No. It's just gotten bad in two years."

"Several bands of bandits, or just one?"

"One. They killed off the others, or made them join. Boss Kuemon is in charge."

Kaze put down his empty bowl of gruel. Jiro pointed toward the pot with his chin, to see if Kaze wanted more. The samurai shook his head no. He found a clear spot and seemed to be settling down for the night, sleeping, Jiro noted, with his sword tucked in his arms. Jiro banked the fire and settled down himself.

"Want a *futon*?" Jiro asked, digging out one of the sleeping mats for himself.

"No. I'm used to sleeping on the ground."

"All right. I have to wake up early to sell charcoal."

"I wake up early, too. By the way, how many years has the new Lord been in charge of this District?"

"Two." As soon as he spoke, Jiro knew the reason for the question. This was why he didn't trust words. It was too easy to say more than you wanted to, even with a single one of them.

Jiro awoke very early the next morning, long before the sun was up. He lay still, listening to the breathing of the still-sleeping samurai. When he was sure that the stranger was sound asleep, Jiro quietly got up and crept to the door of his farmhouse. It was so dark he couldn't see his guest, but he had lived his entire life in the house and knew its every cranny. At the door he paused once again to listen for the slow, rhythmic breathing of the ronin and heard it. Reassured, Jiro took the stick out of the sliding wooden door that jammed it shut at night. Then, with painstaking care to assure he wasn't making a sound, he slid open the door.

Once outside, Jiro slid the door shut with equal care. Then he stealthily made his way from the farmhouse and the village.

Kaze continued his slow breathing as he listened to Jiro's receding footsteps. He expected Jiro to make his way to the privy. That would almost always be to the south of a farmhouse. Kaze had noticed a *nanten* bush growing south of the farmhouse, something usually planted next to a privy as a symbol of ritual purification, so he was sure that's where the facilities were. But the charcoal seller was walking west, not south. That meant he was walking into the surrounding woods.

Kaze lay still, slowly listening to his breathing, and tried not to be curious about the strange nocturnal journey of the charcoal seller. He counted over a thousand breaths before Jiro painstakingly slid the farmhouse door open again and crept inside. In the dark, Jiro made his way back to his spot on the farmhouse's platform floor and settled back to sleep, congratulating himself on making his nightly trip without the samurai noticing.

The next morning, Kaze shared a breakfast of hot miso soup and cold porridge from the night before with Jiro without complaint. The breakfast passed without any comment on the charcoal seller's peculiar behavior. Kaze finished his food, then he put on his *tabi* socks and started strapping on his hemp sandals.

"Looking around the village again?" Jiro said, frankly curious.

"I've seen the village. I'm moving to the next village."

"You're leaving?" Jiro said, alarmed.

"Yes. There's no reason for me to stay."

"But the Lord hasn't decided what to do about the murder." Fear made words tumble from Jiro's mouth.

"The murder has nothing to do with me."

"But the Magistrate told you to stay here."

"Your Magistrate is nothing to me. He's too stupid to even understand what happened. He will never find the murderer. *Domo.* Thank you for your hospitality. Good luck."

"But the Magistrate will be mad if you leave!"

Kaze shrugged.

"You may meet bandits on the road."

"Then that is my karma. Domo."

Kaze stuck his sword in his sash and strode out of Jiro's hut. Jiro rushed to the door, watching the samurai walk down the path that led through the village using the economical gait of a man used to covering long distances. Jiro was fearful of the samurai's leaving, yet not quite sure what he should do about it.

Once out of the village, Kaze enjoyed the sweet air of the mountains, scented with pine and the memory of summer grass. The sky was sunny, and although he had gained no news of the girl, he was not discouraged. He would not quit. This last village meant one less place to look. If she was alive, sooner or later he would find her.

To demonstrate his powers of concentration, Daruma, the Indian monk who founded Zen Buddhism, sat in a cave and meditated for nine years while staring at a wall. Kaze's Sensei would often relate that story when Kaze grew too restless with a lesson or exercise, but Kaze could never see the example applying to him. He could be still, but he could not be idle.

He had searched for the girl for two years. During the search he had wandered the cities and back roads of Japan, constantly moving. Inactivity, not a lack of patience, was why the lesson of Daruma was never incorporated into his heart. It was two years since he saw her, and at that age girls grow quickly. He wondered if he would recognize her. Would there be some spark of her parents shining in her face as she matured, or could he walk past her on a village street and not recognize that he had found the object of his search?

Just as swordsmanship was a matter of a hair's width, luck in life could be a matter of brief seconds. A man could turn and an arrow or musket ball fired at him could miss. If he turned a fraction of a second later, he would be dead. Even if she did look like her parents, perhaps Kaze would be turning a corner just as she was stepping out a door and miss her. Perhaps she would be moved to a village just as Kaze had left it. There were so many possibilities, but Kaze knew he could not just sit idle and wait for luck. He believed in the Japanese proverb that said waiting for luck is like waiting for death.

As he walked along the path, Kaze looked at the splashes of blue sky peeking through the woven branches of the trees. It was a constantly changing mosaic that recalled the intricately painted patterns on the expensive Satsuma porcelains he knew from his youth. His quest weighed on his soul, but he reflected that his life was not without its pleasures, especially as he walked along an empty road, smelling the coming autumn and listening to the sound of his sandals crunching the pine needles that had drifted across the path. He was about to start humming an old folk song when he stopped abruptly and stared into the trees lining the road. Something caught his eye.

## CHAPTER 5

*A butterfly roosts.*
*Unexpected elegance*
*on a bobbing leaf.*

It was a subtle thing, but he was a man used to living off subtleties. The trees along this patch of road were thick and overgrown with brush, yet deep in the woods, through the tangle of branches, Kaze had seen a flash of red, then gold. He stared intently, seeing if he could spot the colors again, but saw nothing except the dark tree trunks.

Leaving the road, he started making his way into the trees. Silent as any hunter, he carefully stepped over brush and glided from point to point, penetrating the woods with a maximum of stealth and a minimum of sound.

A short distance from the road, he stopped. There the woods opened up into a large clearing. The grass in the clearing was trampled down, forming a space roughly the size of eight tatami mats. In this space, standing alone, was a *Noh* dancer.

The dancer wore a rich kimono of red and gold. The crimson silk was embroidered with a pattern of golden maple leaves, tumbling from one shoulder and fluttering their way to the kimono's hem. Stepping through this dry autumn shower, a brown embroidered doe gently peeked from the back of the kimono to the flank of the dancer, looking about warily with wide eyes. The lushness of the kimono's color was what Kaze had spotted through the trees.

On the face of the dancer was a *ko-omote*, the traditional mask of a maiden: oval, serene, painted white with red lips and high, expressive eyebrows. The mask was surmounted by a black wig with long, lustrous human hair pulled back into a bun, adding to the illusion that the Noh dancer, who was a man, was really a woman.

The dancer moved with slow grace, his movements controlled and stylized. Kaze, who had not seen Noh for many years, was entranced. Noh was part dance, part drama, and part music. In the silent performance being pantomimed before him, the music and stylized singing and speech of the Noh ensemble were missing, but the grace of the dancer remained.

He was moving in a precise, measured triangle, and Kaze realized that it was *Dojoji*, a Noh play about a dedication ceremony for a large bronze bell at Dojoji temple. An enchanting female *shirabyoshi* dancer climbs the mountain to the temple, only to be revealed as a vengeful spirit who turns herself into a frightening serpent when trapped under the bell by the priests of the temple. It's a spectacular performance, with a costume change for the principal dancer when hidden in the bell, metamorphosing from the robes and mask of the maiden to the glittering costume and fearsome mask of the serpent.

The dancer walked through the small triangle again and again, varying the walk by small degrees. It was the part of the play where the dancer makes the long climb up the mountain to the temple, a part that extends for many minutes in the actual performance. Here the precision and skill of the dancer was taxed to keep the action interesting to the audience, and Kaze was delighted by the finesse shown as the dancer made small variations in these apparently repetitious movements.

When the dancer was done, he straightened up, and Kaze realized that this was just a practice and that the complete Noh would not be danced. Still, the skill shown was extraordinary, and Kaze stepped into the clearing and said, "Superb! I have never seen *Dojoji* danced better."

The dancer stiffened and turned in Kaze's direction. "Excuse me," Kaze said. "I do not wish to disturb your privacy, but I couldn't stop myself from praising your skill at Noh." Kaze made a deep, formal bow to the dancer.

Without responding with words, the dancer gave Kaze an equally formal bow, but it was done with a grace that made Kaze feel thick and awkward.

"Thank you for the pleasure of your dancing," Kaze said. He turned around and made his way back to the path. Without looking back, Kaze started down the road again.

Kaze had seen many strange sights in his lifetime, but the silent Noh in a hidden mountain clearing had a dreamlike quality to it. Behind the mask, Kaze could not tell what the man was like, but perhaps that was the best way to be these days: silent and wearing a mask.

The world was changing, and not for the better as far as Kaze was concerned. After three hundred years of constant warfare, Japan had known a brief period of peace under Hideyoshi, the Taiko. But even Hideyoshi couldn't stand a period of warriors dying of old age in bed, and he had attacked Korea with an eye toward eventually conquering China. After some initial successes, the entire Korean war had turned into a disaster, with many of Hideyoshi's closest allies perishing in his foreign adventure. Hideyoshi himself remained in Japan, and he died of old age in his bed. Yet Hideyoshi's death marked a dangerous time for his heir and his allies, for Tokugawa Ieyasu was sitting patiently in Japan's richest region, the Kanto, waiting.

Ieyasu waited as Hideyoshi's allies drained themselves of young blood in the ill-fated Korean adventure, while Ieyasu himself adroitly avoided getting deeply involved. Ieyasu waited while Hideyoshi declined in health with only a very young son as heir. Ieyasu waited while the Council of Regents, of which he was a member, decayed into bickering and dissension instead of helping Hideyoshi's young heir rule Japan. And finally, after a lifetime of waiting, Ieyasu took action and risked it all in a battle involving over two hundred thousand men. He defeated the forces loyal to Hideyoshi's heir at the battle of Sekigahara, setting himself up to become the undisputed ruler of Japan.

Now Hideyoshi's heir and widow were holed up in Osaka Castle, like badgers retreating into a lair, and the rest of the country was embroiled in chaos as the Tokugawas inexorably extended their control over the country, casting numerous samurai, who had been loyal to the losers at Sekigahara, free to wander the countryside as ronin in search of new employment. Kaze had no idea how many samurai were now masterless, but it could easily be fifty thousand or more. These men must find employment with some lord or they would lose their hereditary status as samurai—literally, "those who serve."

Kaze found the large number of ronin wandering the country a convenience in some ways. It allowed him to blend into the crowd because the sight of a ronin anyplace in Japan was not at all unusual now. Normally Kaze's instincts would be to go to Osaka to fight for Hideyoshi's heir or to commit seppuku and follow his Lord into death. But he was not free to follow his instincts. In fact, he was not free at all.

When Kaze had been walking for an hour, a pair of eyes watched him much as Kaze had watched the Noh dancer, hidden in the woods and unseen. As soon as the watcher was sure of what he was seeing, he pulled away from his observation post and scrambled down a slope. At the bottom of the slope two men were sitting on the ground, playing dice. They were dressed in a colorful assortment of clothes and had two spears and a sword stuck into the earth next to them.

One slammed down a scruffy wooden dice cup and lifted it quickly. "Damn!" he said as he stared down at the dice.

His companion gave an evil, yellow-toothed grin. "This isn't a lucky day for you." He scooped up a few coppers that were on the ground between them.

The first man glowered. "If I find out you've been cheating, I'll slice your guts open."

"They're your dice and you've been throwing them. Look," he said, pointing up the slope, "maybe the pup is coming to tell us that your luck is changing. Maybe a nice rich merchant, or maybe a succulent virgin!"

"Someone is coming!" the young lookout reported to the two bandits as he slid to a stop at the bottom of the slope.

"Of course, baka! But who's coming?"

The young man, Hachiro, scratched his head. "I think a merchant. Or maybe a samurai. I'm not sure."

"Fool!"

"If it's a samurai, let's let him pass," the man with the yellow teeth said.

"No. Samurai or not, I'm going to recover my loses. Coming?"

"All right. But let's give the youngster a chance to kill his first man." He looked at the young lookout, who now had an expression of confusion and fear on his face. "Take one of the spears. We'll keep him occupied. All you have to do is sneak up behind him and stick him in the back. Shove hard. Sometimes you hit a bone. Got that?"

"Are you sure . . . ?" the young man said.

The bandit with the yellow teeth hit the youngster on the side of the head, knocking him to his knees. "Do you want to be a bandit or not?"

Looking up with tears in his eyes, the young man nodded yes.

"Good! If this is the life you've chosen, you might as well do it right! Understand?"

Once again the youth nodded.

The man yanked one of the spears out of the ground, and his companion took the sword. They started scrambling up the slope to the road, setting up an ambush. The youth, rubbing the side of his head, picked up the second spear and made his way to a position where he could circle around and come up behind the man on the road.

As Kaze walked uphill on a long straight part of the road, he realized he could be easily seen from the rise ahead. Around him, the air was still and heavy, and the songbirds were not singing. That, by itself, was not proof that there were others ahead of him, but it served to heighten his senses. Although he didn't change his stride or slow down, out of habit he listened intently and scanned the side of the road ahead. His alertness was rewarded with the sound of small rocks rolling down the hillside that formed the down-slope portion of the dirt road.

He walked past the location of the sound. Suddenly, ahead of him, two men stepped out of the forest holding weapons. One had a spear and the other held a sword. So he was surrounded, although he wasn't supposed to know it yet.

"Oi! Hey, you!" one of the men ahead yelled gruffly.

Kaze stopped, watching the two men closely, but not making any aggressive moves. When Kaze said nothing, the man seemed to grow agitated. "Do you hear me?" the man demanded.

"Yes, I hear you," Kaze replied. "It's hard not to hear such a sweet voice as yours. And so polite, too."

The man frowned. He looked at his companion for guidance. His friend said, "Are you being smart with us?" He showed large yellow teeth when he talked.

"I wouldn't care to be smart with men such as you. In fact, being smart with you would be dumb."

"What's that mean?" the one with yellow teeth asked.

"As I've said," Kaze replied.

The two men looked at each other again, puzzled. Then the first to speak said, "Do you know who we are?"

"Why don't you tell me?"

"We're part of Boss Kuemon's gang. We control the roads around here, and you'll have to pay us a toll to walk on them."

"What toll?"

"All your money, of course!"

Behind him, Kaze could hear a shower of pebbles as someone scrambled up the hillside and onto the road.

"Is that all?"

"What else have you got?"

"Aren't you going to try to take my life, too? The one standing behind me is shaking so much that I can hear his bones rattle. Surely he must be thinking about something like killing me to make him shake so." Kaze heard a gasp behind him. Then he heard the person behind him step back. Good.

"If we have to, we're not afraid of killing you!" Yellow Teeth said.

"That's right, we've killed before."

"Oh? How many times?"

The one with yellow teeth puffed out his chest. "I've killed three men! All were smart mouths like you, who didn't give me their money!"

"And I've killed four!" his companion said.

"Seven men. That's certainly a life's work to be proud of. Your mothers did a service when they brought you into this world. And how many has the one behind me killed?"

"I've killed lots," said a young voice from behind Kaze. It had a quaver to it.

"You sound too young to have killed many men," Kaze said without looking behind him.

The two men in front of him laughed. "Pretty good, samurai," Yellow Teeth said. "Even this stranger can tell you're a virgin at killing men, boy. An experienced killer would have run this smart mouth samurai through long ago. Like this!"

Yellow Teeth lunged forward with his spear. Kaze stepped to the left and grabbed the shaft of the spear with his left hand as it passed to his right. Spinning in a complete circle, Kaze drew his sword with his right hand and had it swinging in a deadly arc when he completed his spin. The blade caught the man with the sword, who was rushing forward to help his companion. The sword bit deep into his neck and thorax, sliding out as the man's momentum carried him forward.

Kaze let go of the spear and brought his sword upward into the side of the spearman. The razor-sharp blade cut into the man's side, slicing deeply just under the rib cage. The man staggered backward, holding onto his side with a surprised look on his face. He lost his footing and fell backward onto the road.

Kaze quickly turned. He was facing a youth holding a spear in trembling hands. Behind him, Kaze could hear the hiss of air burbling from the sliced neck of one man and the groans of pain from the other. Both were dead, or soon would be, and Kaze just had to be careful that the man cut in the side didn't have the strength to make a last effort to kill him.

Kaze's eyes met the young man's. "Well?"

The youth dropped his spear and started running down the road, propelled both by the downhill slope and a jolt of terror. Kaze shook his head and turned to view the two bodies. The entire incident had taken seconds.

Kaze walked over to the man cut in the side. He was desperately trying to hold the pieces of his belly together while his lifeblood gushed out. Kaze put his sword at the ready, prepared to give the coup de grâce. "Should I?" he asked.

The man looked terrified and violently shook his head no. Kaze lowered his sword, wiped it clean on the man's clothes, and put it back into its scabbard. Then he dragged the man to the side of the road, where he could lean back against a tree out of the sun.

He went to the man with his neck cut but saw that he was already dead. By the time he returned to the man with the cut side, he was dead, too. Kaze looked down at the dead bandit and reflected on the human tendency to sustain a few more miserable seconds of existence in this troubled world. Sometimes it didn't make sense to him, especially since men would be reincarnated and live again. He sighed. He desired to be free to live or die as he wished, instead of tied up by debts of honor and obligation.

Before she died, the Lady had said, "Find my daughter." It saddened Kaze to think of that night and all that led up to it. Instead of the serene beauty he associated with her, the Lady's body was twisted and ravaged by the torture she had endured. Her face was haggard and lined with pain, and Kaze was desperate to find some warm, dry shelter for her. Instead, she was lying in the rain under a crude bower Kaze had constructed from tree limbs. After rescuing her from the Tokugawas, he had eluded the men with the banners with the family crest that looked like a spider: eight bent, white bamboo leaves surrounding a white diamond, all on a black background.

Walking in the dark storm, he had carried her deep into the mountains and, although he was weary, he wanted to continue fleeing the pursuing guards. But he realized she needed rest and had taken the risk of stopping to build a shelter to protect her from the hard rain. Kaze dared not build a fire and was considering asking permission to lie next to the Lady so his body heat could warm her when she had started speaking.

"I don't know how, but if she's still alive I want you to find her. It's my last wish and my last command to you," she said. She looked at him with feverish eyes, black from strain and pain. The translucent whiteness of her skin was caused by cold and her weakened condition, not by carefully applied rice powder, as it would have been in happier days. It gave her a ghostly appearance.

Kaze couldn't speak. He bowed formally in response to the Lady's order. Hot, wet tears flowed down his cheeks and mingled with the icy raindrops striking his face. The Lady extended a weak hand. It trembled with the effort to keep it in the air. "Give me your wakizashi." Surprised, Kaze removed his short sword from his sash, putting it in her hand. The weight of the sword caused her hand to drop to the ground, but she clutched the scabbard fiercely. At first Kaze thought the Lady had lost heart and was going to use the short sword to commit suicide, but then she said, "This represents your honor and the ability to take your own life. It is now mine until the girl is found."

Now the sword reposed in the Lady's funeral temple, waiting for him to reclaim it. That was how many villages and towns ago? And how many faces of little girls had he looked at, hoping to see a glimmer of the Lord or the Lady in that face? She was seven when he started, and now he was asking about nine-year-olds. Would he be asking about ten-, eleven-, and twelve-year-olds before he could find her? But ahead was another village, and maybe in this village he would find what he was seeking. Then his life would be his own again, along with his honor.

He looked around for the bandit's sword and went to pick it up. Using this weapon instead of his own sword, he started scraping out two shallow graves. When he finished burying the men, he looked at the trees lining the road until he found one that suited his purpose. Using the bandit's sword, he cleanly sliced a limb off, then took a second cut at the limb's stump to cut a piece of straight tree branch as long as his hand. He took out the small knife embedded in his scabbard and set to work, his hands moving with practiced economy as he carved the wood. From the rough wood emerged Kannon, the Goddess of Mercy. With a few final slices of his knife, he finished the folds of her robe and then gazed into her serene face. It was the face of the Lady, not as he had seen her last, but the way he wanted to remember her.

Placing her by the side of the road where she could look upon the graves of the two bandits, Kaze continued his journey.

*Dark night, ghostly moon.*
*A leaf flutters to the ground.*
*Demons on the road.*

It was early afternoon by the time Kaze walked into the next village.
The thatched roofs, the dusty streets that turned to mud when it
rained, and the weathered wooden walls all looked familiar to him.
Every village in Japan was starting to look the same to him. But like
Suzaka, Jiro's village, Kaze could see that this one, Higashi, was more
run-down and tattered than he was used to.

Unlike Jiro's village, Higashi boasted a tea shop where travelers
could get a meal and spend the night. It was located where three
roads met, and on the indigo-blue half-curtain that hung from the
top of the doorway, the name HIGASHI TEAHOUSE was painted. It
wasn't poetic or imaginative, but Kaze decided that as a name it had
the virtues of simplicity and clarity. He stepped into the shop.

In the entrance was a square area with a dirt floor. It was surrounded by the raised wooden floor of the teahouse. Kaze sat on the
edge of the floor and untied his traveling sandals. A serving girl in
the shop spotted him and came to the entrance. With a deep bow
she shouted, "*Irasshai!* Greetings!"

Kaze nodded an acknowledgment and bent down to remove his
footwear. When he straightened up, he was greeted by the sight of

the girl holding out a pair of clean cotton tabi to him, an unexpected touch. He removed his dirty tabi and put on the clean socks.

He followed the girl into the back of the teahouse. "Do you want a private room or the common room, samurai-sama?" the girl asked. Kaze considered his financial position and weighed it against his wish to be alone. His desire for solitude won.

"A private room."

She escorted him into a small, four-mat room. He sank down to the tatami, shifting his sword to a more convenient position.

"Sake?" the girl asked. Kaze noticed that she had grabbed the loose sleeve of her kimono and was twisting it between her fingers. He wondered if it was just a habit or if she was nervous about something.

"No. *Ocha*. Tea. Before you go, can you tell me if there has been anyone new to this village in the last few years? I'm trying to find a nine-year-old girl. She might have been sold as a servant."

The girl gave him a puzzled look and said, "No, samurai-sama."

"All right. Just get the tea."

The girl scurried off while Kaze settled in. The thin paper walls did nothing to dampen sounds, but the teahouse was very quiet. Kaze thought he could have saved a little money because it sounded like the common room in the teahouse was as empty as his small private one. He sighed. Thoughts of money weren't a worthy occupation for a samurai. Usually this was left to the samurai's wife to worry about. A gripping sadness clutched at Kaze's heart with the mere thought of a wife. His wife. His dead wife. Like the Lady, she was gone, too. He took a deep breath and tried to clear his mind.

The girl returned with a teapot and cup. She placed them before Kaze and poured the tea. As soon as she put the teapot down, she started worrying the sleeve of her kimono again. "Do you want something to eat?" she said. "The rice isn't made yet, but we have some delicious *oden*."

"Oden is fine. Bring it immediately. I'm hungry."

The girl rushed off to get his order. He picked up the cup and sipped at the hot, bitter tea. One good thing about his current life was that it had taught him to appreciate simple things: the joy of a cup of hot tea served without the ritual of the tea ceremony or the taste of a simple stew like oden.

He could hear the rapid shuffle of the girl's feet as she returned with his order. Suddenly, through the thin paper walls, he heard the girl stumble and the crash of a bowl hitting the floor. "Oh," he heard the girl utter.

Soon there was another, heavier set of feet approaching. It stopped, and the high-pitched voice of a man could be heard.

"Stupid! What's the matter with you?"

"I was just rushing because the samurai said he was hungry and—"

"Look, you've broken the bowl!"

"But I—"

"Damn it! I'm tired of your clumsiness! I don't know why we ever bought you."

"I'm sorry, but I was—"

"Don't talk back to me!" Kaze heard the smack of a hand hitting a face, and a sharp, surprised yelp from the girl. Kaze tried to block out such unpleasantness and took another sip of his tea. Like all good Japanese, he willed himself not to hear what could be easily heard through the thin walls.

A second, louder smack was heard. This time the girl cried out in pain. A third hit, and now the girl seemed frightened as well as in pain. Kaze sighed. He got up in one fluid motion and opened the shoji screen door of the room. A few feet away the serving girl was cowering on the floor, backing away from a bow-legged man dressed in a blue kimono. The man raised his hand to hit her again, and Kaze quickly crossed over to him before he could bring his hand down. Kaze grabbed the man's wrist.

Almost automatically, the man tried to jerk his hand away from Kaze's grip. Kaze tightened his fingers around the man's wrist and held the hand immobile. Surprised, the man looked around to meet Kaze's glare.

"I'm very hungry," Kaze said evenly to the innkeeper. "Please bring me another bowl of oden. You can add the price of the broken bowl to my bill."

The innkeeper opened his mouth to speak, then shut it. The anger drained from him as Kaze continued to glare at him. He stopped pulling at Kaze's grip and said, "Of course, samurai-sama. I was just upset with the clumsiness of the girl. She broke a dish yesterday, and with business the way it is I can't afford to pay for such clumsiness."

Kaze released the innkeeper's wrist and walked back to his room, closing the shoji screen after him. After a pause, he heard the innkeeper say, "Well, don't just sit there crying. Clean things up, then go get another bowl of oden."

Kaze picked up his teacup and took another sip. He was halfway done with the cup when the shoji screen opened and the serving girl came in with a tray containing another bowl of oden. Her face was still red where she had been slapped, but her tears were wiped dry. Kaze took the chopsticks off the tray and picked up the bowl. Holding it close to his mouth, he took a piece of steaming *daikon* radish and sucked it in.

The girl sat watching Kaze eat. With a second piece of vegetable in his mouth, Kaze said, "Well?"

The girl gave a clumsy bow. "Thank you, samurai-sama."

Kaze brushed aside the remark. "The punishment was out of proportion to the crime, but you were clumsy."

"I know, samurai-sama. It's just that we're all on edge here. Even the master is scared. That's why he hit me. He's not normally a mean man. He's just upset like the rest of us."

"Why is everyone upset?"

The girl looked over her shoulder and almost whispered, "The master doesn't want us to talk about it. He says it will hurt business."

"There is no business, except for me, so why don't you tell me?"

Once again, the girl looked around. Then she said, "Two nights ago we saw a terrible sight. A demon rode through the village."

Kaze believed in demons, just as he believed in other spirits and ghosts. Everyone did. But he had never actually seen a demon, and he found it strange that this girl said she had. "What kind of demon?"

"It was horrible. It had a red face with two horns, like this." She put her hands to her forehead and made little horns with her fingers. "It had long white hair and wide shoulders. It was riding a black horse and carrying off a poor soul to hell."

"What do you mean?"

"A man was strapped across the horse!"

"This demon rode a horse?"

"Yes, it was awful! It came thundering through the village and rode off down the road. We all saw it, and we've been scared ever since. No one knows when it will come back—maybe this time for one of us!"

Kaze put down his teacup and studied the face of the girl before him. She was perhaps eighteen or nineteen, with a coarse peasant's face. She had a strip of cloth wrapped around her forehead as a sweatband, and her kimono was old but clean. The fear in her eyes was palpable, and it was plain she believed what she was saying.

"Is that so . . ." Kaze said, letting the last word trail off to indicate he was a bit skeptical.

"*Honto desu!* It's true!"

"And the demon came riding through this village?"

"Yes."

"And several people saw it?"

"That's right, samurai-sama. I'm not making it up. Almost everyone in the village saw it. We heard this horse in the night and looked out to see it. Since then, the master's been reciting sutras every spare moment he can find to ward off evil spirits from this house. Most of the village has been doing the same."

"Where did the demon go?"

"No one knows for sure. Did you happen to see it on the road?"

"No. I just came from Uzen prefecture. I'm on my way to Rikuzen prefecture, but last night I stayed in Suzaka village."

"Oh, then you took the wrong road at the crossroads."

"What do you mean?"

"You remember the crossroads where four roads meet?"

"Yes, I remember it very well."

"One of the roads is from Uzen."

"That's the road I came on."

"Yes. One of the roads goes deeper into the mountains, toward Mount Fukuto. Another road goes to Suzaka village, and the fourth comes here, Higashi village."

"So you don't have to go through Suzaka to get to here?"

"No. That's where the District Lord has his manor, but most people don't go through Suzaka. That's why it doesn't even have a teahouse. Most people go directly from the crossroads to here."

"So the roads form a kind of triangle, connecting the crossroads, Suzaka village and Higashi village?"

"Yes."

"And up ahead is a branch in the road where I can continue toward Rikuzen or go back to the crossroads?"

"That's right."

"Is that so . . ." This time Kaze's intonation conveyed that he was genuinely interested in what the girl was telling him. "I understand that the Lord of this District has only governed it for two years," he continued.

"Yes. That's Lord Manase. He got the District as a reward for killing the famous general Iwaki Sadataka at the battle of Sekigahara. He took the general's head to Tokugawa Ieyasu himself and presented it and got this District as his reward."

"The District doesn't seem very peaceful."

"It's terrible! Ever since Lord Manase took over things have gone from bad to worse. The teahouse business gets less each year because people are afraid to travel through here. No one is safe. Everyone is suffering!"

"Is that so?" Kaze said. The words were the same as before, but this time the tone conveyed sympathy.

The girl then leaned forward, almost whispering. "Tonight I'll come visit you in your bed. We'll have to be silent, so the master won't know, because I'll do it for free. I wouldn't charge you, samurai-sama."

Kaze studied the stumpy body and rough, red face of the serving girl and swallowed what he was going to say. Instead, in a kind tone, he said, "I won't be staying the night. I want to return to Suzaka village."

"But it's late," the serving girl protested. "You'll have to travel in the dark! The roads are full of bandits, and the demon might still be about."

"Yes, I know."

When Kaze finally got back to Suzaka, it had been dark for several hours. As he approached Jiro's hut, he could see the glow of the fire peeking through some gaps in the door. Kaze rapped on the hut's sliding wooden door and said, "Oi! Jiro! Wake up! It's the samurai. I've returned and want to spend the night."

Kaze heard movement in the hut. Then he heard the stick that prevented the farmhouse door from sliding open being removed. The door was shoved ajar slightly.

"Jiro?" Kaze said. There was no response. He waited for a few minutes, but there was no more sound from inside the farmhouse. Silently, Kaze loosened his sword and slid it out of its scabbard. With his free hand he slid the door of the farmhouse fully open.

Inside, he could see the glow of the charcoal fire in the firepit and smell the bubbling porridge in the pot. Otherwise, he could detect nothing in the darkened farmhouse.

Cautiously, Kaze stepped into the hut, saying, "Jiro?"

A net dropped down on his head, trapping his sword arm under its heavy skein. Kaze brought his sword up and had sliced through two ropes of the net when the first blow hit. It was heavy, like a club.

It staggered Kaze and forced him to one knee. He was attempting to stand when the second blow hit. Kaze twisted, but the enfolding shroud of the net prevented him from dodging the heavy fall of cudgels. One blow hit him on the side of his head, and he saw a red flash. Before he could absorb this, additional blows pummeled his head, forcing him into the black sleep of unconsciousness.

## CHAPTER 7

*My footprints on a*
*Black sand beach. A rising tide*
*Erases the past.*

**K**aze woke to the sounds of a man groaning in pain. It took him a few befuddled moments to realize that the sounds were coming from him. He stopped the groans and sucked in a breath of air to clear his head.

He was sitting hunched up in a wooden cage barely large enough to hold him. He felt his face with his fingers, wincing at especially tender spots. Good. His neck, cheek, shoulders, and face were bruised but apparently not broken.

He looked around and could see that the cage was in some kind of small courtyard. Next to him was another, similar cage. Inside the cage was Jiro, his knees drawn up and his head hanging down.

"Oi! You!" Kaze said to get his attention. Jiro looked up. His expression was one of despair and infinite sorrow. Instead of being moved to compassion, Kaze grew angry. Jiro had already given up. "Why are we here?" Kaze demanded.

Jiro made no reply. He just hung his head down again.

Kaze snorted in disgust and looked closely at his cage. It was old but of surprisingly good construction. He lifted his feet and pushed against the door with all his strength. Nothing. He looked around the cage once more to make sure there wasn't a weak spot but satisfied himself that trying to break out of the cage was a fruitless effort. He would have to wait until they took him out of the cage for some reason. That might not be for days, so he got himself as comfortable as possible and tried to relax, husbanding his strength.

He closed his eyes. He couldn't help but think of what his Sensei, his teacher, would have said about his current predicament.

"Baka! Fool! You knew there was something suspicious and you still went stumbling in like some rank amateur! It's disgusting."

"Yes, Sensei. But the net was unexpected. It . . ."

Of course, the Sensei would then skewer him with a look of contempt. In the old days, Kaze would drop to his knees and bow with his head touching the ground.

"You know the lessons," the Sensei would say. "What lesson is appropriate for this?"

"Expect the unexpected."

"Of course. Careless!" Sensei had a way of saying "careless" that made it sound worse than the foulest oath Kaze had ever heard a drunken castle guard utter. Kaze would never have a response after Sensei said this word. He could only wait in silence to see if he would be forgiven. Somehow, he always was.

"I don't know why I continue to waste my time with someone so stupid," the Sensei would eventually say. Then he would sit Kaze down and carefully explain to him how he could avoid the situation in the future. Besides the tactical advice on how to handle the situation at the hut, the Sensei would have undoubtedly also told him that he could stay out of this kind of trouble by simply minding his own business and staying focused on what he was supposed to do. It never prospered a man to pursue problems that were not his own.

Kaze wished his Sensei were still alive because he often needed advice and now had no resources to get it. It would be embarrassing to have to confess to him his current situation, but he would gladly trade that embarrassment just to hear his Sensei scold him once again.

Keeping his eyes closed, Kaze listened intently for the sound of anyone approaching, but he let his mind drift to when he first met his Sensei.

He was eight. A group of boys his age were trudging up a narrow mountain path. The boys were giddy with thin mountain air tinged with the smell of adventure and freedom. It was early winter and a light dusting of snow covered the ground, even though it was not exceptionally cold. Gaunt black branches hung over the twisting path as the boys engaged in a steady chatter composed of youthful spirits and high expectations.

"I hear he's a master of *kumi-uchi* and *tachi-uchi* style of fencing," one boy said excitedly.

"Of course he's a master. He killed fourteen men in individual duels before he retired to these mountains."

"I'm going to kill a hundred men! It'll be a case of the student surpassing the master!" another boasted.

"He hasn't accepted a student for a long time," Kaze cautioned.

Lord Okubo's son, who was higher ranked than Kaze, looked at him and said, "He may not accept *you,* but he's certainly going to accept me. It will be an honor for him to have an Okubo as a student."

Kaze, who had already shared some military training with Okubo, knew to say nothing. Okubo was a year older, but Kaze had still bested him at everything, including a schoolboy fight in front of the temple where they took writing instruction. The larger Okubo was still smarting from that and could use only his superior social position as a weapon.

"How far up the mountain is his hut?" puffed fat Yoshii. Although he was the son of a samurai, his parents indulged him, and his weight and lack of physical training made the journey a tough one.

"I don't know," Kaze admitted. "It's supposed to be at the end of this trail."

"I'll be glad to get there," Yoshii said. "I could use something hot to eat and some time warming myself by the fire."

"Don't you know anything?" sneered Okubo. "When we get there we're supposed to get on our knees and bow to the door of the Sensei's hut. It shows we're serious about getting him to train us. If necessary, we're supposed to stay there all night to show him how serious we are."

"All night?" said Yoshii.

Okubo wrinkled his nose in disgust and picked up the pace. The other boys, including the puffing Yoshii, hurried to catch up. Kaze didn't mind the faster pace, but he was sure Okubo was doing it just to be cruel to Yoshii.

Presently the boys came across a wider patch of road, where the snow was laid like a pristine white futon. They plowed through the ankle-deep snow for several steps before Kaze stopped and said, "Chotto matte. Wait a minute."

"What now?" Okubo said, stopping. "First that pig Yoshii and now you. If we keep stopping we'll never get there. What?"

"Look." Kaze pointed to the road ahead.

For a long distance ahead of the boys the road was not the smooth white surface it had been. It was disturbed by marks in the snow.

"I don't see anything," Yoshii said.

"Look at the road," Kaze instructed.

Yoshii stared intently, then confessed, "I don't know what I'm supposed to be looking at."

"The road is disturbed."

"I can see that."

"But what is it disturbed by?"

The boys gathered around one of the marks in the snow. It was long and narrow, with three claws in the front and a fourth claw, like a rooster's spur, in the back. From a lifetime close to nature, they were sensitive to shifts in weather or the tracks of animals. They had hunted with their fathers and the other men of the clan. The large tracks were like nothing they had seen before.

"Is it a bird?"

"Have you ever seen a bird this big?" The tracks were longer than the length of a katana.

"Is it a lizard?"

"That's even sillier than a bird. A lizard would have to be the size of a dragon to make a track this big." An awful stillness descended as the word "dragon" was uttered.

Kaze looked around. "The tracks come from the side here, then go down the road for quite awhile, then go off into the trees ahead. Let's follow them."

"Are you crazy?" Yoshii spluttered.

"I've never seen anything like this before, and I want to see what it is."

"I'm not following this thing!"

"Me, either!"

"We've got to get to the Sensei's hut," Okubo said. "We don't know how far it is, and we might not even get there before dark."

"Dark?" Yoshii uttered.

"Maybe. We don't know how far it is."

"I'm going back to town," Yoshii said. "My parents can send me to one of the schools there. I don't have to be up in these mountains with a crazy hermit just to learn *kendo*." Silence greeted Yoshii's declaration. Even Okubo didn't take the opportunity to sneer at the pudgy youngster's desire to return to the town. Emboldened by the lack of criticism, Yoshii went one step further. "Is anyone coming back with me?" he asked.

Several of the boys looked at each other, and finally one said, "That sounds like a more sensible idea to me."

"Yeah."

"Me, too."

"Fine," Yoshii said, surprised at his newfound position as a leader. "Let's head back. It doesn't do for us to be up here in the dark. Only the gods know what is up here in these mountains." And, without a word of goodbye, he turned on his heels and started back down the mountain trail with considerably more speed than he showed coming up it.

The boys who agreed to return with him looked surprised but scurried to catch up.

"Cowards!" Okubo shouted. "Scared because you see tracks in the snow! Disgusting!" He looked at Kaze and said, "Why don't you hurry up and join them, too?"

Kaze observed mildly. "I just pointed out the tracks in the snow. I didn't say I wanted to turn back."

"Well, you should turn back, along with the rest of the cowards!"

Kaze said nothing, observing Okubo.

"Why don't you say anything?"

"I have nothing to say. I'm just waiting for us to move on."

"Do you think I'm afraid to go on?" Okubo asked.

Kaze cocked his head to one side, shrugged, and continued his journey down the path without comment. Okubo looked at the three other boys who remained, then started down the path after Kaze. They all walked in awful silence, devoid of boyish laughter or taunts. Trees that were merely gaunt in winter now took on a sinister look, and the dark shadows in the woods were scanned with nervous glances as the boys closed ranks into a tight pack. The cawing of a winter crow made the boys jump, then giggle with nervous relief when they saw the bird.

About a half hour before dark, they reached the end of the road and found a rough country hut. The hut had a thick thatched roof and walls formed by stacked logs. A door of uneven wood dominated the face of the structure, and it seemed to have no windows. It was the kind of crude shelter a woodcutter or charcoal burner might have, not the grand abode of a master fencer.

"Is this it?" Okubo asked.

"It must be. We're at the end of the trail."

"Are we supposed to bow now?" one of the boys asked.

Okubo didn't respond, but he dropped to his knees and bowed facing the door of the hut. Kaze stared at Okubo's back, looking at the white family mon near the neck on Okubo's black outer kimono.

It looked like a white spider, with bent bamboo leaves surrounding a diamond. The other boys, including Kaze, did the same and Kaze tried to clear his mind and meditate. Meditation would not anesthetize you from the effects of the snow, but through meditation you could learn to ignore it.

Night fell, and the mountain cold started creeping through their knees and feet, chilling each boy to the bone. The boys had already been taken on mock military maneuvers in the field. They were used to being outdoors, even in winter, and they had been toughened by a life lived close to nature. Still, they weren't used to kneeling in snow for long periods of time. It was an uncomfortable and stressful end to a disturbing journey.

From inside the hut, they could hear the banging of pots, so they knew someone was home. As it got darker a sliver of light peeked out from under the bottom of the door. The smell of smoke mingled with the crisp pine air of the mountains, creating a tantalizing smell headier than any incense. Kaze could imagine what it was like to be in that hut, huddled around the fire with a warm quilt wrapped around him. Almost immediately he cursed himself, using the boyhood curses he had picked up when he was around older men. It did no good to imagine what it would be like to be warm. It only increased the torture of being in the snow. Instead, following the lessons he was taught about the Zen style, he cleared his mind and tried to think of nothing, simply existing in the universe and ignoring the cold that was steadily taking over his limbs.

The movement in the hut stopped, but the door remained closed. In a few minutes the light from under the door was extinguished.

"Do you think he knows we're here?" one boy asked.

"He wouldn't be much of a Sensei if he didn't."

"Do you think he'll let us in?"

"I guess not. Maybe he wants us to stay out all night to show how determined we are."

"It's an insult to leave an Okubo out here this long!"

"Are you going to knock at his door?"

"Of course not. I have my pride to think of. I'd lose face if I did something like that. Why don't you knock?"

"I have pride, too."

"But you should—"

Okubo's comment was cut short by a strange sound. It was a whipping sound that in the silent mountain night echoed very loud.

"What's—"

"*Yakamashii!* Shut up! Listen."

The swish, swish sound continued.

"What is that?"

"I don't know. It sounds a little like a riding crop moving through the air before it strikes the horse."

"Where's it coming from?"

Two of the boys got up from their bow and looked around. Suddenly, with a shaking finger and an equally shaky voice, one of them pointed and said, "Lllooook!"

All the boys, including Kaze, looked in the direction the boy was pointing. There, in the darkness of the woods, they could barely make out a white shape in the faint starlight. It was at a level more than twice as high as a man's head, it was the size of a large bird, and it flitted between two trees with alarming speed. A swishing noise accompanied its movement.

"What's that?"

"I don't know. I've never seen—"

"It's a ghost! I know it's a ghost! Lord Buddha protect me! It's some kind of mountain spirit that will kill us all! Those weren't dragon tracks, they were demon tracks!" The boy who made this identification jumped to his feet and rushed to the door of the hut. Two others were right behind him, panic lending both speed and strength to their cold-numbed legs. They started pounding on the door.

"Let us in!"

"Open the damn door!"

"Lord Buddha protect me! Please, Sensei, let us in!"

The pounding had no effect, and the door remained solidly closed. "Look, the way to the trail is open! Let's run!"

The three boys started rushing pell-mell toward the trail that brought them to the hut, which was in the opposite direction from the apparition.

Kaze, still on his knees, glanced over at Okubo. The older boy's face was so pale that he looked like a ghost himself. But he made no move to run. Whether this was caused by bravery, fear, or pride, Kaze couldn't tell. For Kaze, it was simple caution. He wanted to see more before he went running into the night in terror.

Instead of seeing more, he heard more.

"BLOOD!" A deep, hollow voice came from the woods where the boys had seen the spirit. It reverberated in the mountain air with an unnatural resonance. "I want blood! Give me blood!"

Kaze stood up. He wasn't ready to run yet, but he wanted to prepare to run if he had to. Okubo misinterpreted Kaze's action. As soon as he saw Kaze move, Okubo jumped to his feet and bolted with the rest. Kaze risked a quick glance over his shoulder to see Okubo flying down the trail, then he returned his attention to the woods.

"I want *your* blood! Give me *your* blood!" the booming voice said, but Kaze saw no signs that the owner of that strange voice was doing anything to collect on its demand. He stood there, straining every sense he had to see, hear, or smell something from the woods, but now in the darkness it was silent. Kaze didn't return to his bowing position, but he didn't run, either.

The rest of the night was spent in silence, save for the rustling of an owl's wings as it flew above the hut with the night's prey in its claws. Kaze had never experienced a night where silence could build so much tension. He had sometimes been given mock guard duty on maneuvers and had once been caught sleeping at his post. He still remembered the beating he got for that transgression, administered by the hands of his own father. He never fell asleep again at his post as guard, but he had always found himself fighting the tug of dark sleep while he stayed awake. That night the cold and the terror and potential for new terrors to come drove all thoughts of sleep from his body, and when the dawn came the next morning, Kaze was relieved to see the surrounding woods turn from black to gray to colors with the increasing light.

A few minutes after the sun was finally in the sky, the door of the hut opened and a spry old man came out. His hair was long, white, and shaggy, and his clothes were like a simple peasant's, except for the two swords stuck in his sash. His eyes were sharp and arresting, like the eyes of a hunting hawk. His hands were large and powerful, and despite the man's age Kaze could see he still had tremendous strength in his arms and shoulders. Kaze dropped to his knees and bowed.

The man walked over to Kaze and stared down at him. "I suppose you want to be a student?"

Kaze wanted to ask if the old man had heard or seen the ghostly happenings of the night before, but decided to stifle his questions, at least for now. "Hai! Yes, Sensei!"

"Do you know how to use an ax to chop firewood?"

"Yes, Sensei!"

"Then come on. You might as well make yourself useful while I decide if I want a student."

CHAPTER 8

*The past calls to the
present. A memory of
the young bird's first song.*

**K**aze spent an hour chopping firewood. The full-sized ax was heavy and clumsy, but he kept at it gamely despite his fatigue and the difficulty. He was proud of the pile of firewood he had managed to create when the Sensei returned. The Sensei looked at the pile of wood but made no comment. All he said was, "I suppose you'll want some breakfast?"

"Yes, Sensei!"

"Then follow me." The Sensei led Kaze into his hut, where a big pot of *okayu,* rice porridge, was bubbling over the fire. The hut was sparsely furnished and almost devoid of personal possessions. The major exception was a sword stand in one corner, where a long katana and a shorter wakizashi were stored. Like every boy of his age in the warrior class, Kaze fancied himself a judge of fine swords. These were exceptionally fine. They were swords much finer than the everyday swords worn by the Sensei and even finer than the swords Kaze's father kept to wear on very special occasions.

The Sensei walked over to a corner of the room, and Kaze thought he was going to get a bowl for the okayu. Instead, the old man picked up a piece of firewood. Turning suddenly, he threw it at Kaze.

Shocked, Kaze nimbly stepped to one side as the firewood

bounced against the wall behind him and clattered to the floor. The Sensei looked at Kaze for a moment, then calmly proceeded to pick up a wooden bowl and a pair of hashi, as if flying pieces of firewood were the prelude to every meal. "Here," he said, handing the implements to Kaze. "Help yourself."

Kaze warily took the bowl and hashi from the Sensei, but the Sensei made no additional aggressive moves. "Find me when you're done eating and I'll give you a kendo lesson. You're not my student yet, but it won't hurt to see how stupid you are at learning." Glancing at the piece of firewood that had been thrown at him, Kaze sat down to breakfast wondering what kind of teacher he had sought out.

His questions about this Sensei increased with the lesson, because the Sensei started Kaze's formal instruction in the way of the sword by teaching him how to tie the sash on a kimono.

"In ancient times, we used to hang our swords from our sash with cords," the Sensei began. "Now it is our custom to place our swords in our kimono sash. You have been wearing swords for ceremonial occasions since you were small. On those occasions the swords were for show. In battle the swords will be for survival. You have to learn to carry them as a samurai. Proudly, but also in a practical manner. You can't carry them too loosely, or they will slip. You can't carry them too tightly, or the sash will constrict your wind and cause you annoyance. Today you will learn how to tie the sash of your kimono in a proper fashion. It is a small thing, but from small, fundamental things the foundation for greater things is built. After you learn this lesson, you will observe how other samurai tie their sashes. That observation will teach you if a man is grounded in fundamentals or if he is just displaying his swords in a flashy manner."

Under the Sensei's instruction, Kaze tied and retied his kimono sash until he could do it perfectly. He had to admit that carrying the two swords of the samurai tucked into his sash was now more comfortable, but he couldn't see what this had to do with sword fighting.

"Can I ask a question, Sensei?" Kaze said at the end of the lesson.

"What is it?"

"When will I be taught things that have to do with kendo?"

"Baka! This does have to do with kendo. Everything I teach you has to do with *bushido*, the way of the warrior. This morning you learned a lesson before breakfast. A *bushi* must keep fit, even if it's through something like chopping wood. You should also learn calligraphy, art, and poetry, but a bushi can't simply occupy his time with artistic pursuits while waiting for the next war. He must do things to stay in good physical condition. At breakfast you were taught another lesson, a famous one, when I threw the piece of wood at you. Bushi must remain alert and expect an attack at any time. Have you ever heard that?"

"Yes, Sensei." Kaze anticipated another attack from the Sensei. That was what was usually done when students were taught this lesson, and he knew it. The student is told to expect an attack at any time, then he is asked if he understands that. When he says yes, the Sensei launches an immediate attack to illustrate that the lesson is fact.

"Do you understand that?"

"Yes, Sensei!" Kaze readied himself for the launch of some kind of attack, like the flying firewood. Instead, the Sensei merely continued with his lecture. Kaze was almost disappointed.

"In life things will happen to you and you must draw the lessons from them. You will not always have someone there to explain them to you, and you must learn to learn on your own. Do you understand that?"

"Yes, Sensei."

"Good, then go gather up some of the firewood you chopped this morning so we can make dinner."

A simple dinner was eaten in almost total silence. After spending a sleepless night and a long day, Kaze could barely keep his eyes open. The dark hut and the flickering fire lulled him to drowsiness as surely as a mother's lullaby. Kaze was given a futon and a quilt and shown a place to sleep in one of the outbuildings near the Sensei's hut. "I'll tell you by tomorrow if I want you for a student," the Sensei said as he left.

Kaze dropped into a deep, exhausted sleep. The sight of dragon footprints and flittering ghosts and unearthly voices calling for blood entered his dreams. The frightening events of the night before twisted his dreams into a nightmare, and he was certain he could feel the presence of a demon or malignant spirit right in the room with him. Suddenly, a sharp pain across his arm and shoulder jolted him out of sleep.

He sat up confused and bleary-eyed. He looked around and there, sitting next to him, was the Sensei. A clay lamp was by the Sensei, and he held a stick of bamboo. He was looking at Kaze.

Kaze rubbed his shoulder and was about to protest being hit with the stick. Then he shut his mouth. After a moment's silence, Kaze said, "Be prepared for an attack at any time."

The Sensei nodded. "Good! Very good! You're not as thick and stupid as you seem. I'll take you as a student. Chop some firewood when you wake up, and after breakfast we'll continue your training."

Kaze smiled. One of his first lessons was to expect attack at any time, and yet he had still been captured at Jiro's hut. He expected an attack, but he didn't think about the nature of the attack. From his circumstances, he knew the attacker must be the local Magistrate. He held the slow, stupid Magistrate in low regard. Yet even stupid men can kill you if you are careless. Kaze hoped that this time he would survive so he could benefit from that lesson in the future.

The sound of footsteps snapped him out of his reverie. He opened his eyes. People were coming.

## CHAPTER 9

*An apparition*
*Echoes the sounds of the past.*
*Past becomes present.*

"**S**ooo yooou caaptuured thaaat samuraiiii." Kaze couldn't see the speaker yet, but the voice had the high pitch and long, chanting quality of court nobles. It surprised Kaze to hear it in this rural District where a court noble would not be found, but he had heard enough nobles to know that the accent was an affectation and not something the speaker was raised with.

"Yes, Manase-sama." The voice of the officious Magistrate.

"Good. Well, let's see them," Manase said, using the same sing-song inflection.

The two men entered the courtyard. The Magistrate was wearing the same kimono he wore when Kaze first saw him, but Manase's costume was a surprise. Manase wore a brightly colored kimono with several rich robes. At his sleeves and the hem of the robes, the thick layers of cloth formed a dazzling rainbow that almost illuminated the drab courtyard. On top of Manase's head was a tall, black-gauze cap, like that of a noble, with a black ribbon coming down around his chin to hold the peaked cap in place. The cut of the robes was old-fashioned, and the District Lord looked like the image on a very old scroll painting stepping off the silk and coming to life.

Manase stopped several feet from the cages. The Magistrate seemed surprised at the District Lord's abrupt halt, so Manase explained.

"I don't like to get too near." He gave an exaggerated sigh. "These types always smell so bad!"

"Yes, yes, my Lord. We can—"

Before the Magistrate could finish, Kaze decided to take a chance. "I am Matsuyama Kaze," he said in a voice as clear as his painful face would allow. "Although my current circumstances are strange, Lord Manase, I want to repeat my praise for the fragment of *Dojoji* I saw yesterday. I hope some day to see a complete performance."

The Magistrate bustled up to Kaze's cage. "Here, here you. You shut up until you're spoken to! Daring to address the Lord—"

"Magistrate."

The Magistrate halted in midsentence and looked at Manase. "Yes, my Lord?"

"Take that man out of that cage and get him a bath and fresh clothes."

"But my Lord—"

Manase gave a quick, but graceful, flip of his hand. His voice had a tinge of impatience to it. "Do as I order."

"Of course, of course, my Lord. Fresh clothes and a bath. Right away!"

Manase turned and left the courtyard. The Magistrate also left, but in a few minutes he returned with two guards. They were as badly equipped and loutish as the two guards Kaze had seen at the crossroads. In fact, on closer inspection, they were the guards he had seen at the crossroads.

The Magistrate fumbled in the sleeve of his kimono and came out with a large brass key. It was a rectangular bar of metal with notches filed along one end. He gave the key to a guard, who stuck it in the lock of Kaze's cage and opened the door.

Kaze unfolded himself from his cramped confinement. As he got to his feet, he felt himself swaying slightly, the legacy of his beating and a night spent stuffed into the cage. He closed his eyes briefly, centered himself, and stopped the swaying.

The Magistrate grabbed Kaze's arm. It wasn't to support him but to escort him like some small child or prisoner. Kaze shook off the Magistrate's hand and glared at him.

The jowly cheeks of the Magistrate were set in hard slabs. His small eyes were like two tiny black pearls in a sea of flesh. They radiated unadulterated malevolence toward Kaze.

"Come on, then," the Magistrate said, walking out of the courtyard.

As Kaze followed he reflected on the danger of taking anyone too lightly. The Magistrate was a buffoon, but buffoons can be especially dangerous because they will kill out of stupidity. Life is so fragile and brief. It can be snuffed out by a misplaced step or a lack of caution or failing to properly assess the measure of a man.

Kaze was taken to the kitchen area of the manor and fed. The manor was set up as a large rectangle, with several open courtyards in the middle. The courtyards were edged by covered verandas with raised wooden floors and tile roofs. This was the typical design of most country manors, and Kaze was familiar with the general layout without ever having been in Manase Manor before.

Kaze was then given a bath in a wooden *ofuro* bathtub. The bathtub was chest-high and as wide as the armspan of a man. The wet, fragrant wooden slats of the tub were fitted together so cunningly that no caulking was needed to keep it watertight. Along one wall was a bench, where the occupants of the tub could sit while they relaxed in water up to their necks. A small fire in a copper box was stoked by a serving woman. The box protruded into one wall of the ofuro and heated the water to a satisfying degree of scalding pleasure.

Kaze stripped down and allowed the serving woman stoking the fire to help him scrub down before he got into the tub. He used a wooden scraper and a rag to remove the dirt, wincing in pain but not crying out as the cleaning tools were applied to the dark bruises that mottled his skin. Being naked at an ofuro before a strange woman was something that held no erotic connotations for Kaze. Since childhood he had taken baths in this fashion, with servants of one type or another helping him. The woman scrubbing his naked back was as much a fixture of the ofuro as the bench seat or pile of wood to heat it.

When he was fully clean, the woman dipped water out of the ofuro and rinsed the dirt off him with bucket after bucket of steaming water. Then he climbed up on a small stool and stepped into the scalding water, sinking into the tub and sitting on the bench, letting the water lap at his chin. Kaze let the steaming hot water wash away his aches from the beating and night in the cage.

"Ahh, that feels wonderful," Kaze said.

The woman made no comment but just looked down sullenly.

"This is a fine ofuro," Kaze tried again.

"Hai. Yes." The woman murmured it so softly that Kaze almost didn't hear her reply.

He closed his eyes and put his head back against the edge of the tub. "Your master must enjoy this ofuro." The woman made no answer, but instead busied herself shoving some more wood into the copper box.

"Doesn't he enjoy this?" Kaze asked, curious.

Again answering so softly that Kaze had to strain to hear her, the woman said, "The Lord doesn't use the ofuro much." The thought of a Japanese not using an available bath was alien to Kaze, and he paused to contemplate what this meant about the District Lord. He speculated that perhaps the Lord was a devotee of Dutch learning, that strange set of beliefs and superstitions brought by the smelly Europeans. Kaze had never met one of these strange creatures, but they were notorious for not bathing like civilized human beings. These large, hairy barbarians brought with them a whole slew of fantastic stories about the customs of their homeland. Most people would be ashamed of the things the barbarians seemed proud of, and the stories about them that Kaze had heard alternatively fascinated and disgusted him. They were notorious liars, and Kaze thought that anyone who would follow their outlandish customs or believe their silly tales must be feeble-minded. Still, Tokugawa Ieyasu kept several around him, and so did Nobunaga and Hideyoshi before him, but Kaze thought they must be kept as pets, the same way one would keep an interesting dog.

He tried to engage the serving woman in more conversation to find out about Lord Manase's household, but she responded only with a few grunts and bobs of her head. Since becoming a ronin, Kaze had become accustomed to a style of treatment he had not been exposed to previously. Even the peasants treated him with less respect, though he was still a samurai. Yet Kaze wasn't sure if the servant's reticence was rudeness or something else.

She did provide Kaze with a copper mirror when he requested one, and Kaze studied the damage to his face. It was puffy and purple in spots, but Kaze dismissed the beating as work done by amateurs. He had been in worse fights, fights where he couldn't move for a week after the battle was over, and he had been the winner.

The kimono that Kaze was given after the bath was a deep indigo blue with a white crane on the back. The crane pattern was created by protecting areas of the cloth with a thick paste, then putting the cloth in an earthen jar filled with dye. The cloth was left to sit for weeks, staining the fibers a deep blue, as blue as the deepest lakes or the Inland Sea itself. Later the cloth was removed and the paste cleaned off. A white pattern on a blue cloth was the result. This pattern was a very delicate one. The crane, a symbol of long life and prosperity, showed the outline of individual feathers.

Kaze's own clothes, which were simple utilitarian things, were taken to be cleaned. They would be ripped apart at the seams, washed in a stream, put on special frames, starched, and then resewn when they were dry. The various panels of the kimono would be swapped around to even out wear on the garment.

After the bath, Kaze was fed miso soup, rice, and pickles. Finally, Kaze was taken into Lord Manase's presence. As he followed the serving girl leading him, Kaze noticed that the manor was in need of repair. A few errant tiles were seen peeking over the edge of the roof, and some of the shoji screens had holes where crude paper patches had been applied. Despite Manase's fine kimonos and sumptuous Noh outfits, the District did not seem a prosperous one.

Kaze was shown to an eight-mat room that functioned as Lord Manase's study. The room was dark, and Kaze could see that wooden shutters were used instead of shoji, leaving Manase to sit in a perpetual gloom as light filtered through the shutters in compressed slits. Manase was sitting on a *zabuton* cushion with a folded paper scroll spread out before him on the floor. Kaze could see that the scroll was an old one and that the writing on it was in *hiragana*, the fluid cursive script, often used by women, that spelled words phonetically. Kaze sat on the tatami mat a respectful distance from Lord Manase.

Without looking up, Manase asked, "Have you ever read *The Tale of Genji*?"

"Many years ago."

"What did you think of it?"

"Lady Murasaki was a genius."

Manase looked up in surprise and give a tittering laugh. He covered his mouth with his hand, just like a maiden. Kaze noted that Manase had his teeth blackened, like a Court noble in Kyoto. It puzzled and disturbed Kaze to see this rural District Lord adopting the language, clothes, and customs of the Court. It seemed out of place and presumptuous.

"A genius! A woman genius!" Manase gave another high-pitched laugh. "I can't say I have ever heard of a woman being called a genius before." Manase's face had a light dusting of rice powder on it. His eyebrows were shaved, and small false eyebrows were painted high on his forehead.

"I judged her work, not her sex. No man I know wrote about life six hundred years ago with such passion and interest."

Manase nodded his head. "In that I suppose you're right. I've tried to read all I can about the courtly life of that period, and I keep coming back to *The Tale of Genji* over and over again. If a woman can be a genius, she was one, but it's strange to hear you call her that."

Kaze said nothing.

Manase folded up the scroll and said, "You're also a devotee of Noh."

"I used to be, in times past. It's been many years since I've seen a Noh play. That's why it was a real pleasure to see you that day."

"And how did you know it was me?"

"A Noh dancer learns balance and grace. His walk can be quite distinctive. When you were practicing *Dojoji* I was able to observe your walk for a long time. When I saw you enter the courtyard I saw the same walk."

Manase laughed again. "That's a useful trick, identifying a man by his walk."

"It can be useful on a battlefield. You can see someone from far away and still tell who he is."

"Surely the crest on his helmet will tell you that."

"No, not always. A man can wear any helmet. Sometimes the crest on the helmet doesn't identify the man. It's a popular ruse in war to have someone else wear a leader's helmet to confuse the enemy."

"But I was able to identify General Iwaki Sadataka by his helmet. I would have been a complete fool to kill the wrong man and take his head to Tokugawa-sama."

Kaze had a hard time picturing this dandy killing anyone, much less a famous general like Iwaki, but the manor they were sitting in showed that the Lord had been rewarded for something.

"If that happened, who do you think would be more surprised?" Kaze asked. "Lord Tokugawa or the man who lost his head because it was found under the wrong helmet?"

Manase gave his high-pitched, tittering laugh again. "You're a droll fellow. I like you! It's so deadly dull in this little backwater. Like your name, a fresh wind is always welcome."

Kaze nodded. "How did you come to kill General Iwaki, if I may ask?"

"It was during the battle of Sekigahara," Manase said in the tone of a man reciting something he's said many times before. "Sekigahara was a confusing battle with two hundred thousand warriors present. In the morning the forces against Tokugawa-sama outnumbered his troops, but he had made secret agreements to get support from many of the lords who were supposed to be fighting against him. At the proper time, these troops would turn on their own army and help the Tokugawas. In addition, Tokugawa-sama had made arrangements for several other lords to remain neutral and not enter the battle at all. Despite that, it was a desperate battle, and it wasn't decided until the forces who had agreed to turn against their own army did so.

"Toward the end of the battle General Iwaki became separated from his guards. I managed to come across him when he was alone and kill him." Manase gave a flip of his hand. "The General was an old man but still skillful with the sword. I was lucky to kill him."

"He was separated from his guards?"

"Oh yes. The guards were quite mortified by their carelessness. I understand they all committed *seppuku* on the battlefield to atone for their lack of fidelity."

"This is the first time I've heard of a general getting separated from his guards."

"I said Sekigahara was a very confusing battle. Armies were first on one side, then the other. It was hard to know who was fighting whom, and enemies in the morning were allies by that afternoon."

"Yes, I know."

"Were you at Sekigahara?"

Kaze laughed. "Oh, I've never been in such a famous battle. Sekigahara changed Japan, because the forces that supported the late Taiko's widow and heir were defeated. Now the widow and the Taiko's young son are entrenched in Osaka Castle, and Tokugawa-sama is the real ruler of Japan. Rumor says he will soon declare himself Shogun, so you received this district from the hands of a future Shogun. I'm just a ronin, and one who is frankly a little envious that you had a chance to distinguish yourself in battle and receive this district as your reward."

Manase looked petulant. "It's a miserable little 150-koku district and far removed from all the things I love." In theory, Manase could provide many fighting men if he was called to do so by the new Tokugawa government, although usually he would be asked to take to the field with only a fraction of the theoretical total. It was a small district compared to some of the fifty-thousand- and hundred-thousand-koku districts ruled by major lords, but Tokugawa Ieyasu was notoriously tightfisted.

"If I may be impolite and ask, where is your original home?" Kaze asked.

"I come from Ise," Manase said, naming an ancient district at the edge of the Inland Sea. "I long for the shimmering waters of Ise Bay and the taste of fresh sea bream. I felt closer to the Gods there. His Majesty, the Emperor, comes to Ise to consult with the gods Amaterasu-o-mikami and Toyouke-no-o-mikami at their home in the Grand Shrines."

"Those shrines are made of unpainted *hinoki* wood, Japanese cypress?"

"Of course."

"Were you ever there for a *sengu-shiki* ceremony?"

"When I was a young man. They do it only every twenty years, and thousands of pilgrims come to see it."

"During the ceremony they actually dismantle the shrine buildings and construct entirely new ones?"

"Yes. The pilgrims and the populace get bits of the shrines as talismans. Oh, the happiness to get a bit of the sacred shrine is something to behold."

"You must miss it terribly."

Kaze was surprised to see a tear well up in Manase's eye. "Oh yes," he said. "This rural life has very few compensations."

Kaze sat in silence while Manase recovered himself.

"This conversation has taken a melancholy turn," Manase said. "I had intended to take advantage of the rare sight of a cultured man in this backwater." He pointed to a large block of wood in the corner of the room, as thick as the span of a man's hand. "Would you like to play a game of *go*? Only the imbecile Magistrate plays here, and he hardly gives one a game."

Kaze nodded and slid across the mat to the go board. He moved it between the two of them and took one of the brown, covered, monkeywood bowls from the top. Kaze took the lid off his bowl as Manase took a second bowl from the top of the board. Inside were white go stones made of shell: pearlescent, thick, and expensive. Manase's bowl held black stones, equally thick. The top of the board was crisscrossed with nineteen lines, forming a grid.

Since Manase had black, he moved first. He took a stone between the tips of two of his fingers and set it down on an intersection of the grid with a decided snap, a move that made a pleasing "click" sound on the thick go board. The board had a sound hole and small legs on the bottom to magnify and enhance this sound.

The opening moves, which followed standard patterns called *joseki*, went quickly as the two men snapped down stones. Go is a game of position and territory. Once a stone is placed it can't be moved except to remove it from the board if it is completely encircled by the enemy's stones. The winner secures the largest territory, either through strategy or "killing" the opponent's stones.

Early in the game Manase made a move that invited Kaze to start a fight along one side of the board. Without comment, Kaze declined the gambit and played a stone at a bigger point; a place that secured more territory for him. "I would have thought you were a fierce fighter," Manase commented after Kaze made his move.

"Fighting without purpose is the activity of fools," Kaze said.

"Meaning?"

"*Gomen nasai.* I'm sorry. I meant that I am willing to fight when the stakes are right, but I must know what I am fighting to accomplish."

"You wouldn't fight just because your Lord told you to?"

"Of course, a samurai's first duty is to obey his Lord. But I could be more effective in fighting if I understood what the objective is."

"How do you reconcile that with unquestioned obedience?"

"I am not questioning; I am simply understanding the purpose."

"A strategist," Manase said teasingly, placing a stone that started an attack on Kaze's territory.

"No, a realist," Kaze said, responding with a stone that threatened to encircle Manase's attacking stone.

Manase stopped to ponder the board for a few minutes. "I misjudged you," Manase said. "I mistook your calm nature for a lack of fighting spirit. Now I see you're quite willing to fight when it suits you." He placed a stone down to support his attacker.

The battle on the go board continued to ebb and flow, with both players locked in a struggle to assure the survival of their stones. Manase would constantly offer Kaze a perceived opening, but, upon study, Kaze would see that the moves were cunning traps designed to get him to commit to a course of action that would eventually lead to disaster.

After Kaze refused one such gambit, Manase gave his affected laugh and said, "It's quite frustrating playing you."

"Why?"

"You never accept my invitations." Manase clicked down a stone.

"I will when the time is right." Kaze answered with a stone of his own.

"When will the time be right?" Another stone.

"There is a time for everything." Kaze paused to study the board. "Patience is the coin that buys the proper time." He placed his stone.

"In that you are like Tokugawa-sama," Manase said.

Kaze, who disliked being compared to the new ruler of Japan, said, "Why do you say that?"

"Haven't you heard the story they've recently made up to show the character of the last three rulers of Japan?"

"No."

"It's really quite amusing. They say Nobunaga-sama, Hideyoshi-sama, and Tokugawa-sama were looking at a bird on a limb, and they wanted the bird on the ground. I'll kill it, Nobunaga-sama says, and that will bring it to the ground. I'll talk to it, Hideyoshi-sama says, and convince it to come to the ground. And I will sit, Tokugawa-sama says, and wait until the bird wants to come to the ground itself."

Kaze had to laugh. The story was both irreverent toward the leaders of Japan and illustrative of their characters. "But," Kaze added, "at Sekigahara, Tokugawa-sama stopped waiting. He attacked, and he won." Kaze placed a stone to start an attack on Manase's position on the go board.

The play of the stones became increasingly rapid, with the click of pieces played sounding quicker and quicker as the battle between the two men was joined. Go was a common game for a warrior because it taught the need for proper timing of attacks, the value of evaluating the biggest move, and the virtue of anticipating an enemy's response. It held a fascination that prompted the proverb, "A go player will miss his own father's funeral."

Despite Manase's maneuvers and stratagems, Kaze played a calm and steady game, and by the end Kaze had a fifteen-point advantage and victory. "You're a stronger go player than I imagined," Manase said, as he scooped stones into his bowl.

"I was just lucky."

"There is no luck in go. Like *shogi*, Japanese chess, the game is all skill. It's not like dice or war, where luck is everything."

"There's no skill in war?"

Manase placed the lid on his bowl. "Only the skill to take advantage of the opportunities that luck has brought you. Now that you have beaten me at go, we're even."

Kaze gave him a quizzical look.

"It was my strategy to use a net to capture you," Manase explained. "I knew the Magistrate and his miserable guards could never capture someone as strong as you were described to be without some kind of clever stratagem. Now that I've met you, I see I was right."

"That strategy was a good one. I'll remember it."

"Yes, I'm sure you will. We'll have to see about some other game to see who the eventual winner will be between us."

"Such as?"

"Oh, poetry composition or something similar. Please be my guest for a few days. I've already instructed the Magistrate to return your sword to you. If you stay, it will give me a chance to study you and see what would be the best thing to challenge you with next."

"Thank you. I will stay briefly, but I can't impose on you. I'll be just as happy to continue staying with the charcoal seller."

Manase giggled, his humor, which had been soured by the go game, seeming to return. "Oh, that's quite impossible. You see, I intend to crucify that charcoal seller."

*The caterpillar*
*spins a cocoon. What knowledge*
*from a fuzzy head!*

"**W**hy do you want to crucify the charcoal seller?" Kaze asked, surprised.

"Oh, for the death of that merchant at the crossroads."

"But the charcoal seller didn't do that."

"You found him standing over the body yourself."

"But the man was killed with an arrow. The charcoal seller had no bow."

"He probably hid the bow. You know that weapons have been forbidden to peasants since the time of Hideyoshi-sama's great sword hunt, which is almost twenty years now. The recent war between the Toyotomis and the Tokugawas has allowed the peasants to gather arms again, so I know they all have their secret cache. They claim they need them for defense against bandits, but peasants are notoriously greedy. They'll often kill if there's a few coppers in it for them. You just interrupted the charcoal seller before he could rob the merchant."

"Perhaps the charcoal seller interrupted a bandit—"

"Oh, don't go on," Manase said. "If the charcoal seller didn't kill that merchant, then I'm sure it was someone else from this village. Killing one peasant is as good as killing another. It serves as a lesson to all of them. Please don't bother me with this talk about the charcoal seller again. It's quite boring. Instead, come with me. I want you to meet someone."

Manase rose, and protocol required Kaze to stand, too. Kaze noticed that Manase wore trousers that were long and trailed behind him. His feet in the trouser legs rubbed against the tatami mats, making an exotic swish-swish sound as Manase walked. It took practice to walk in this kind of pants, and they were normally reserved only for officials of the Imperial Court. Kaze followed behind, his cotton tabi gliding silently. The sound of the long legs of Manase's trousers rubbing across the tatami reminded Kaze of happier days, in a life long before his current wandering state.

Kaze couldn't enjoy the sound made by Manase's passage, however. He had come to like the charcoal seller, and Manase's plans to crucify Jiro did not sit well. Kaze was not repelled by the thought of death. He had been raised to believe that death is just a part of the natural cycle of life and rebirth all men must go through. With hundreds of crimes carrying the penalty of death, he had also seen countless executions and had even ordered several himself.

What bothered him was the prolonging of death. He knew some men derived pleasure from the suffering of others, and he wondered if the strange District Lord leading him through the passages of the seedy villa was such a man. Kaze believed that death, when necessary, should come cleanly and quickly. There were good ways to die and bad ways to die, and crucifixion was not a good way to die.

Some lords who favored crucifixion also favored the novel Christian cross, an invention that came into Japan with the smelly Christian priests and pale, Western traders who were little more than pirates. But given Manase's proclivities toward old things, Kaze was sure that a traditional Japanese cross would be used: Two poles set into the ground to form an X, the arms of the victim tied to the top of the X so he was hanging. The pull of the earth would settle the victim's lungs and other organs, and the man would die an agonizing death of slow asphyxiation. For a small, wiry man like Jiro, that kind of death could take many long days.

Kaze wondered what was the best tactic for saving the old peasant's life, but before he could formulate an idea, Manase came to a shoji screen door and stopped. "Sensei?" he called softly, placing his face next to the door.

From behind the screen, Kaze could hear a low murmuring, like someone reciting a sutra. The murmuring stopped for a moment, then an old, cracked voice said, "Is it time for a treat?"

Manase gave that high, tittering laugh of his and slid back the shoji screen. He entered with Kaze in tow. "No, Sensei," Manase said, settling down on the tatami mat. "Later on the servants will give you mashed *azuki* beans sweetened with honey, but right now I want you to meet a guest of mine."

Kaze sat down slightly behind Manase and looked at the curious creature before him. He was a very old man with wisps of scraggly gray hair clinging to the side of his head and an equally thin and scraggly beard. His eyes were covered with a white sheen that made the man blind. His kimono was clean but patched in numerous places.

Seeing Kaze's gaze on the kimono, Manase leaned over and said in a low voice, "He won't give up that kimono. He claims all other kimonos are too rough and scratchy. How amusing!"

"I can hear that," the old man said. "I may be blind, but I can hear very well, don't you know. Why have you disturbed my studies?"

"Of course, Sensei," Manase said in a placating voice. "It's just that we get so few visitors worth talking to that I thought I'd introduce you to a samurai we have staying with us, Matsuyama Kaze."

"Matsuyama Kaze? What kind of name is that? It sounds like an odd name to me."

"It is an odd name, but it suits a strange fellow," Kaze spoke up. "I am glad to meet you, Sensei. Please be kind to me." The last phrase was a common greeting instead of a real request.

"Be kind? Be kind? First let me see your lessons."

Kaze looked at Manase for guidance. "He sometimes thinks he's still teaching," Manase said. "He goes in and out with great frequency, thinking he's in the past and then remembering he's in the present. Just have patience. His mind will return to the moment after he's drifted a bit."

"My young Genji, my shining prince, how can you expect to take up the mantle of courtly duties if you don't study? Do you want to embarrass your household and all your ancestors? People will laugh at you!" The old man shook a withered finger in Kaze's direction.

"I have no doubt people will laugh at me," Kaze said kindly. "I apologize to you, Sensei, for not having my lessons completed."

The old man's head snapped up, like a snoozing sentry suddenly startled by the coming of his captain. "Lessons? What lessons? Is someone here to meet me? Do you want to study the classics? I'm blind now, but I can still recite them from memory. I say them over and over again so they will not flutter from my mind like an escaping bird."

"I am Matsuyama Kaze. I am glad to meet you, Sensei."

"I am Nagahara Munehisa." He put his hands before him on the mat and gave a short bow. "I used to be classics master in the household of Lord Oishi Takatomo. I once had the honor of reciting part of the *Kojiki* before His Imperial Majesty, the Emperor."

"Nagahara Sensei, that is a great honor indeed. You must be a scholar of exceptional merit to recite our oldest history before His Majesty."

"You are too kind. It was the Imperial Household that asked for the *Kojiki*, but the *Genji* is my real love."

"I am honored to meet such a distinguished scholar." Kaze placed his hands before him on the mat and gave the blind old man a deep bow, even though the old scholar could not see the compliment.

"Ah yes, the *Kojiki*, the *Kojiki*. The remembrances of Hieda no Are, an old, old woman. Like the *Genji*, another tale from a woman.

She was sixty-five when her legends were recorded. Did you know I'm sixty-three?"

"No, Sensei, I didn't."

"Yes, I'm . . ." The old man paused, a confused look coming over his face. Suddenly he seemed quite stern. "So you would rather see the horse races than study your classics? Bushido is more than swords and horses and armor, young master. Bushido, the way of the warrior, is also about knowing the classics of Japan and even China. To be a superior man, you must be a cultured man. And a young lord in your position must be a superior man. I am your teacher, your Sensei, and I am responsible for you. Do you want others to laugh at you, bringing shame to both you and your household? You are a most willful boy, sneaking out to see those races!"

Kaze looked at Manase for guidance. The District Lord took a fan from his sleeve and started cooling himself. He had a look of complete indifference on his face. Kaze returned his attention to the old man and said, "Yes, Sensei. Thank you for correcting me."

The old scholar didn't seem to hear Kaze's reply. Instead he started mumbling to himself again at a rapid pace. Kaze couldn't make out all the words, but he caught "Heike" and "battle" and "mirror in the seas." Kaze thought he must be reciting the story of the ancient battle between the Minamoto and the Taira for the leadership of Japan.

Manase gracefully stood to leave, and protocol required Kaze to follow. In the hallway outside the Sensei's room, after the shoji screen door was closed, Manase gave his little laugh again and said, "How boring. He's gone again. He'll recite for quite some time. He's afraid of forgetting the things he used to be able to read, so he tries to recall them to memory by repeating them over and over. He keeps forgetting more and more of the stories, however, and then tries even more desperately to remember what he has left. When I first bought him, he could recite the most marvelous stories, especially from the era of Genji. That was almost six hundred years from today, but that old man could make it seem as alive and modern as if the world of Genji were just outside the walls of this villa."

"You bought him?"

"Oh, yes. A man was leading him around the countryside like a performing bear, putting on shows where he would recite stories and get paid a few coppers. I paid off his handler and brought him into my household. He really was a classics master in Lord Oishi's household, but he gets less and less useful to me. Lately he just wants sweet treats like some kind of child, and his ability to concentrate and carry on an interesting conversation gets less and less." Manase sighed, "I suppose that eventually my only link to the world of Genji will be the books I have, because that old man will go completely crazy or die."

"You seem especially interested in the world of Genji."

"Yes. That's how I try to live my life."

"But that was six hundred years ago!"

"But it was the pinnacle of our life and culture. The people of Japan have been in a decline ever since. I still try to follow the customs and beliefs of the age of Genji. That was a time when there truly were shining princes, and men of refinement could pursue the highest aesthetic interest. After three hundred years of constant warfare our heritage was lost. No wonder old courtly arts and customs are dying, and rough, swaggering bushi rule."

"You mean Lord Tokugawa?"

Manase caught himself. "Certainly not! Tokugawa-sama is a most cultured man. I'm talking about other lords."

"Of course. How stupid of me. Please accept my apologies for not properly understanding your comments."

"Well, yes. I accept your apologies. I was just upset because the old man slips deeper and deeper into his private world, depriving me of the entertainment I bought him for."

"I can see where that would upset you." Kaze stared blandly at the District Lord.

"Well, I must attend to some duties now. Please stay for a few days. Despite your strange ways, you're an amusing fellow in this dreary backwater."

"Can I ask one final thing before you go, Lord Manase?"

"What is it?"

"If I find the villager hiding a bow, would you let the charcoal seller go?"

Manase studied Kaze for several seconds. "You are a most peculiar fellow. The peasants hide their weapons, and it would take weeks to search all their filthy huts to see where they put them. That charcoal seller will be crucified in a few days, and I won't delay things for a foolish search. But I'm a reasonable man, and if you can somehow find out what weapons the villagers have in that time, then of course I'll arrest the one with a bow and crucify him instead. As I said, it's all the same to me which villager is killed for this murder. It might as well be the one who actually did it."

## CHAPTER 11

*Tears drip like blood on*
*a ghostly face. Obakes*
*dwell inside my soul.*

It was a quiet night as Kaze made his way from Manase's villa to the nearby village of Suzaka. Leaving the villa had been absurdly simple. Manase posted a sentry, but Kaze found the sentry comfortably asleep, sitting on the ground and leaning back against a gatepost, announcing his slumbering status with a raucous snoring.

The mist that had painted the ground the first morning Kaze entered this district was back. It was a gossamer blanket that captured the faint light of the stars and the brighter light of the waxing moon, entangling both in the swirl of its ephemeral weave. Kaze cut through the undulating blanket, the passage of his feet tearing puffy-edged holes in the surface.

Kaze looked over his shoulder and sought the image of the rabbit in the moon that Japanese children were taught to look for. He could see the familiar ears and eyes, and he smiled in recognition. He stopped for a moment to look up between the flanking pines to glory in the wave of stars that crested over the treetops and flooded the heavens. Nowhere did the stars seem so close and attainable as they did in the mountains. Kaze's curious mind wondered why the stars seemed so flat and dull in cities like Kyoto.

The trees that bordered the path to the village meant that Kaze had no worries about losing his way in the dark. Besides, with the instinct that all people close to nature must develop, he knew the general direction to the village even without the trees to guide him. He started off again, enjoying the journey.

The night had an unnatural stillness to it, a trait Kaze had noticed before when conditions were like this. It was as if the damp air smothered the normal sounds of the forest, leaving a void in the air waiting to be filled. As he walked, that stillness was pricked by a sound so faint he had to stop to make sure he actually heard something. It was from up ahead, where the road curved so Kaze couldn't see what was hidden beyond the corner. He still couldn't make out what it was, but there was most definitely a sound.

Kaze reached down and smoothly loosened his sword, the sword moving past the sticking point that kept it firmly in the scabbard with a satisfying click. Walking silently, Kaze approached the corner that was flanked by dark trees. As he came to the curve in the road, he was able to comprehend the sound he had heard. It was a woman crying. Curious, Kaze rounded the corner to see what was ahead of him.

There, crouched down in the middle of the road, was a high-born woman wearing a white kimono, the color of death and mourning. Kaze could easily tell her station in life from her long hair and the cut of her kimono. Her face was buried in her hands, and her hair cascaded down around her shoulders. Kaze could hear most definitely that she was sobbing. Through a trick of starlight, the form of the woman seemed almost as misty and ephemeral as the silver blanket covering the ground around her, and Kaze rubbed his eyes because the edges of the woman seemed to blur into the night. Kaze's eyes were especially acute, so the shifting shape of the woman made him uneasy.

He walked toward her slowly, his eyes trying unsuccessfully to focus on the form before him. Because of her eerie luminescence, he was able to make out her shape easily, and there was something so familiar about the slope of her shoulders and the way her head was bent forward that Kaze stopped walking.

He opened his mouth to speak, but his mouth was dry, and only a soft whisper emerged. The woman apparently didn't hear him, for she made no change in her posture. The dryness of his throat surprised him, and he suddenly realized that a chill had taken hold of his bones unlike any cold he had experienced before. It was a dry, inward chill that was so intense that Kaze found himself trembling from it.

Kaze took a deep breath, and the air around him tasted dry and flat, like the dead air in an old abandoned monastery or barn. He studied the shifting shape of the woman once more and, with an awful certainty, he knew who was before him.

"My heart has no hindrance," Kaze said to himself, reciting the *Heart Sutra*. "No hindrance, and therefore no fear." He took another gulp of that dead, flat air and, repeating the *Sutra* to himself, he called upon his courage and approached the woman.

Stopping a few feet from the figure, he bowed deeply, keeping his back straight. "I am here, Lady," Kaze said, greeting the obake, the ghost, of his dead mistress. The obake ceased her sobbing, and Kaze took this as a sign that he could straighten his bow. The figure before him still had her face in her hands, and Kaze was at a loss about what to do next. Suddenly, the figure looked up and removed the hands from her face. Kaze's soul froze.

Instead of the serene face of his dead Lady, the same face he carved on the Kannons he habitually left behind him, he saw that the obake was faceless. No eyes, no nose, and no mouth; just a soft lump of flesh. Yet, even without a face, he heard her sobbing and he saw the drops from wet tears glistening on her kimono.

Kaze stood motionless before the apparition, not daring to breathe. A fear more real than any he had known gripped his heart, yet he stood his ground and didn't flee. No hindrance, and therefore no fear, he told himself. No hindrance, and therefore no fear. This obake was the spirit of the Lady, someone he served when she lived, and someone he still served through his searching, even though she was dead. There is no reason to fear her now, even though she was a faceless entity.

"How can I help you, Lady?" Kaze said, summoning up all his courage. He was pleased that his voice sounded more normal than before.

The obake unfolded from the ground, rising like a puff of white smoke until it was standing before Kaze. It raised a hand in a languid motion, the arm floating upward gently until it pointed down the road.

"You want me to go with you?" Kaze asked, his heart chilling at the possibilities.

The obake continued to point down the road.

"There's something down the road?"

The obake remained motionless.

"You want me to leave?"

The apparition lowered its arm.

Kaze sighed, a gripping anxiety replacing fear. He dropped to his knees and bowed before the obake, his head cutting through the low-lying mist and touching the earth. It somehow felt comforting to be so close to the damp ground in the presence of the obake, and the contact with the planet gave Kaze the courage to go on. "I know you want me to find your daughter," he said. "Please excuse my lack of attention to my pledge! But Lady, something is very wrong here. The Lord I served, the man you were married to, always taught that it was our duty to maintain harmony within ourselves and in our society. That harmony has been destroyed here. All of Japan is in upheaval as the Tokugawas impose their will, but I feel there is some chance for me to restore harmony to this little piece of Yamato. I don't know the cause of the disharmony, and I don't know if I can correct it, but Lady, I would like to try. If I fail within a few days, I will continue my search. But for now, my Lady, please let me try!"

Kaze remained motionless, waiting for some sign from the obake that his request was granted or denied. The stillness that surrounded him was suddenly broken by the sound of a cricket in the woods. Kaze looked up, and the obake was gone.

Kaze tried to stand and couldn't. His heart was tripping in his chest and his body felt weak, as if he had a three-week fever. The air now tasted damp, but alive. He noted with wonder that the mist, which covered the ground, was rapidly shrinking into the earth, flowing into ripples and crevices and tiny folds as if it were water. He closed his eyes, centering himself and willing the chilling numbness of fear away. No hindrance, and therefore no fear.

Soon his breathing became slow and rhythmic, and the weakness in his limbs was replaced by growing strength. He stood, adjusting his sword in his sash. Then, with a firm step, he started off down the path to the village.

Kaze felt guilty about pausing in his search for the child to try to free the charcoal seller, but he now knew the Lady understood and was giving him permission to try to find harmony for this village. He wondered about the demon seen in the next village and wondered if this place was unusually active with spirits.

From his earlier exploration he knew the village layout. It was a compact collection of huts and farmhouses holding perhaps two hundred people. Like most villages of its size, it was organized alongside a dusty main street, with huts and houses flanking the street.

Kaze stood at the edge of the village, still calming himself and also enjoying the calm while he could. Behind him, in the woods, he could hear the song of a nightingale. It comforted him, and he tried to focus his attention on what he was about to do, not what he had just experienced. Then he took a deep breath and took his sword and scabbard out of his sash. Holding the sword in the middle of the scabbard, he ran to the door of the first hut in the village.

"Wake up! The bandits are attacking!" Kaze used the butt of the scabbard to bang on the house door.

"Nani? What?" a sleepy voice from within the hut called out.

"The bandits! They're attacking. *Hayaku! Hayaku!* Hurry! Hurry! Grab a weapon and come out here!"

Kaze ran across the street to the next hut. He started pounding on the door.

"Wake up! Wake up! Bandits are attacking the village! Grab your weapons and come outside!"

Without waiting for an answer, he ran back across the street to the next house in line. There he repeated his warning and ran to the next house. As he zigzagged across the street he noticed the men of the village tumbling out of their homes onto the main street. A few carried newly lit torches, and in the flickering yellow light Kaze could see that all were carrying weapons of some type. As he progressed through the village the crowd in the main street grew larger and more confused.

"What—"

"Where's the bandits?"

"What's going on?"

"Are they attacking?"

"Where's the attack?"

Kaze looped around to catch the village houses that weren't on the main street. By the time he finished his circuit of the village, a large crowd of men and women were huddled together in the center, milling around, clutching weapons, and looking nervously into the dark.

Puffing from his exertions, Kaze strode into the mass of people and started pushing his way though the crowd.

"What's going on?"

"It's that samurai who was at Jiro's. . . ."

"Where's the bandits, samurai?"

As Kaze shouldered his way through the forest of people before him, he looked at the weapons they were holding. A few clutched farm implements, but most had spears, swords, and naginatas. He made his way through the milling group, ignoring all questions, until he reached the center of the crowd and saw a pudgy hand holding a bow. He walked up to the owner of the hand and confronted the sweating face of the Magistrate.

"S-s-see here, s-s-s-samurai, w-w-w-what's going on?" The Magistrate stuttered in fear.

Kaze saw a handful of arrows in the Magistrate's other hand and pulled one out of the man's shaking fist. The remaining arrows tumbled to the ground. Kaze walked over to a man with a torch and studied the arrow in the flickering light.

"W-w-what's going on? Here, here, answer me!" the Magistrate demanded.

Kaze finished his inspection of the arrow, then looked around the crowd slowly to make sure there wasn't another man with a bow that he missed.

"T-t-tell me!" the Magistrate commanded.

Kaze raised one hand in the air to quiet the crowd.

"People of Suzaka village!" Kaze shouted. The milling group immediately hushed. Kaze looked at the concerned faces around him, then said, "Superb! Your courage and martial manner have driven away the bandits that were planning to attack this village. *Omedeto!* Congratulations!"

Kaze started marching off, and the crowd opened up before him like the tall grass of summer falling away when you walk through an open field. As he made his way back to the manor, Kaze could hear the buzz of an excited village receding behind him.

The peasants milled about, discussing the possibility that the new samurai was mad. Some thought that perhaps the samurai was right and that they had scared off an attack by brigands, but others scoffed at the notion that Boss Kuemon or any other brigand would be scared by any group of peasant rabble. As the excitement of the novel night wore off, groups of peasants started drifting back to their homes.

Ichiro, the village headman, was one of the last to leave. Shaking his head over what the samurai was up to, he wearily went back to his house, where his wife and children had gone back to sleep long before. He placed his naginata in the corner of the main room of the house and looked at it speculatively for a few minutes. Then he went to a corner of the room and moved several bales of rice, clearing a section of the floor. He removed several of the loose floorboards and dug down into the earth, removing an old section of matting that had been covered with dirt as camouflage. Underneath was a shallow hole, lined with old rice-stalk mats.

Ichiro got a twig from the kindling stack and lit it from the still-smoldering charcoal in the hearth. Using it like a crude candle, he examined the contents of his secret cache. In the flickering orange light, the oil on the weapons gleamed with a malevolent sheen. Two swords, a dagger, and a bow were nestled together in the shallow depression. Ichiro took the dagger from his forbidden armory and replaced the mat.

## CHAPTER 12

*Hanging between earth
and eternity, I grab
for earth and for life.*

The next morning, Kaze was escorted into Manase's presence. Kaze had found his own clothes, newly cleaned, starched, and resewn, waiting for him when he got up, and this was what he was wearing.

Manase was once again dressed in several sumptuous robes, forming a layered collection of color. He was sitting on a small veranda, looking over a garden of large rocks and shrubs. Kaze knew that in Heian Japan, the time of *The Tale of Genji*, the refinement of a woman was judged by how she layered her many multicolored kimonos. The delicacy of color, the transition of one color and pattern to the next, and the careful sculpting of overlapping pieces of cloth were all signs of sensitivity and refinement. He wondered if the same applied to a man, because Manase's robes were all carefully layered and arranged to present a pleasing cascade of color.

"I understand you caused an annoying commotion in the village last night," Manase said, without turning to look at Kaze.

Kaze gave a deep bow, even though Manase was not looking. "I apologize for disturbing the tranquillity of your District," Kaze said, "but I wanted to see the weapons the peasants had. Sounding the alarm was one way to see those weapons without engaging in a tedious search. A warrior always grabs the weapon he's most comfortable with when he's put in sudden danger."

Manase gave his high-pitched laugh. "How clever! You are a highly entertaining man. What did you find?" Manase asked when he stopped laughing.

"The only person in the village who grabbed a bow was the Magistrate."

Manase turned around and gave Kaze a look of surprise that was magnified by the false eyebrows painted high on his forehead. "You think the Magistrate killed that traveling merchant?"

"I don't know. The arrows used by the Magistrate were not the same as the arrow in the man at the crossroads. That arrow had a dark shaft and unusually fine fletching of gray goose feathers. The Magistrate's arrows were crude things by comparison. Perhaps bandits did kill that man, and they were disturbed before they could rob him. I just don't know why they would bother to dump the body at the crossroads."

"So now you think bandits killed that merchant?"

"He wasn't a merchant."

"What?"

"The murdered man was a samurai." The death of a samurai was much more serious than the death of any merchant. Merchants were actually in one of the lowest social classes. Only the *eta,* outcasts who handled unclean things like slaughtering animals and tanning hides, were lower on the social strata than merchants.

"How do you know he was a samurai?" Manase demanded.

"His sash was tied to hold two swords. I pointed out the sash to the Magistrate, but he either couldn't see that or refused to see it."

"Are you sure?"

"Yes. The sash was loose where the two swords fit."

"But I was told the dead man looked like a merchant."

"I don't shave my head, so without my sword I would also look like a traveler or merchant of some kind and not a samurai," Kaze pointed out. Samurai typically shaved the front part of their heads, letting the rest of their hair grow long. The long hair was gathered and greased into a topknot, held in place by a dark cord. Kaze's hair was left to grow and gathered in the back, but he did not shave the front part because of the inconvenience and the expense.

Manase seemed to muse to himself, "How interesting. A samurai was killed. And you think it may be my own Magistrate who is the murderer."

"I'm not sure who the murderer is, Lord Manase. It could also be the bandits."

"But surely bandits wouldn't attack a samurai."

"They attacked me."

"What? When?"

"The other day. I walked to Higashi village, and three bandits attacked me on the road."

"What happened?"

"Two bandits stopped me on the road, and a third tried to sneak up behind me to kill me. The murdered man was shot in the back, so maybe bandits tried the same ruse with him, only they were successful."

"How did you escape the bandits?"

"I didn't escape. I killed two. The third was young, so I let him escape me."

"You killed two of them?"

"Yes. I buried them by the side of the road, because I was told that was the custom in this District."

Manase pulled a fan from the sleeve of his kimono and started waving it briskly. "Oh, this is all too much for me," he confessed. "Since it was a samurai killed, we of course must make a better investigation of the circumstances of his death. How can you tell if it was the Magistrate or the bandits who killed him?"

"I'll try to find out more about the bandits, to see if they use bows in their attacks."

Manase snapped the fan shut. "Please continue your investigations, Matsuyama-*san*. I'm not a cruel or unreasonable man. If you can bring evidence to me that someone else murdered that man at the crossroads, I won't crucify the charcoal seller. In the meantime, I'll keep the peasant safe here, enjoying my hospitality."

"You can help by assigning some men to assist me in finding the bandit camp," Kaze said. "That would make the search go faster."

"All right," Manase said. "I'll order the Magistrate to put together a search party to help you."

The next morning Kaze was shaking his head in disbelief. "These are the troops?" He looked at the ragtag band of militia before him. He expected professional warriors and instead he got armed peasants.

"Here, here, I thought we were just going to find the bandit camp, not fight them," Nagato said. "These men will be fine for just finding it." The Magistrate had come to the gathering point on a horse, but the thick forest ahead meant he would have to walk from here. Across his back was a quiver, and in his hand was the bow that Kaze had seen when he had rousted out the village.

Kaze was still skeptical, but the point of the search was to locate the camp, not destroy it, so he had to admit grudgingly that Nagato might be right. "Fine," he conceded, "What direction do we search first?"

"North," Nagato said quickly.

"Is that the direction we're most likely to find the camp?"

"Yes."

Kaze, not knowing the local geography, decided to go along with the Magistrate. If he was wrong, there would be time to search in other directions later. "All right," Kaze answered.

"Good, good," the Magistrate said. "You men form a line, but stay within shouting distance. We'll start north and continue until midday. The bandit camp can't be farther than a half day away. If we haven't found it by then, we'll return here."

And search another direction tomorrow, Kaze silently added.

"Where are you going to be?" Kaze asked the Magistrate.

"I will be on the right wing. You take the left wing." Normally the leaders would be in the center of a formation of men, but if the Magistrate wanted to try "the double-headed blossom" formation, where two leaders were on the wings, it didn't bother Kaze.

"*Yosh!* Let's do it!" Kaze said, walking to the left so he could take up his position.

The men strung out in a long line, with Kaze at one end and Nagato at the other. There was a large gap between each pair of men so the search party could cover as much ground as possible. With the distance between them and the obscuring brush and trees, each man could see only one or at most two others on each side of him.

Kaze started forward, glimpsing the searcher to his right occasionally when the trees thinned out or when he was on a small hill. The day was sunny and the last residual heat of a humid summer clung to the trunks of trees, making the air thick and still. The heavy underbrush made progress difficult, and occasionally Kaze had to make a detour to keep moving forward. He soon lost sight of the searcher to the right. He was farther than hailing distance, but he had no intention of shouting if he found any sign of the bandits anyway. With this group of peasant militia, he didn't want to alert the bandits or get into a fight with them.

He kept his eyes open for the signs of a path or some other indication that humans were in the area. Thus far he had seen nothing of interest, except that a bamboo forest was growing to his left, encroaching on the territory of the pines and cryptomeria. Even in nature, there are wars for territory, Kaze thought.

Because of the heat, he paused for a moment, sitting on the large gnarled root of a tree to rest. He pulled a small earthenware bottle from his sash and took out the peg that sealed the top. He tilted his head back to pour cool water into his mouth when he heard the familiar whistling sound of an arrow in flight. Kaze had been in battles where the sky was black with deadly shafts, and he knew that sound.

Not pausing, Kaze simply tumbled backward off the root of the tree, falling behind it as the arrow struck the trunk with a solid thunk. Kaze had no time to see how close the arrow would have come, because from the woods there came a lusty shout from the throats of many men. From the undergrowth a dozen men emerged, all dressed in stolen cast-offs like the bandits he had met on the road. They brandished spears and swords, and their headlong charge would converge on Kaze's position in just a few moments. Kaze rolled to his feet and started running. He had been ambushed.

Kaze drew his sword. He was sure he would have heard that large a group of men getting into position, so they had been waiting for him. He had been set on a path designed to have him run into them. What he didn't know was who had betrayed him: the Magistrate, Lord Manase, or someone else.

In an instant he was out of the pine forest and running into the bamboo forest. The stalks of bamboo were as big around as a man's arm, and the floor of the forest was littered with the nubs of bamboo shoots and slippery leaves. Kaze dodged through the stalks, darting right, then left, feeling the shiny bamboo stalks graze his shoulders as he made his way through the wild growth. In the thick growth he could never see more than a few feet before him, so he didn't bother checking over his shoulder for his pursuers. He didn't need to, because he heard the shouts of his attackers growing progressively fainter behind him. He was outdistancing them.

Suddenly he burst out the bamboo forest and saw the earth drop away before him. He tried to come to a rapid halt, but the slippery bamboo leaves clogging the ground made his feet fly out from under him and he skidded over the edge of a precipice. He dropped his sword before it could go flying over the edge and clawed at the lip of the crevasse. He risked a quick look down and saw that he was hanging from the edge of a fissure formed by some past earthquake. Below him the bottom of the fissure was a great distance, and the rocky floor looked uninviting and dangerous.

Willing his fingers to dig into the hard earth at the edge of the crevasse, he hung there for a few long moments, uncertain if his grip on the edge would save him or if the earth would give way, sending him to the bottom. It held.

Pulling himself back onto the bank, Kaze heard the shouts of the approaching men. The ambush had been carefully planned. Kaze was now trapped on the edge of a tear in the earth that was too wide to jump, with his attackers about to burst upon him in a few seconds. Kaze picked up his sword and made a quick decision.

He positioned himself next to a bamboo stalk growing at the edge of the fissure and drew his sword back with both hands. In his mind, he pictured the sword on the other side of the bamboo stalk, cleanly cutting it. He brought the sword down with authority and made his mental image of the completion of the stroke a reality. The stalk was now cleanly cleaved, and it fell forward, spanning the fissure with a narrow bridge, no wider than a man's arm.

The stalk was glossy, smooth, and slippery and looked too thin to cross on. Kaze was reminded of an acrobat he had once seen, who walked across a stretched rope using a bamboo and paper umbrella for balance. Kaze had superb balance, but he wasn't sure he could negotiate this thin and tenuous bridge. The voices of the men chasing him were near, and it seemed he had no option.

Taking a deep breath and holding his sword out for balance, Kaze started running on the stalk to cross the ravine. The flexible bamboo shaft bowed dangerously when he got to the middle, causing Kaze to momentarily lose his balance, teetering on the edge as the rocky floor of the fissure waited for him. He fought to control both his mind and body, centering himself literally and figuratively, pulling himself back upright on the fragile bridge. Wishing he were barefoot instead of in sandals so his feet could get a better purchase, Kaze made his way up the sloping bow of the bamboo and onto the other side. With a quick, one-handed swipe of the sword, Kaze cut the thin top of the bamboo, causing the stalk to fall into the fissure, eliminating the possibility that anyone, no matter how foolish or skilled, would follow him across. In an instant, he stood in the bamboo growing on the other side of the chasm.

Kaze's pursuers came to the edge of the fissure, but since they knew of its existence, they had slowed their pursuit and didn't fall over its edge. They scanned the bottom of the chasm to see if they could find Kaze's body, but noticed nothing. Puzzled, they concluded that Kaze must have somehow eluded them in the bamboo forest. They turned around and formed a search party of their own to see if they could locate him.

As they did this, Kaze was already walking near the bank of the fissure, looking for a place where he could climb down into the chasm and climb up the other side. He was more interested in seeing the arrow that precipitated the ambush than in completely eluding the men.

After a great deal of searching, he found a place where he could climb down one side of the fissure and back up the other. When he finally made his way back to the location of the ambush, the sun was starting to move toward the horizon. Kaze was careful in his movements, taking time to assure himself that he wouldn't stumble into another trap. When he finally came to the tree where he had stopped for water, he waited in hiding for several minutes to make sure the way was clear. He was glad he did.

In the forest he could hear the sound of two men arguing, the voices getting more heated as they approached the ambush site.

". . . but he got away!"

"That wasn't our arrangement."

"I won't pay for nothing!"

"Now, now. I did what I agreed to. I must be paid!"

"I'll pay you nothing."

"We had an agreement, an agreement!"

"But why should I—"

"If you want me to do more—"

"How about half?"

"No, all!"

"Half!"

"Two thirds?"

"All right."

"Done, done!"

Nagato emerged from the forest and stopped. A muscular man with a potbelly and shoulders covered with tattoos appeared next to him, pulling out a pouch that was tucked into the side of his loincloth. Nagato still carried his bow and the half-naked man was carrying a spear. He stuck the spear into the earth and opened the pouch. The clink of coins could easily be heard as the tattooed man counted out coins into Nagato's eager hands.

Nagato's betrayal neither surprised nor offended Kaze. In these times no person could be trusted, and Nagato had the kind of character that made him even less trustworthy than most. What offended Kaze was the sight of a samurai acting like a greedy merchant, snuffling around a peasant with money like a pig in heat.

When the money was paid, the tattooed man said, "I have to find my men. They'll search all night for that damn samurai if I don't tell them to stop. There'll be other days, if that dog's head doesn't have the sense to leave here." He continued walking into the forest toward the bamboo grove.

The Magistrate stopped and slowly counted the money paid him. Then he took a cloth from his sleeve, put the coins into it, and wrapped them carefully before tucking them into the sash that held his swords. He walked over to the tree where Kaze had been sitting just a few hours before and tugged at the arrow embedded in it. The arrow was sunk deep into the bark. The Magistrate was not careful, and Kaze could hear the sharp crack as the shaft snapped in two.

"Damn!" the Magistrate said. He threw down the broken arrow and stomped off into the woods, leaving Kaze alone once again.

Kaze showed patience and waited until he wouldn't have more visitors. Then he approached the tree. He saw the water bottle he abandoned when he tumbled backward and retrieved it. He had taken it from Jiro's hut, and Jiro would want it back. Then he picked up the broken arrow shaft that the magistrate had abandoned and studied it thoughtfully.

*Love knows many names.*
*Alone in the darkened woods,*
*all names sound silent.*

The next morning, Kaze wandered into the courtyard and approached the cage that held Jiro. The night before, he had blandly told Manase that the search had failed and that he would have to think of another stratagem for finding the bandit camp. Nagato was there as well, and he fidgeted constantly, waiting for Kaze to mention the ambush. Kaze didn't. Instead, he started a long conversation about the relative merits of *haiku* poetry versus the longer *tanka* form of poetry. Manase loved it and kept up a lively conversation with Kaze for hours. During this whole time, Nagato was compelled by protocol to sit perched on his folded legs, supporting his considerable weight by resting on his heels and knees. He was soon in agony, praying for the boring conversation to end. But every time it looked like the discussion was about to finish, the ronin samurai would bring up some other subtle poetic point, and he and Manase would pursue that point for endless minutes. In his pain he cursed the samurai and couldn't understand why he would pick this occasion to engage the Lord in such a long discussion and not bring up the ambush. By the end of the evening, Nagato could barely get up to walk home.

As Kaze approached Jiro's cage, he wrinkled his nose at the stench. They didn't let Jiro out to go to the bathroom. Jiro had tried to perform his functions in one corner of the cage, but in such an enclosed space his actions were more of a gesture than an effective measure.

The old charcoal seller looked up at Kaze with tired eyes.

"Are they giving you water?" Kaze asked.

Jiro nodded an affirmative listlessly.

"How about food?"

He shook his head no.

Kaze reached into his sleeve and pulled out a large rice ball wrapped in leaves. He handed it through the slats of the wooden cage into Jiro's trembling hands. Jiro ripped open the leaves and started to eat the rice ravenously.

"Careful," Kaze admonished. "It would be stupid to choke on a rice ball before I can do something to get you out of here."

Jiro was so surprised that he stopped eating. For the first time his eyes had some life to them. Tears started forming.

"Stop that crying," Kaze said brusquely. "I hate pathetic people. There are too many of them in our land now, and it gets wearisome. Do you know where the bandit camp is?"

"No."

"Then you are going to stay in this cage a long time. I need to find that camp to see something. It might help me to get you out."

Jiro thought a minute. "Aoi," he said.

"Love?" Kaze answered. *Aoi* meant love.

"Not the word love. Aoi is a woman's name. She's the village prostitute. A widow. This is a poor village, but she has too much money and too many fine things. Only the bandits have money. Maybe she gets her money from them."

Kaze looked at the hunched-up figure and said, "A few days in a cage has loosened both your mind and your tongue. That's a good suggestion. Maybe you should make a similar cage for your house after I get you out of this one." He started walking out of the court-yard.

"Careful," Jiro called after him.

Later that afternoon, Aoi stepped out of her hut and looked up and down the village street. She knew that in a place as small as Suzaka, her comings and goings would be noticed by others, so in her arms she had a basket for gathering wild mushrooms, with a cloth covering its contents. Acting nonchalant, she wandered out of the village into the surrounding hills and woods.

She wandered for several minutes, taking a meandering route that skirted the edge of the village. She was in no hurry, and she carefully selected a route different from the last one she took to the camp. She had been schooled in precautions, and the lessons had been punctuated with curses and dire threats about what would happen if she led anyone to the camp.

In the woods, the afternoon was still and quiet, and the dry scent of the trees was a subtle combination of pine and pitch and dried sap. Although her view through the trees was limited, Aoi would stop occasionally to look around, to make sure no one was on her trail. For some reason she felt uneasy and skittish, even though this was a common journey for her. Despite her caution, she saw and heard nothing out of the ordinary.

After walking into the forest for an hour, she stopped and placed her basket down. She lifted a cloth in the basket and pulled out a colorful cotton kimono. Shrugging out of the plain kimono she was wearing, Aoi donned her working clothes. Tying the sash of her kimono snugly around her hips, she carefully arranged the collar to show the nape of her neck to its best advantage. The nape was considered elegant and erotic, and Aoi wished she had white powder to dust on her face, neck, and shoulders to spruce up her fading beauty.

When she was young, she worked the fields with her parents and nine brothers and sisters. They all sweated in the hot summer and froze in the bitter cold of winter and, like all farmers, they had the capricious weather to contend with. When Aoi was thirteen, her family faced an especially hard winter. Their dried daikon radishes were depleted, and a meal consisted of a handful of millet cooked in a common pot. They faced the prospect of slowly starving to death, one by one.

So, without telling her what they were doing, Aoi's parents took her up a snow-clad road to the village of Suzaka. There, after a few days' negotiation, they sold her to an old farmer for enough food to keep the rest of the family alive for a few months.

Aoi's mother cried bitter tears as they left her in the custody of the old farmer. "He's your husband now. Be a good wife," was all her mother could say as they left her.

"Come on," her father said, tugging at Aoi's mother's arm. "At least we didn't sell her to a brothel just so we could make more money off her. She'll be a respectable wife."

Aoi stood and watched her parents leave, a flood of tears clouding her vision. The hard grip of the farmer pinched her arm to make sure she didn't run after her parents. When her parents were out of sight, Aoi was put to work cleaning the farmer's hut. The farmer closed the door of the hut and sat watching her work. When the cleaning was done, she made dinner for the farmer. Aoi was not allowed to eat with her husband, so she watched greedily as he shoveled mouthful after mouthful of food down his gullet. Her mouth watered at the sight of so much plenty after such a long time of want. After her new husband was done eating, Aoi was able to wolfishly eat her fill, something she hadn't been able to do for months.

The millet and brown rice gruel was hot and satisfying, and Aoi had sweetened it with chunks of daikon radish and sweet potato. She took bowl after bowl of the gruel, reveling in the sensation of having an abundance of food that she didn't have to share with brothers and sisters. She ate so much that before she was done, her stomach was churning with the unfamiliar sensation of excess food packed into it.

Suddenly, Aoi bolted to her feet and pushed open the door of the hut. The farmer, thinking she was trying to run away, made a grab for her, but she managed to elude his grip and burst out of the doorway. But Aoi was not intent on escaping. She was just trying to make it to the privy before she threw up from all the food she had packed into her belly. She didn't make it.

She fell to her hands and knees halfway along the path to the privy, heaving up great gobs of undigested food onto the grass that lined the path. The farmer caught up with her and reached down to grab her hair so Aoi couldn't escape once she stopped throwing up. After many long minutes, Aoi's stomach emptied itself and she was able to sit, her mouth sour with her recently expelled dinner and her head hurting from the farmer pulling at her hair.

When she was able to wobble to her feet, she made her way back to the hut, the farmer right behind her, still grasping her hair. Aoi felt dizzy and sick and would have gladly curled up in a corner and fallen asleep. Instead, the farmer pulled out a dirty sleeping mat and roughly forced Aoi to lie on it. Then, with shaking hands, he pulled the clothes off Aoi and fell on her.

As a country girl, Aoi knew the basics of procreation from watching animals. She also knew about the male anatomy from living in close proximity with so many brothers, often diapering her younger brothers when they were babies. But none of Aoi's girlish knowledge prepared her for what the farmer did to her, and she lay there with the taste of vomit in her mouth, a large, smelly body pressing down on her, and a newfound pain between her legs. She cried more tears, until the flood of them washed down her thirteen-year-old face like a stream.

When Aoi was fifteen, she made a cuckold of her husband for the first time. Like all agrarian people, the peasants of Suzaka were keenly in tune with the rhythms of life. The rising and the setting of the sun marked their workdays. When winter came and the high snows drifted into the mountains, they cherished their meager allotment of light as they sat in their darkened houses, bundled against the cold and preparing material for the coming spring. In winter they would make tools or hand-carve bowls or plait grass rope, all useful implements for the daily chores of life.

Suzaka, being a mountain village, always had a rather meager rice crop, and the people were heavily dependent on dry crops like millet, as well as the gathering of ferns, bracken, and wild mushrooms from the surrounding forest. This made Suzaka a very poor village, because in Japan rice was money. The wealth of a lord was measured by how much tax in rice was due him from the peasants of the district. When services were not exchanged or bartered, portions of rice were more commonly given than coins.

Only merchants, samurai, and the rich dealt in copper, silver, and gold, and to the common peasant, richness was equated with baskets of rice grains that could be planted or eaten.

Throughout the year an enormous number of small festivals and observances were honored in the village. When times were good, these observances became parties, often degenerating into wild bouts of drinking, with amorous couples sneaking into the forest for a romantic tryst. As with all farmers, the parties were full of earthy humor, with bawdy songs and dances that often imitated both rutting animals and people.

When times were bad and food was short, the religious observances were still held, but they were somber, not wild occasions. In the Land of the Gods, each home's hearth, well, and kitchen had its own collection of protective deities, and when hard times and famine were felt, each and every God was implored to make the next cycle of life less harsh and less hungry.

Aoi's husband was old and taciturn and had lost physical interest in her after the novelty of her young body had worn off. During the second Higan celebration of Aoi's marriage, she slipped off from the revelries with a young man of eighteen, who already had a wife and a child. He and Aoi coupled for a few minutes in a quiet meadow in the woods. To Aoi's surprise, although her partner was more pleasing physically than her old husband, she didn't find the act itself more pleasing. To Aoi's genuine pleasure, however, the man gave her a roughly carved comb as a present when the act was done. The possibility that lying with a man might result in tangible goods was not something she had actually worked out, and that crudely carved comb was the genesis for a career as a part-time village prostitute.

She was seventeen when her husband found out how Aoi was getting a whole collection of combs, clothes, and extra spending money that he finally noticed, but to Aoi's surprise the old man didn't seem to care. All he said was "*Shikata ga nai*. It can't be helped."

When Aoi's husband finally died, she was twenty-three. She continued to farm the land and slept with villagers and the occasional traveler. She rebuffed all efforts to find her another husband as she continued to bed the husbands of others. As the bandits grew strong in the area, they became her most lucrative customers, and Aoi's business increased to the point that she no longer had to do any farming to get food.

One thing she didn't like about visiting the bandit camp was that she was expected to sleep with Boss Kuemon before she could sleep with any of his men. The actual act with the bandit leader took only a few minutes because it took only a few fake moans on Aoi's part to get him to perform with the quickness of a rabbit. It wasn't sleeping with him that she objected to. Aoi's objections were based on the fact that Kuemon never paid her. He said it was a tax in kind for allowing her to ply her trade to the rest of his men.

Aoi straightened up and adjusted the sash on her kimono. Then, plastering a mechanical smile on her face, she put her old kimono into her basket, picked up the basket, and walked the remaining few hundred yards to the little ravine that held Boss Kuemon's camp.

Boss Kuemon came out of the log hut that served as his shelter and headquarters. He was wearing only a loincloth, and he idly scratched his round belly. On his shoulders and back he had a large blue Chinese dragon tattooed, and he liked to walk around half-naked to show off the artwork that adorned his body. His shoulders were thick and muscular, and when he walked across the camp he had the distinctive, bent-legged, rolling gait of a palanquin porter.

Kuemon's father had been a palanquin porter, and, for the first twenty-two years of his life, Kuemon had followed his father's trade, often literally following his father's footsteps as his father took the front of a palanquin pole and Kuemon took the rear.

The palanquin was used to transport cargo or people. Two porters would hoist a long pole on their shoulders, each facing forward. In the middle of the pole was a small platform, hung from the pole by ropes. For a fee, people could ride on that platform while the porters shuffled off in a rolling jog, carrying the passengers to their destination. In a mountainous land with almost no improved roads, the palanquin was more practical than a cart and cheaper than a horse.

In the normal course of things, Kuemon would have remained a porter his entire life. But things were hardly normal in Japan. First, after three hundred years of constant warfare, one particularly powerful warlord named Oda Nobunaga almost succeeded in uniting Japan. Oda was assassinated, and one of Oda's generals, a man called Hideyoshi, the Taiko, seized power and, through diplomacy and war, did unite Japan. The astounding part was that Hideyoshi was a peasant. This was a lesson not lost on Kuemon. Where numerous hereditary warlords failed, a talented peasant was successful.

Kuemon considered himself talented. He was a good fighter and a leader of men. He abandoned his life as a porter and took up the life of a brigand. He was not sorry for his choice. Now he had a nice band of men, and he made a living a thousand times richer than any palanquin porter could make.

Hideyoshi was dead and, slowly but surely, Tokugawa Ieyasu was tightening his control on the government while Hideyoshi's son and widow remained cowering behind the thick walls of Osaka Castle. Kuemon decided Ieyasu would kill Hideyoshi's son when he was ready. It's what Kuemon would do.

Despite understanding what Ieyasu would do, Kuemon did not identify with the new head of Japan. Ieyasu was an aristocrat, not a peasant. Although he affected the spartan ways of the warrior, Kuemon had heard that Ieyasu claimed a newfound family link with the Fujiwaras. This convinced Kuemon that the days of peasants rising to generals were numbered and that birth would become paramount under a Tokugawa regime. The Fujiwaras were one of the families that could claim the ancient title of Shogun, and that meant Ieyasu had a preoccupation with the trappings of birth and an interest in claiming the ancient title for himself. Because of his low birth, Hideyoshi could never claim this title, and he had had to accept the less important title of Taiko.

Kuemon's men all called him "boss," and that was title enough for him. The title of boss was more than he could ever hope for as a palanquin porter.

"Someone approaching!"

The voice of Hachiro pierced the peace of the camp, and every head went up to hear the identification of the interloper. Hachiro was not good for much, as his recent encounter with the samurai who killed two of Kuemon's men showed, but he was useful for odd jobs like standing sentry, guiding people, running messages, or tending the camp. That damn samurai had eluded Kuemon's trap, but Kuemon was a patient man, and he would have a chance to kill him again.

"It's Aoi!"

Kuemon smiled. The tart from the village. Initially, Kuemon had insisted that she sleep with him to avoid paying her for her services, but now Kuemon was convinced that she slept with him because she liked it. He puffed out his chest like a courting pigeon and awaited her arrival in camp.

## CHAPTER 14

*Troops, weapons, martial*
*music: All are blinding puffs*
*of shifting black smoke.*

The next morning a tired but richer Aoi left the bandit camp as Kuemon gathered his men together. Since two men had been killed by a traveling samurai, the men no longer wanted to stake out roads in small bands. Now they insisted on sticking together. Kuemon found this arrangement inefficient and cowardly, but he wisely acquiesced. He thought that in a few weeks the fear generated by their slain comrades would disperse, or perhaps they would kill that samurai, and things would return to normal.

Hachiro was left on guard as the rest of the men departed. Hachiro was the eighth child of his parents. In fact, his name, Hachiro, meant "number eight." He had attached himself to the bandits because it represented one of the few ways he could better his lot in life, but he was slowly learning that he didn't have the ruthless mettle it took to become a successful brigand.

In his tale of how the samurai easily killed the two bandits, Hachiro had neglected to mention his failure of nerve in spearing the samurai in the back. In this band, a failure of nerve would mean expulsion or death, and he wasn't willing to face either. So he stood with a spear at his guard post trying to look fierce as Boss Kuemon and the ten men in his band went off to stake out a road.

As the bandits disappeared, stillness fell on the narrow canyon that hid their camp. Hachiro sat on a patch of grass and put the spear down next to him. The sun was warm and caressing, and the pine scent of the trees that covered the slopes of the canyon formed a delicious perfume. Hachiro was tired. He had spent the last of his meager share of the bandit's plunder on the woman from the village, and he felt both sleepy and sated because of this.

Hachiro was one of the last to use her, and he had stayed up most of the night waiting for his turn in excitement and nervous anticipation. Now that she and the bandits were gone, the glow from sleeping with her mixed with the warm sun, pine scent, and lack of sleep combined into an irresistible anesthesia. He knew that Kuemon would order him beaten if he caught him sleeping on sentry duty, but he also knew that it was unlikely that Kuemon or anyone else would be back before afternoon. Hachiro laid back and decided to take just a short nap. In seconds he was sound asleep.

Ever patient, Kaze let the youth settle down and get into a deep sleep before he moved. With the silence of an experienced hunter, Kaze made his way past the boy, careful not to let his shadow fall on the boy and possibly disturb him.

Aware that there might be some men left in the camp, Kaze carefully made his way from one crude shelter to the next. Finally, in what appeared to be the leader's log hut, he found the group's armory. He looked over the band's ragged collection of weapons and found what he had hoped. He took a sample and left.

A few hours later he presented himself to Lord Manase and placed an arrow down before him. Manase was sitting in his study, once again dressed in several sumptuous, layered kimonos.

Manase looked down at the arrow with great interest but didn't pick it up. His painted eyebrows high on his forehead always gave him a quizzical look, but this time the look was backed by words. "What is it I'm looking at?" he asked.

"The samurai at the crossroads was killed by a rather distinctive arrow. It had a dark brown shaft and very fine fletching done in gray goose feathers. This arrow is identical. I took this from the bandit camp this morning."

"Is that so?"

"If the Magistrate has preserved the arrow that killed the samurai, you could compare them for yourself."

"I don't think he did," Manase said. In response to Kaze's expression, he added, "But I believe you that the arrows are identical. So what is your conclusion?"

"It's not likely that two people would have arrows as finely made as this one in—"

"In a backwater like this?"

"I was about to say in an area that doesn't look like there would be a great need for arrows as fine as this," Kaze said.

Manase laughed. "You've gone to a lot of trouble for one peasant. Why?"

"Just a whim."

"You are a strange fellow. The villages are full of peasants, and one less wouldn't be a terrible loss. Besides, the man is old."

Kaze shrugged. "You said that if I brought you proof that he didn't kill the samurai you would release him."

"Yes, of course. I'll order him released."

"Thank you, Lord Manase."

"So the bandits killed another man. This time it was a samurai. They're getting to be quite annoying now."

"I know where their camp is. I could lead you there if you wanted to wipe them out."

"Me?"

"Or your men. You mentioned your district was a hundred fifty koku, so it should be easy to gather enough men to take care of them. There are around twelve bandits."

Manase shifted uncomfortably.

Kaze waited for Manase to speak. The silence between the two men extended for a painfully long time. Kaze finally said, "I would accompany the force, if you like."

Manase laughed a nervous laugh. "That offer has made me a little uncomfortable."

"I meant no offense. If you want your men to handle this alone . . ." Kaze let the sentence trail off, in the characteristic Japanese way to invite comment from the other party in a conversation.

"That's not the reason. It would be good for you to accompany anyone going to attack the bandit camp. Unfortunately, I really don't have any men besides the Magistrate and a few guards."

Kaze couldn't understand what Manase was saying. As the head of a 150-koku territory, he was supposed to maintain many fighting men.

"You mean your men are off in the service of the Tokugawas?"

"I mean I don't have any men besides the Magistrate and the guards."

Kaze was stunned. Manase had ignored the most fundamental duty of a District Lord to his master: the maintenance of samurai who could be called up for battle.

"This is rather embarrassing," Manase continued. "This weary provincial domain doesn't have the resources to properly maintain the lifestyle of a gentleman." Manase waved his hand at his expensive kimonos. "In fact, I've actually had to borrow money to purchase the proper quality of essential materials, such as equipment for the tea ceremony. As a result, some things have had to be"—Manase sought for a good word—"deferred. Of course, I will create the proper contingent of samurai when the time is appropriate, but right now I just have the Magistrate and a few men. You've seen some of them. They are not fit for the kind of mission you are proposing."

Kaze sat immobile, fighting to keep his emotions off his face. Revealing his emotions would offend Manase, and Kaze still needed Manase's goodwill. But it was a struggle to maintain his composure because Manase had admitted to a dereliction of a duty so basic that it defied Kaze's entire view of the world and how it should be properly structured. Each common samurai owed allegiance to a lord, unless he was a ronin like Kaze. But even ronin sought employment in the service of a lord. The lords owed allegiance to greater lords, and those Lords owed allegiance to a clan. It was a neat military pyramid that could collapse if the foundation was not maintained. If the Tokugawa government called on Manase to deliver his fighting men for service and he failed, then it would mean death for Manase.

"I'm sorry to hear that it will be impossible to field a proper force to wipe out those bandits," Kaze said, choosing his words carefully. "Twelve men are too many for me to take on alone, but those bandits are ruining the economy of this District. Perhaps there is something I can do if I spend some time thinking about it."

*Lies men tell women.*
*Lies women tell men. Somewhere*
*precious truth must live.*

**K**aze approached the hut door and called out, "*Sumimasen!* Excuse me!"

There was a scurrying noise inside, and after a few minutes the door slid back and a sleepy-eyed face poked its way into the sunlight. Although it was afternoon, it was obvious that Kaze had roused Aoi from her slumbers. When she saw who it was, Aoi's eyes widened. "Chotto matte, kudasai. Please wait!" she said.

She poked her head back into her hut, and Kaze waited for a few more minutes as Aoi scrambled around, fixing her hair and putting on a better kimono. As he waited, Kaze put down the earthen jug he was carrying and looked around the village. Several faces, which were watching him from open windows or half-opened doors, retreated to the darkness of their houses as he looked in their direction. Kaze sighed. A small village has too little to keep it busy when the local economy is bad. The hut's door slid open.

"Samurai!" Aoi said, stepping outside her hut and bowing deeply. "How can I serve you?" She put a sly smile on her face.

Kaze lifted up the jug he brought with him, and said, "I thought we might drink together. It gets lonely in such a small village, and I've heard that you're good company."

Aoi stood to one side and bowed again. "That would be nice," she said. "Please enter, and I'll stir up the fire to get hot water going. I would love to drink with you."

Kaze ducked into the low door of the hut and looked around, letting his eyes accustom themselves to the gloom of the hut. Like most peasants' huts, the interior had a raised wooden floor with two cutouts with dirt floors. One cutout was by the entrance, so people could sit on the edge of the raised floor to take off their sandals, and the other was in the center of the hut, where a charcoal fire could be built for warmth and cooking. The fire was just glowing embers and white ash, showing that Aoi hadn't even made her morning meal yet, but the hut was still filled with lingering hints of smoke.

Kaze sat on the wooden floor and removed his sandals. He placed the jug of sake next to him, and when Aoi had stirred up the fire, she scurried over to pick up the jug. She removed the cloth cover and wooden stopper from the jug and poured some of the sweet sake into a flask. She placed the flask into a metal pot of water that she had hanging over the fire. She looked at Kaze and smiled, then she filled a second and third flask, placing them into the water.

Aoi prepared a small plate of food. "It will just be a minute for the sake to warm," she said. "Please sit down and relax." She put a zabuton cushion on the floor.

Kaze moved to the cushion and sank down. Aoi moved to his side, placing the plate before him.

"What a surprise," she said. "I've seen you in the village. It's hard to miss such a handsome and manly samurai!"

Kaze said nothing. Aoi leaned into him, the edge of her kimono negligently hanging open so Kaze could see the curve of her breast. "I've been hoping you would visit me," she said in almost a whisper. She placed her hand on his arm. "You are so good-looking, and a gentleman, too. The whole village knows you saved the life of the charcoal seller." She sighed. "I'm sure all the girls fall in love with you! Handsome, kind, and I'm sure virile and generous!" She rubbed his arm softly.

"No," Kaze said, extracting his arm from her grasp. "Not handsome, not a gentleman, and too poor to be generous. And today, not even virile. I just wanted some company while I drank my troubles away."

The smile dropped from Aoi's face. Kaze took a small, paper-wrapped bundle from his sleeve and placed it down before her. It made a pleasant clink as the coins stacked inside the paper hit each other. "Of course, I intend to pay you for your company." The smile returned to her face.

"Oh, you don't have to do that," Aoi said as she scooped up the bundle and placed it in her sleeve. "It's my pleasure to drink with you!"

"I'm glad," Kaze said, amused. "I feel like some company today."

Aoi returned to the kettle and tested the temperature of one of the flasks. She looked over her shoulder, "Not really warm enough yet," she said, "but let's start anyway!" She took the flask out of the water and brought it and two tiny sake cups to Kaze on a woven tray.

She poured two glasses of sake from the flask and handed Kaze his cup, holding the cup with both hands, bowing slightly, and saying, "*Dozo!* Please!"

Kaze took the cup and sipped the tepid wine. "Ahh!" he said, smacking his lips. "I needed that!"

Aoi filled Kaze's cup again before picking up her own. She tossed hers down with a practiced hand. "*Oishi!* Tastes good!" Aoi said. She picked up the flask and poured herself another drink. "Now, if I can't make you feel better in other ways, why don't you at least tell me your troubles?"

Kaze looked at her over the rim of his cup. "It's very frightening." He finished his drink and held his cup out for Aoi to refill it.

"What's frightening?" Aoi asked, puzzled. She pick up the flask, shook it slightly to judge the amount of liquor still in it, and filled Kaze's cup.

"All the things that are happening."

"What's happening?"

Aoi expected Kaze to talk about the brigands and the attempt on his life, which the brigands had told her about. Instead, he leaned toward her, his voice a hoarse whisper, and said, "Ghosts!"

Aoi, who was in the process of fishing another flask out of the pot of warm water, paused. "Ghosts?"

"Yes." Kaze shook his head. "It seems to get worse every place I go, and I think this District may get to be the worst yet."

"What are you talking about, samurai-sama?"

"On the way here I passed through a village where a *kappa* had stolen a child. Do you know what a kappa is?"

Aoi, her eyes wide, shook her head no.

"It's a disgusting creature, all slimy and white. It looks like a jellyfish made into a man. It lives in water or wet places, such as in deep ponds or the still water under a bridge. It has a saucer, made of flesh, growing out of the top of its head." Kaze touched the top of his head to illustrate his point.

"What for?"

"The saucer contains water. As long as the kappa is near water, he can't be defeated, so he carries some with him always. The only way to kill him is to knock him off his feet, so the water spills out of the saucer. Then you can kill him."

"You . . . you've seen such a creature?"

"Of course. I once killed one, but the one in the village near here was too strong for me. I had to leave him, despite the fact that he will steal more children."

"What do they do with the children they steal?"

"No one knows. The children are found dead, floating in a pond or river, usually drowned, but no one knows what the kappa does with them." Kaze looked around, as if making sure they were alone in the hut. "I think they mate with the children before they drown them, and that's where new kappa come from."

Aoi put her hand to her mouth.

"But that's not the half of it. In this district much worse things are happening."

"What?"

"Didn't you hear about the demon?"

"You mean the story about the demon that rode through Higashi village?"

"It's not a story. I talked to someone who saw the demon. It had fierce eyes, a twisted mouth, blood-red skin, flowing white hair, and two horns, like this." Kaze brought his two fists up to his forehead, using his little fingers to indicate tiny horns growing out of his head. "It was awful. A truly bad omen. It was riding a big black stallion, and people say lightning flashed as the horse's hooves struck the earth. It was out gathering victims and had the soul of an adult strapped across his horse, carrying the poor man to hell."

"Honto? Truly?"

Kaze nodded gravely. Then he sighed. "It's a terrible time. This is the wrath of heaven. Under the Taiko we had peace, but the Tokugawas have started their reign with the death of thirty thousand or more. That's just at one battle: Sekigahara. Think how many more have died and will die soon. The Tokugawas are hunting down all who oppose them and killing them. All that blood! All those souls crying out for vengeance! All those ghosts wandering the land, unable to find rest because of their violent end. No wonder demons are now abroad in our country."

"Are demons worse than kappa?"

"Of course. You can kill a kappa and you can protect your children by keeping them away from water and damp places. But demons can go everywhere and they can't be killed. They will break down the door of a hut if they want the person inside. As demons start snatching souls, one by one, other ghosts and monsters will be stirred up. It wouldn't surprise me to see dragons and other hideous creatures wandering the land. It will simply get worse and worse until the spirits of all the dead are appeased through the sacrifice of the living."

"You've seen such things?"

Kaze's pleasure at spinning tales was momentarily clouded by the memory of his encounter with the obake of the Lady. "Yes," he said darkly.

Aoi was no fool. She had long since learned to distrust men and their pronouncements. But the way this samurai affirmed his contact with the supernatural sent chills up her spine. She stared at his tight lips and set jaw. She looked into dark eyes that seemed to know something that stretched beyond the parameters of this life and extended into the period between incarnations. She froze, uncertain about what to do next. Finally, she whispered, "Honto? Is that true?"

As if returning from a dream, Kaze's eyes refocused and looked at the frightened woman. It was what he was trying to achieve, and now it was no longer fun. "Honto," he said.

"What can we do?" Aoi said, her eyes wide.

Kaze shrugged, finishing the sake in his cup. "I don't know. I simply report what I know to be true. In fact, there are rumors that dragon tracks have been spotted in the next district. Once dragons take over a district, there is nothing to do but leave or be eaten."

Aoi, who had been perched attentively on her calves, collapsed to the side, sitting despondently with anxiety and fear. "What can we do?" she asked once more.

"I don't know," Kaze said. "No one has the answers for such terrible times. Under the Taiko we had relative peace and stability. The Taiko had his failed Korean adventure, but at home we did not have wars and we had order. Now with the Tokugawas our entire social order is upset. Their government extends its control into every aspect of the land, usurping rights that are not theirs. It's even rumored that Ieyasu will declare himself Shogun." Kaze paused, then sighed. "Do you know what I'm talking about?" he asked, not unkindly.

Aoi shook her head no. To her, talk of the rulers of Japan was like talk of the Gods. They were remote and mystical figures. The talk of ghosts and demons had more immediacy and reality to her. It was much more likely that a ghost would alight in this remote village than a ruler of Japan.

Instead of continuing, Kaze held out his cup. It took Aoi a few moments to react, but finally she picked up the sake flask and reached to pour another drink for Kaze. The rim on the cup made a chattering sound as the shaking flask bumped against it.

## CHAPTER 16

*Young buds don't always
grow in sunshine. Sometimes they
must survive winter.*

It took her several days to work up the courage to visit the bandit camp again. At first she resolved never to return to the forest and hills, but the samurai had said that demons would break down your door if they wanted you, so she told herself that she wasn't running any greater risk by going to the bandit camp than by staying at home. Besides, the lure of money tugged at her much more strongly than her fear of ghosts, demons, and dragons.

Still, this time she made no concessions to the need to hide the camp. She didn't wander through the woods, and she didn't carry a prop like a mushroom-gathering basket. She didn't pause to see if someone was following her, but she did look around constantly, straining to see or hear the first inkling of a ghost.

By the time she got to the camp, she was so sick with anxiety she didn't bother feigning the mechanical smile that always adorned her face when she visited. Kaze, who was sitting on a high limb in a comfortable tree, saw her rush past below him, and he smiled.

The next morning, Boss Kuemon was mad. He came out of his hut after a pleasant sleep instigated by sex with the woman from the village, and he found his men sitting around in small groups, talking about ghosts and demons. He scoffed at the talk, but saw in the eyes of his men a kind of fear that prompted him to demand the cause of such foolish talk. "Aoi" was the answer.

The woman had already left, so all Kuemon could do was stomp around the camp shouting at his men to stop being so weak and foolish. He thought briefly of banning the woman from the camp, but he considered his free "tax" and the morale of his men and decided that action was the best course. Rousting everyone but Hachiro, the kid he used for a sentry, Kuemon took his men out to look for prey.

By late afternoon the men returned, and the talk of demons and dragons was mostly forgotten. Hachiro was sent to the spring for fresh water to make the evening rice. He took a wooden bucket and walked through the woods, down to the pool of water the camp used.

The dying sun slanted through the trees, sending ribbons of golden light cascading across the tree trunks. The woods were ripe with the smell of drying pine needles and the familiar sounds of the forest. Hachiro happily whistled a folk tune as he swung the empty bucket in time with the music. He started singing.

> *Little, little fire.*
> *Big, big flame.*
> *Bubble, bubble,*
> *Take out the big fire.*
> *Even though the kettle cries,*
> *Don't take off the cover!*

It was a silly song, one sung by mothers to teach their daughters how to cook rice. Hachiro had heard his mother sing it many times to his sisters, with all the children laughing and squealing with delight at the admonition at the end. In the close, homey atmosphere of the Japanese farmhouse, all members of the family wove bonds that created a tight fabric. The thought of his mother and family made the young man stop, the last words of the song catching in his throat. Tears formed in his eyes, and he whispered, "*Okaasan*. Mother."

War had come to Uzen, Hachiro's home province. And because war was just another name for madness, when it came to Hachiro's village it created madness for all who lived there. The day of madness was like any other day in Hachiro's young life. He started the day with a communal breakfast with his family, his mother serving soup and leftover rice to his silent father and his noisy siblings. Hachiro felt there should have been some foreshadowing of the events to come, some disturbing dream the night before, some premonition while he ate, or even some ominous clouds or claps of thunder. There was none of this.

The day was ordinary in every respect. He fought with his sisters, and his older brother disciplined him by cuffing him on the side of his head. It was an affectionate slap, enough to show Hachiro that his brother cared to discipline him but not enough to hurt. To punish him for his rowdiness, the older brother said Hachiro should go to the bamboo forest and gather bamboo shoots. This brought gales of laughter from his sisters and caused his face to burn red. Gathering *takemono,* bamboo shoots, was women's work.

Hachiro voiced protest, but his older brother stood firm. In the hierarchy established in the family by gender and birth order, Hachiro was very low. He should have accepted his brother's pronouncement without comment, but instead he tried to appeal to his father.

Hachiro's father was a stern, silent man who, nonetheless, loved his children. In some ways he conformed to the idealized view of Japanese fathers recounted in the village's folktales.

"*Niisan,* Older Brother, says I have to gather takemono like a girl," Hachiro protested.

Hachiro's father lifted the soup bowl to his lips and slurped down the final dregs. Looking over the edge of the bowl, he said, "If you're going to tease and fight with your sisters, then you should do women's work."

The family had waited until the father had made his pronouncement, and the confirmation of the sentence triggered additional waves of laughter. Hachiro didn't see what was so funny about his father's statement, but he knew better than to challenge or question it. Under Confucian principles, the father was the master of the household, and the master had spoken.

Hachiro took a basket and the funny little hooked knife used to cut bamboo shoots and stomped out of the house. The bamboo forest was a good hour away from Hachiro's village, but he had walked for only ten minutes or so when he heard the distant sound of shouting men behind him. He paused for a second, unsure of what all the noise meant, then turned to run back to the village.

Hachiro came to the top of a hill and could see the village was under attack. Troops had swooped down on the clustered farmhouses, setting fire to them by throwing lighted torches on the thatched roofs.

Fire was the most feared force in Hachiro's life. He had already lived through several shakings of the earth that knocked articles off shelves and made sliding wood and paper doors pop from their tracks. He had lived though times of lean harvests and hunger, although the old people of the village laughed at the complaints of youngsters, telling them they were seeing nothing compared to conditions of true famine. He had lived through a war, although he wasn't sure what the war was about or which side the Lord of his District was on. Only fire, with its terribly swift destruction of homes, had brought real terror into Hachiro's life. And now he was learning that fire was just a minor by-product of what men could do.

Uncertain, Hachiro stood at the top of the hill and watched the scene unfolding below him. The troops attacking the village carried banners with a diamond surrounded by six bent bamboo leaves. This mon was unfamiliar. It was white on black cloth and looked like a malevolent insect. Outside the village a cluster of horsemen stood, watching the attack. In the center of the cluster was a tall, thin man with a black-winged helmet. In his hands was a black war fan, a metal fan used by generals to direct troops on the battlefield. The large size of the fan made the signals of the general easier to see.

The thin man seemed to be in charge, giving signals to direct different groups of troops in their attack on the village. He stood on the stirrups of his horse and waved a large group of troops toward a previously untouched corner of the village. Hachiro realized that the men were moving toward his house.

Transfixed by panic and fear, Hachiro saw the troops fan out and enter each of the houses. In some cases the doors of the houses had been barred, but the men easily kicked them down and entered. He saw a half dozen men entering his own house, and his heart stopped. Hachiro wanted desperately to know what the men who had entered his house were doing. To his sorrow, he suddenly found out.

He saw his mother rapidly backing out the door to his house. This strange sight was explained as the shaft of a spear followed her out of the house, then a soldier. Hachiro thought the man was just chasing his mother out of the house with the spear, until she collapsed several paces from the door. Then he realized that the point of the spear was embedded in his mother's stomach and that she was holding the shaft, backing away in a desperate attempt to remove the weapon from her body.

"Okaasan!" Hachiro shouted.

His mother hit the dirt in front of the house, and the soldier leaned into the spear, driving it deeply into the writhing body of the screaming woman. Hachiro also heard the screams of his sisters coming from the house.

Galvanized into action, Hachiro dropped the basket and gripped the bamboo knife tightly. He started running down the hillside toward his house and the body of his mother. Before he had taken two steps, his foot hit a root, sending him tumbling down the hillside. He felt the sting of the knife biting into his side. Then his head hit a rock and blackness descended.

When he woke, he thought he was in hell. One eye seemed stuck shut from the dried blood that came from the gash on his head. But through the half-open other eye he could see only darkness and orange flames. He smelled acrid smoke. When he opened his parched lips, a bitter white ash entered his mouth. That set him coughing, and the coughs aggravated both the pain in his head and the pain in his side. He reached down and felt sticky blood on his flank.

If he had been carrying a regular knife, instead of the tiny, hooked takemono knife, Hachiro would be dead. Although the bamboo-shoot knife inflicted a nasty gash, it didn't penetrate enough to hit a vital organ. Still, with the darkness, flames, smoke, pain, blood, and dizziness, Hachiro was not sure that he wasn't dead. He tried to sit up to see what was around him, but he was so weak he could only roll over. Then he slipped into blackness again.

After he returned to consciousness, he had enough wits about him to realize the darkness was simply night. The smell of smoke and taste of ash was still strong, but the dancing orange flames were gone. He sat up and felt weak from loss of blood and his head wound. He slumped forward a few minutes, catching his breath and building his strength. Then he thought of his mother. What had been a village a few hours before was now a collection of embers. Hachiro realized the flames of hell he had seen were the flames of the village. In a way, it really was hell.

He stumbled to his feet and swayed unsteadily. Holding his side and walking slowly, he made his way down the hill and toward what was left of his house. The fire had burned down to just embers, and the dull glow from the collapsed beams provided scant light. As he approached, he saw a shapeless form in front of the house. He fell to his knees and reached out to touch the cold body of his mother. With trembling fingers, he stroked her hair and cried tears of pain, loss, and anger.

When the sun came out, he made his way to the stream next to the village to get a drink. When he approached the water, he recoiled in terror. His image, captured in the sluggish waters of the stream, was a frightening specter of dried blood, bruised flesh, and matted hair. He realized that he must have looked dead to the troops that destroyed his home village, which is why he survived.

He never found out which side or whose troops slaughtered the village. He didn't even know why or if the troops even had a reason.

With his family killed and his village destroyed, Hachiro fled to the mountains. There he was stopped by Boss Kuemon's brigands and captured. At first he was used as a kind of slave, but soon he was adopted more like a pet. The brigands had even decided that they would teach him to be a killer, but thus far they had been unsuccessful.

Hachiro sighed. Now he was involved with men he had been taught to fear, carrying messages for them. Since neither Kuemon nor Hachiro could read, these were verbal messages, often with puzzling content. Hachiro wondered what kind of life his karma had led him to, and he decided he must have been very wicked in a past life to deserve this fate. He started walking again.

He reached the spring, looked around at the tranquil woods, and brightened up a bit. The clear water made a cheerful sound as it burbled from the earth. Hachiro's stomach was full, something that wasn't always true in the life of the farmer. Despite the work and abuse, maybe this life of the bandit was not too bad.

He looked down at the spring to dip his bucket in. His eyes widened in disbelief, and for a few agonizing moments he was paralyzed with surprise and fear, unable to run and unable to cry out. Then, dropping the bucket, he ran back to the camp as fast as his legs could carry him, shouting for help.

Fifteen minutes later a noisy group of men returned to the spring. They were making jokes and talking loudly among themselves. Hachiro was being dragged by the arm by one of the men, who pushed the youth toward the spring and demanded, "Well, baka! Where are they?"

Hachiro pointed down at the soft mud that surrounded the spring. "There!"

The men gathered around and looked at the mud. Deeply imprinted into the black earth were the footprints of some giant creature. The laughter and talk died.

"It looks like some kind of giant bird," one man said in the silence. "It has three front toes and a spur out the back."

"Maybe it's a lizard."

"Have you ever seen a lizard that big? Each footprint is longer than my forearm."

"Well, have you ever seen a bird that big?"

"Has anyone ever seen dragon prints?"

"Dragon prints? Have you ever met anyone who's seen a dragon? Don't be ridiculous!"

"Ridiculous? Me? Listen, you son of a union between a dog and a pig, did you ever see anything as big as these prints? Why not a dragon?"

"Does anyone know what a kappa's tracks would look like?"

"A kappa? How big would a kappa have to be to leave tracks like this?"

"Maybe they have big feet."

"But what is it?"

"The tracks come from the forest, where the pine needles hide them. It went to the spring for a drink, then it turned around and returned to the forest. See! Right here. The tracks fade out as it went back on hard ground."

"Look, here comes Boss Kuemon. Maybe he'll know what this is."

Kuemon approached the knot of men and said, "What's all this foolishness? Are you letting a baby-faced boy spook you? First the woman and now the boy. I've never seen such a bunch of weak-minded baka!"

"But look! Hachiro didn't imagine the tracks. They're still here."

Kuemon walked up to the spring and stared down at the tracks. He stared for a long time, the rest of the men waiting for his judgment. Finally, one of the braver bandits prompted, "Well?"

Tearing his eyes away from the tracks, Kuemon stuck out his chest and said, "It must be some kind of trick. Or maybe a freak accident of some kind. They just look like tracks. They couldn't be real." He glared at his men. "If one of you is making some kind of joke with these tracks, I'll cut your heart out! Tell me now, before I really get mad! Did one of you do this?"

"No."

"No, Boss."

"It's not one of us. They look real."

"We were all with you. It couldn't be a trick."

Kuemon looked at the faces of his men, trying to detect a guilty party. They were all hardened men, however, and used to lying. Still, Kuemon could see nothing in their faces except questions and fear. Curse that woman, and now this boy.

"Well, whatever it is, I'm not going to let a few tracks in the mud bother me. Hachiro! Pick up the bucket you dropped and fetch the water. We still have to make the evening's rice." Kuemon straightened his shoulders and strutted back to the camp. It bothered him that none of the men immediately followed. They wanted to stay by the spring, staring at the tracks.

In the hills above the camp, Kaze saw the men rushing to the spring. He settled back into a comfortable spot at the foot of two large trees. He didn't have to sneak down to the spring to see what was happening. He knew the effect of the dragon tracks would be as great as when he and the boys first saw them in the snow, so many years ago.

In the bandit camp, the men were silent and sullen. Kuemon didn't like it, and after dinner he decided to give the men courage through drink. "Hachiro! Bring out some *shochu* from my hut," he ordered. "Open a barrel of sake, too!"

The men, sitting around a campfire after their evening meal, looked up in anticipation at Kuemon's order. Shochu was a fiery liquor produced by peasants.

"What's the occasion, Boss?" one asked.

Kuemon laughed. "I've decided to have a party. It isn't every day we see the footprints of ghosts or dragons." He raised his hands high into the air, making claws with his fingers. On his face he put on a grimace worthy of a *kabuki* actor. "I'm the ghostly creature," he intoned as he made his way around the campfire, provoking nervous laughter from the men. "I don't know what I am, but I must be pretty scary to have such big feet! Maybe I'm a ghost. Maybe I'm a kappa. Maybe I'm a demon. Maybe I'm just a stupid bunch of tracks designed to scare old women and weak boys! Boo!"

The tension of the men dissolved in laughter. Kuemon, meeting success, started an impromptu dance, scampering around the fire saying "Boo!" at the men. Soon other men were joining him, striking twisted poses and making blood-curdling shrieks.

Hachiro broke open several jugs of shochu. He poured the contents into cups and handed them around. Then he took a barrel of sake out and broke it open and poured some of its contents into an old metal pot. Instead of putting the pot into hot water, he simply put it over the fire to warm up. In a few minutes he was handing Kuemon a square wooden box that acted as a cup, filled with sake. Kuemon drained the sake in one long drink and demanded more from Hachiro before the others could be served.

"Put more wood on the fire!" Kuemon demanded. "Let's build the fire large to keep away all the spirits and ghosts and demons. Boo!"

The dry wood was piled on, and the fire crackled and hissed as sparks flew up into the night. The shimmering orange light of the fire cast weird flickering shadows that added to the demon imitations of Kuemon and the others.

Most of the men were up and dancing around the fire, holding cups of shochu or wooden boxes of sake in one hand and clawing at the air with the other. All were laughing and making scary sounds.

"Booo! Booo! Watch out ghosts! I can be as scary as you!"

"Look at me! I'm a demon, a scary demon!"

"Ooooh! Ooooh! Watch out for me. Ooooh! I'm a wailing demon."

"You sound more like a woman having sex! Come here, little demon, I have something for you!" The man crudely grabbed his crotch.

Instead of taking offense, the wailing demon sidled up to the taunter and said, "Oh yes! I'm here for you, you big hunk of man. But wait, what's that tiny thing you're holding in your hand? Surely you don't think that small thing will part my jade gates, do you? Why that thing wouldn't fill up a female rabbit! Perhaps I should turn around so you can treat me like a young boy?" He faced away from the fire, bent forward, flipped up the back of his kimono, and exposed his loincloth-covered buttocks to the man. The rest of the group started laughing uproariously.

Encouraged, the wailing demon pushed his rear out even further and said, "Yes, I'm sure you will like this best. But I still can't feel anything. Are you so small that . . . ?" The man's voice trailed off and he abruptly stood up, staring into the forest away from the campfire. The group of half-drunk bandits was still laughing ebulliently, and the object of the joke came up to the wailing demon and gave him a rough shove. The wailing demon staggered forward, but instead of getting mad he put up his hand and hissed, "Look!"

One by one, the bandits stared into the darkened forest to see what the wailing demon was staring at. And one by one, the bandits stopped laughing.

High in the trees the bandits could see a ghostly apparition flitting from treetop to treetop. Even in the darkness of the forest, it could be seen by the starlight. It moved with amazing speed, darting from one location to the next. Its movements were accompanied by a swishing sound that added an aural element to the visual speed.

"What's that?" one man said in a low voice.

Boss Kuemon came from around the fire to get a closer look. "Have any of you ever seen anything like that before?"

The men shook their heads no or murmured a negative.

The white presence suddenly dove to the ground and disappeared.

"Get my sword," Kuemon growled. No one moved. All the men were transfixed, waiting to see if the apparition would reappear.

"Get my sword!" Kuemon shouted. "And you men get your weapons and follow me. I want to get a closer look at that thing."

Still the men didn't move. Kuemon walked up to some and started kicking and cuffing them, knocking them out of their fear-induced stupor. Hachiro brought Kuemon's sword, and a few of the other men grabbed swords and spears, but others, although they grabbed weapons, could not be induced to leave the safety of the fire, no matter how many blows Kuemon rained down on them.

Exasperated and angry, Kuemon finally led the men who would follow him into the woods, seeking out the white presence. After a search of more than an hour, the men returned to the glow of the fire. They gathered around, looking at each other's faces, each not daring to speculate about the strange events of the afternoon and evening or what their fruitless search meant.

"Well, it's probably a trick of the vision," Kuemon said. A few of the men glanced in his direction, but no one would make eye contact, and no one agreed. "Sometimes the eyes play tricks on you," Kuemon continued. "Like mistaking those impressions in the mud for footprints. They were probably—"

"BLOOD!" A deep, ghostly voice echoed out from the forest. The men were galvanized, jolted to a state of taut alertness as they peered into the dark trees. They clutched their weapons in a tight grip and edged closer to the sheltering light of the fire.

"I WANT BLOOD!" The voice came from the darkest part of the forest that surrounded the bandit camp. It boomed out of the darkness with a resonance that was unearthly.

"Come here!" Kuemon hissed. "Form a defensive line! Stay alert. Be ready for an attack at any moment."

From deep in the darkness, Kaze watched the effect of his cry for blood with satisfaction. The bandits were all on the alert now, their nerves frayed and near the breaking point. They would probably stay alert most of the night. Even if they didn't, they would be sleeping in shifts, jumpy and watchful. Kaze smiled.

He untied the piece of white gauze he had attached to the end of a long, thin piece of bamboo. By running through the trees and whipping the bamboo back and forth, he had created the ghostly apparition the bandits had searched for.

Then he picked up the fat, hollowed-out tube of bamboo that he had used as a megaphone when crying for blood. The megaphone had given his voice just the right touch of ghostly reverberation.

He hauled the evidence of his manufactured ghosts with him to a safe, secluded spot in the forest. There he had previously stored the gnarled tree branch, carefully chosen and shaped, that formed a large claw. Tied to the branch was a long piece of bamboo, so Kaze could stand at some distance and make tracks in the soft mud, creating the dragon prints that so frightened both the bandits and a group of young boys. Fluffing up a bed of fragrant pine needles, he snuggled down into a satisfied sleep.

## CHAPTER 17

*Shadows where there is
no light. Demons appear to
prick at our conscience.*

The next morning, Kaze climbed a tree to observe the camp from a safe distance. He could see the men in the camp standing around the burnt-out campfire from the night before, arguing. From a distance they looked like *bunraku* puppets playing out a scene in pantomime. Kaze couldn't hear what was being said, but he didn't need to.

The man he took to be Boss Kuemon was haranguing the other bandits. He had a sword in one hand, and he was marching up and down like a general trying to instill courage into reluctant troops. He would stop occasionally to point to the woods where Kaze had performed his ghostly tricks the night before. Kuemon started marching in that direction, but then stopped when he noticed none of the men were following him.

He returned to the men and started his speech again. Finally, after much cajoling, first one, then a second, then a third and a fourth man joined Kuemon. No amount of hand waving and fist shaking could make the others join in the search of the woods. Shouting over his shoulder as he marched into the woods followed by the four men, Kuemon finally started the search.

The remaining men stood around looking at each other for several minutes. First one, then the next, started talking and pointing to the woods. Then, as if by general agreement, the men ran into the camp, grabbed as much as they could carry, and scattered into the forest in directions away from the searchers. The only one left in the camp was the young boy that Kaze had spared in his encounter with the bandits on the road, the same youth that obligingly fell asleep while on sentry duty. Kaze laughed out loud and settled into a comfortable position on the tree limb to await further developments.

Kuemon conducted a thorough search of the woods, and it was well over an hour before he returned with his four remaining followers. From his vantage point in the trees, Kaze watched as Kuemon exploded like fireworks shot into the night sky to mark a summer festival. Kuemon started by knocking the youth to the ground, then he tore through the camp, discovering what was missing, then he ran back to the boy, who had just picked himself up, and knocked him down again. With a shaking arm, the boy pointed in the direction the other men had run, and Kuemon and the other four ran off in that direction.

Kaze started climbing down the tree, happy with the results of his actions. With ten or twelve men, it would be a suicide attack, in which the best result would be the loss of the leader. Five was possible. The five bandits would return upset and tired from their long night, the fruitless search of the woods, and now the chase after their erstwhile comrades. And Kaze would be ready.

Back in the camp, Hachiro picked himself off the ground and sat for a moment with his head in his hands. Kuemon's blows had set his ears ringing. When the other men looted the camp and ran in fear, Hachiro had been tempted to join. Yet his fear of Boss Kuemon was greater than any fear of the supernatural, and he had waited. With the look of fury in Boss Kuemon's face, he was glad he did.

Hachiro went and picked up a spear. Kuemon told him to guard the camp against man or demon. Kuemon had punctuated his order with a threat to cut out Hachiro's privates and feed them to the demon if Hachiro was not alert and on guard when he returned. The very thought of the threat made Hachiro squirm.

After Hachiro's headache subsided, he realized the source of the discomfort in his belly was actually a call of nature, not the threat from Boss Kuemon. Hachiro went and picked up a handful of leaves for wiping, then made his way into the part of the woods the bandits used as a latrine. Although his need was becoming pressing, Hachiro entered the woods carefully, looking at every tree and bush to make sure some dreadful creature wasn't lurking.

Finally, finding a spot he thought to be safe, Hachiro hitched up his kimono and undid his loincloth. Then he gathered the skirts of the kimono around his waist and squatted down, the spear resting across his knees.

He had just started doing his business when he felt something tickle the back of his neck. He flicked his hand backward to chase away whatever insect was bothering him, but his hand banged against the flat of a sword blade. With a start, Hachiro tried to stand up and grab at his spear. Before he could do so, the spear was kicked out of his lap by a sandaled foot, and a hand on his shoulder forced him back into a squat. "You might as well finish what you started," a husky voice said from behind him. "It will be a long wait for your Boss to come back."

Later that day Kuemon wished he had met a demon. It would take a fight with a demon to drain the anger out of him. He did not catch up to the men who took the cash and other possessions from his camp. True, the bulk of his treasure was still hidden in his hut, but it galled him that the miserable worms, who knew nothing of banditry until Kuemon took them under his tutelage, had stolen from him.

His remaining men were dirty and exhausted from the fruitless chase and the search that morning, but they knew better than to complain during the long walk back to the camp. Every scowl, every snort, every curse he made let the men know that this was not the afternoon to complain about anything to the Boss.

The afternoon was almost ended and the red sun was directly in his eyes when Kuemon returned to the camp. Because of the glare of the sun, he couldn't immediately see who was in the camp as he approached it.

There was a figure standing in the sun with a drawn sword. At first Kuemon thought it was the boy he had set to guard the camp, but as he grew closer he realized that the figure before him was too husky and mature to be the kid. His steps slowed, then he stopped.

His weary men, seeing Kuemon stop, also came to a halt. "Why are we stopping?" one of the men dared to ask.

"Fool! Take out your weapon!" Kuemon matched his order with his own actions, drawing his sword from his sash. Three other swords and a spear flashed in the red sunset as the other bandits brought their weapons to the ready.

The five men advanced cautiously. Kaze noted that they spread out without being told to, so that they would flank him on the right and left. He grudgingly acknowledged that Boss Kuemon had trained his men properly. Kaze was acutely alert to a sudden rush by any or all of the men, but for now he was content to let them come closer, as long as none of them threatened to get behind him.

"Be careful, Boss! He's the samurai I told you about from the road to Higashi." The boy, Hachiro, was tied up securely and sitting where he could view events. Kaze hadn't gagged him because he wanted him to warn the bandits about who he was. He noted a slight hesitation in the steps of three of the men when Hachiro told them who he was. Good. That's exactly what he wanted: a slight hesitation when the moment of truth came.

Kaze shifted the position of his sword, bringing it to the ready position, with both hands on the handle. This action most definitely caused three of the men to lag slightly behind Kuemon. One of the laggards was to the left of Kuemon, the other two were on the other wing. Kaze waited until the stragglers were a full step behind the other men, then he attacked.

The bandits were surprised by the explosive fury of Kaze's attack.

His initial charge sliced the lead bandit across the shoulder and neck because he was too slow in getting his guard up, but instead of jousting with Kuemon, Kaze used the body of the cut bandit as a shield and immediately turned his attention to the two laggards on his left.

One bandit parried his blow, and the distinctive sound of two Japanese swords crossing clanged out in the camp. Instead of striking another blow at this bandit, Kaze took an arcing slice at the second one, the one with the spear, catching him off guard and cutting him through the side.

Kuemon had now stepped around the body of the dying lead bandit, but Kaze spun around and rushed at the bandit who had originally been behind Kuemon. This bandit blocked the first of Kaze's blows, but he wasn't able to block the second, and Kaze's cut caught him across the shoulder and chest. Kaze had a flash of concern as his sword momentarily embedded itself in the shoulder bone of his latest victim, but he was able to wrench it free before Kuemon and the remaining bandit surrounded him.

Kaze nimbly stepped sideways out of the trap set by the two bandits. When he made a half turn, the two men were now standing to the left and right of him, instead of in front and behind. The two bandits hesitated. Kaze, who was now puffing from his expenditure of energy, welcomed the respite.

Kuemon glared at Kaze with a look of pure malevolence. He had wished for a demon to fight, and now he found one in human form. Kaze expected Kuemon to say something to him. Instead, he said to the other bandit, "If we attack together, we'll kill him. He can't handle both of us at the same time."

Kuemon was wrong.

As the two bandits lunged forward, Kaze quickly stepped backward. The spot where the bandits were converging was now empty, and they both had to alter their path to attack Kaze. Instead of attacking him from each side, they were now both in front of him.

Kaze lifted his sword to protect his head and parried the blows of both men, dropping to one knee under the combined force. Kuemon slipped his blade off Kaze's sword and drew it back to take a cut at him. As he did, Kaze lunged forward, releasing the pressure on his blade and bringing it forward. The bandit's blade, now released from Kaze's sword, sliced through empty air as Kaze's cut into the bandit's belly. Hot blood and liquefied stomach contents sprayed out on Kaze as the bandit gave a great groan.

Kaze fell to the earth and rolled away from the dying bandit. With a shout of triumph, Kuemon rushed up to Kaze and chopped down at him. Kaze finished his roll just in time to catch Kuemon's sword with his blade. Kaze kicked his foot out and caught Kuemon on the kneecap, sending him sprawling to the earth. Kaze lunged forward and stabbed Kuemon in the throat, his blade penetrating the larynx and driving deep into the ground. Kuemon clawed at the blade, cutting his hands and making a dreadful, gurgling sound as his blood spurted into the air from a cut artery. He was pinned to the ground by the sword, but he was still struggling to get up so he could deliver an equally mortal blow to Kaze.

Kaze kept his hand on the hilt of his sword, driving it forward so Kuemon could not get up. Kuemon's exertions against the force of the blade grew rapidly weaker, until finally the bandit chief lay still.

Kaze was gasping for breath, but every time he drew in a ragged mouthful of air, it held the awful stench of blood and bile. It gagged him, not only with its physical effects, but with its association with the death and decay abhorrent to Shinto. It was a paradox that puzzled him. As a warrior, he was trained to kill or be killed, and he approached each battle with a coldness that sometimes frightened him. Yet, when it was over, he often had regrets at the consequences of his skill.

During the moments of the fight, nothing else existed for Kaze. He felt more alive than at any other time in his life, including when lovemaking. Every pebble under his foot was distinct and noticeable. Every slight glance by an opponent was memorized. Hard breathing by an adversary sounded like a trumpet. It meant his prey was getting tired and would soon make mistakes or drop his guard. Kaze's mind was wonderfully lucid, racing ahead two, three, or four moves. And the most important thing in the world was winning. It was the only goal, the only existence he acknowledged in a fight.

Afterward, when he had won, the rest of his humanity, which was crowded out by the pressure of the fight, returned. He looked around at the results of his skill and felt a wordless sadness. He understood why so many warriors became priests in their old age.

He had seen other warriors enjoy picnic lunches after a battle, sitting midst the blood, bodies, and hacked-off limbs. That was something unthinkable to Kaze. He enjoyed fighting, but he didn't enjoy death.

He stood up and yanked his blade out of the neck of the dead bandit. He carefully wiped the blade off on the bandit's clothes. There were a few groans from dying men and a peculiar snuffling noise. He looked around to identify the source of the strange noise and saw the youth crying.

Kaze walked out of the camp to the spring where he had made the dragon tracks. He stripped off his kimono and sat in the small pool of water. Its coldness surprised him, but he splashed the water against his body and face to erase the stench of blood. He got out of the pool and dunked his clothes in. As he squeezed his garment, a watery red stain spread in the pool. Kaze wrung out his kimono, and, holding on to it with one hand, he tossed it over his shoulder. Still gripping his sword in the other hand, Kaze casually strolled back to the bandit camp, naked except for his sandals and loincloth, as nonchalant as any man returning from a public bath.

When he got back to the camp, all the bandits were finally dead. The boy was still crying, and he watched Kaze approach him with wide, fearful eyes. Kaze strolled over to where the tied-up youth was lying, and he squatted down on his haunches. He studied the boy's face. It was the broad, blunt face of a peasant. Tears streaked down his cheeks and a bubble of snot filled one nostril.

"What am I going to do with you?" Kaze asked.

The boy made no reply. He was either too fearful to talk or he didn't understand Kaze's question.

"I gave you your life once, back there on the road," Kaze said. "Most people would have understood that the life of a bandit was not for them after that incident, but you immediately returned to this camp. Didn't you understand that you're not like them?"

"They never let me be one of them," the boy blurted out. "I was only allowed to do stupid things, like guard the camp, guide people, run messages, or do the cooking and cleaning."

"You had a chance to be one of them when you were supposed to stab me in the back, and you failed."

"I didn't fail!"

"Don't try to deny that failure. It's something to be proud of, not ashamed. That failure was the reason I let you live."

"I'd have been as bad as any of them!" the boy shouted.

Kaze laughed. "It's a twisted world we live in when a young man tries to claim how bad he is. If I untied you and gave you a sword, would you try to sneak up behind me and stab me?"

The boy looked at Kaze, confused about what to say.

"Relax," Kaze continued. "I'm not going to put you to that test. I'll risk my life, but I won't play with it. First I'm going to gather up all the weapons I can see, then I'm going to release you. Then I want you to dig five graves and bury your comrades. If you do that properly, you shall have your life as a reward. This will be the second time I've given your life back to you. This time don't waste it."

Kaze spread his wet kimono out on a bush to dry, and, by the time he was done gathering up the weapons scattered around the bodies, the boy had stopped crying. Kaze cut the bounds of the boy and set him to work digging graves while he waited for his kimono to dry. Kaze found a tree limb, trimmed it to his satisfaction, and started carving a statue of the Kannon.

"What's your name?" Kaze asked, deftly carving the edge of a robe on the statue he was working on.

"Hachimmmm," the boy murmured, making it hard to hear.

"What?"

"Hachiro."

"The eighth child, or did your parents name you Hachiro as a prank, when you were the first son and should have been named Ichiro?"

Hachiro looked blankly at Kaze, and suddenly realized the samurai was making a joke. He gave a small, tentative smile. "No, I'm the eighth child. There were fourteen in our family, although only seven lived."

"I was a second son, myself," Kaze said. "Why did you take up the life of the bandit?"

The boy stopped digging. "There was nothing else," he said. "Soldiers killed my family. They killed my whole village."

"What soldiers?" Kaze asked, not looking up.

"I don't know." Hachiro thought a moment, then he added. "They carried banners that looked something like a spider."

Kaze froze, then slowly looked up from his carving. "A black banner, with a white diamond surrounded by eight white bamboo leaves, bent in the middle?" he said softly.

Hachiro stopped his work and looked at the samurai, surprised. "Yes! How did you know?"

"There was a tall thin man with a black winged helmet? A helmet with pieces like this?" Kaze put his hands up to the side of his face, still holding the knife with a couple of his fingers. He spread the remaining fingers outward from his face. "He might have had a steel war fan for sending signals to his troops," Kaze added.

"How did you know? Who is he? Do you know why he destroyed my village and killed my family?" Hachiro was excited and forgot to be afraid.

"He is someone in the service of the Tokugawas, and he came to your village because your District Lord was undoubtedly a follower of the forces loyal to the Toyotomis, the late Taiko's family. As for why he destroyed it and killed, that was simply because it pleases him. He needs no other reason."

"Do you know him?"

Kaze's face twisted into a look of pure hatred. "Yes, I know him. It was Lord Okubo. He was a boyhood acquaintance of mine."

Despite his consuming curiosity, the samurai's reaction frightened Hachiro. After a slight pause, he bent down to his work again. Seeing the effect he was having on the boy, Kaze fought to control himself. Finally, after struggling to suppress all the rage the conversation raised in him, he tried to change the subject by asking the boy, "How did you end up with the bandits?"

"They captured me. They told me a farmer's life was too hard. They said that now the Tokugawas have won, there is no need for new soldiers, so there was no way to better yourself."

"Then you should not have bettered yourself. The life of a farmer is hard, but it can be long. The men you're burying all died because of the life they led. If I didn't kill them, they would have been killed by someone else. They were ruining this District. Perhaps Lord Manase would have put together an expedition to wipe them out when things finally became intolerable."

"Oh, Manase-sama wouldn't do that."

Surprised, Kaze asked, "Why?"

"Because Manase-sama needed my master, Boss Kuemon, for money. Manase-sama has borrowed money many times."

Kaze stopped carving. "How do you know that?"

"I used to take the money to Manase-sama's mansion. I was always running errands, exchanging messages, leading people that Boss Kuemon had captured on the road to the mansion, or taking money to Manase-sama." He stole a glance at Kaze. "Manase-sama may be very mad at you killing Boss Kuemon."

"If he is, that will be something I will have to deal with. Right now you have to deal with digging those graves before it gets dark. Hayaku! Hurry up!"

**CHAPTER 18**

*The cock thinks the sun*
*exists to serve its crow. We*
*think we serve our heart.*

"I'll draw a map of the location of the bandit's camp. The Magistrate can go there to see if there's any stolen material that can be returned to its rightful owners."

Kaze was sitting on the worn veranda of Lord Manase's manor. Before him the District Lord sat, practicing his calligraphy. Manase was once again dressed in layers of colorful kimono and he sat with his brush poised over the surface of a roll of fine paper. Next to him was an inkstone with a scene of grasshoppers carved in bas-relief in the head of the stone. In the well of the stone was high-quality ink, freshly ground and mixed with pure spring water.

Kaze could see Manase's efforts on the page. It was a practiced hand, but mechanical in its execution. For true practitioners of calligraphy, technique was practiced until it became unimportant; technique was submerged until the practitioner became one with his art. Then true emotion and character could show through in the art. It was similar to what Kaze had been taught in his use of the sword.

Seeing the mechanical nature of Manase's calligraphy, Kaze realized that he had been teaching himself the arts he practiced and had not been raised in the style he so ardently embraced. Although Manase was a natural Noh performer, his other refinements were recent acquisitions.

"But won't the bandits object to the Magistrate's men stumbling into their camp?"

"The bandits are dead or dispersed."

"Dead?"

"Five of them. The rest have run away."

"Who helped you?"

"No one."

Manase laughed. The high-pitched, tittering laugh was brittle and unnatural. "And Boss Kuemon, the bandit leader?"

"Dead."

Manase carefully put his brush down. He stared impassively at Kaze, his deep brown eyes floating like dual dark suns in the white-powdered sky of his face. Finally, he said, "Excellent!"

Manase shifted position slightly, so he was facing Kaze directly. He gave a slow, graceful bow, which surprised Kaze. "Thank you, samurai-san. This is a wonderful day for this District! Those bandits were becoming very troublesome and bold."

"I thought that, too. This will be a more peaceful District now."

Manase stood and went to the door. He slid it open and called out to a serving girl who was walking by. "You! Call the Magistrate and some of the men immediately!" He returned to his position by Kaze and said, "So the bandits are all dead?"

"As I said, only five of them. The rest have run away."

"And their camp?"

"If you will lend me your brush and give me a piece of paper, I'll draw a map so they can find the camp."

Manase slid the inkstone, brush, and a fresh sheet of paper to Kaze. Kaze picked up the brush but hesitated for a second.

"What's wrong?"

"This is a very fine piece of paper. It seems a shame to waste it on a map."

Manase waved his hand, as if sweeping dust off a counter. "Nonsense! Please use this paper for your map."

Kaze shrugged and quickly drew a map to the bandit's camp on the paper. By the time he was finished, the puffing Magistrate had appeared.

Manase picked up the map and looked at it briefly, then he handed it to the Magistrate. "Here," Manase said.

Looking a bit befuddled, he took the map and looked at it.

"That is a map to the bandit camp," Manase continued. "This ronin was able to do in a few days what you have failed to do for two years. He has killed the bandits or driven them away, and he did it by himself. It makes me wonder what you have been doing all this time, besides collecting a salary from me!"

The Magistrate handed back the map to Manase. Instead of taking it, Manase said, "Fool! Take the map and go to the camp. Search the camp and see if you can recover some of the stolen goods." Manase looked at Kaze and said, "Lately, even I have been a victim of those ruffians. Materials and supplies meant for me were stolen, along with all the other things they took." Manase returned his attention to the Magistrate. "Well?"

Gritting his teeth, the Magistrate got up and left the veranda. Manase clapped his hands, and soon a serving girl appeared. Manase looked at her and said, "Bring me the second drawer from the cedarwood chest." The servant scurried out of the room.

"I must think of an appropriate way to reward you," Manase told Kaze. "Perhaps a banquet or maybe a Noh performance. If that fool finds any money in the bandit camp, I can afford to hire professional musicians and give a proper Noh performance. It will be good to have someone in the audience who can appreciate my art."

The servant returned with a flat wooden drawer from a wooden chest. In it were several fine kimonos. They weren't as fine as the sumptuous kimonos and robes worn by Manase, but they were clearly expensive and much finer than the kimono Kaze was wearing.

Manase paused for a moment, then picked out a kimono with an elegant pattern of pine boughs, hand painted in indigo blue with a red splash of color on the head of a small bird sitting on a limb.

He lifted the folded kimono out of the drawer and set it in front of Kaze. "This is for you," Manase said.

Kaze glanced at the kimono. A samurai being given clothing by a Lord was a special and personal reward. It implied that a ronin like Kaze could join Manase's household, if he wished. Kaze placed both hands before him on the mat and gave a formal bow to Manase. He slid the kimono back to the District Lord, then he bowed again.

After a pause, Manase said, "I see. Too bad."

"I'm sorry," Kaze said.

"No matter, it will still add some excitement to this dreary place to organize the celebrations. Please leave now. I have to plan the program of entertainment."

Kaze bowed and left Manase's study. He walked to the front of the manor house, put on his sandals, and started walking down the path. He didn't look back.

## CHAPTER 19

*Gray of steel, not fog.*
*Life seen through cunning old eyes.*
*Fearsome grandmother!*

**K**aze took the road to Higashi village again, passing the spot still guarded by the Kannon where he had killed the first two bandits, and he arrived in the neighboring village by early afternoon. There was just one inn in the village, and Kaze stopped where he had intervened between the inn's owner and the maid. If the owner remembered the incident, he gave no sign in the profuse greeting he gave Kaze. Since the inn was still deserted, Kaze could understand the man's effusive greeting.

In deference to his dwindling purse and the deserted inn, Kaze elected to sit in the common room instead of a private room. Since he was the only guest, it amounted to the same thing. As he relaxed on the ratty tatami mats of the inn, the serving girl he had aided came in with tea and a hot towel. Upon seeing Kaze, her rough peasant's face broke out into a grin.

"Samurai-sama! You left so suddenly last time that I didn't have a chance to appropriately thank you for your help!"

Kaze said nothing, but he shifted uncomfortably. He judged that he would have to do some deft maneuvering before the night was over. He liked the company of women, but he also liked to select which woman. He also had an aversion to paying for services, although he had no doubts that tonight's services would be free.

The serving girl placed the tea before him and left to fetch some food, giving him a saucy look before she left. Kaze sighed. He reflected that the pleasure he got from righting small wrongs sometimes carried an unforeseen price.

The girl returned with a bowl of okayu with chunks of sweet potato in it. Kaze shoveled a generous portion into his mouth, sucking in cold air with it so it wouldn't burn. The girl sat a proper distance from Kaze, but she was gazing at him with proprietary fondness.

"Nani? What?" Kaze asked.

"Nothing, samurai-sama. I just didn't expect to see you again."

Kaze grunted a noncommittal response.

"When you left I thought that if the demon didn't get you, for sure the bandits would get you," the girl continued.

"The bandits shouldn't be a concern anymore."

Puzzled, the girl asked, "Why?"

"Because Boss Kuemon is dead, and his men are either dead or scattered. It should be peaceful around here, at least for a while. Maybe business will pick up."

"Really? Boss Kuemon is dead? Truly?"

"Yes, truly."

The girl got up, saying, "Excuse me. I have to tell my master this. He'll be so happy!"

Kaze nodded and continued eating his okayu. A few minutes later the master of the inn returned with the serving girl. "Is it true?" the innkeeper said. "Boss Kuemon is dead?"

"Yes," Kaze answered.

The innkeeper broke into a huge grin. "What great news! The food is no charge, samurai-sama! This is wonderful for this District. Lord Manase has finally gotten some men together and taken care of that Kuemon."

"Yes, he did," Kaze said.

"He must have hired troops from outside to do this. That ridiculous Magistrate couldn't have taken on the likes of Boss Kuemon."

"I suppose so," Kaze said.

"Well! Excuse me, samurai-sama, but I have to hurry and tell the rest of the village the good news." The innkeeper scurried out of the room, leaving the serving girl.

"Well, if the food is free, I'll have another bowl," Kaze said.

The smiling serving girl took his bowl and rushed off to refill it in the kitchen. When she returned, she reclaimed the spot where she could goggle at Kaze, making him feel uncomfortable. To make conversation, Kaze said, "Have you seen that demon again?"

"No, not since that night. That's why I was so worried about you when you returned to Suzaka village."

"Why was that?"

"Why, because the demon was on the road coming from Suzaka village."

The question of which road the demon was seen on had never occurred to Kaze. "Was he going to Suzaka village or coming from it?"

"Coming from it. Why?"

"Curiosity is a fault of mine. Indulge me. And you say there was a man strapped to the horse?"

"Oh yes, we could all see that."

"Was the man alive or dead?"

The girl considered that for a few seconds. "I don't know, samurai-sama," she finally said.

"Was he moving or screaming?"

"No, samurai-sama."

"Then he would be very calm for a man being hauled off by a demon."

The girl cocked her head and gave Kaze a puzzled look. Kaze didn't bother to explain his sarcasm. Instead, he asked, "Did anyone see where the demon went?"

"He went toward the road to Rikuzen prefecture."

"But that road is also joined by the road that leads back to the crossroads from Uzen prefecture," Kaze said.

Frowning, the girl asked, "Why would anyone coming from Suzaka want to take that route if they were trying to go to the crossroads?"

"Why, indeed," Kaze said.

"Hey, is anybody here?" a voice called out from the entrance of the teahouse. It was a female voice, but gruff and very loud.

The serving girl had a surprised look on her face because of the appearance of new guests. She quickly got up and left the room to greet them. The girl spoke softly, but Kaze could hear the loud voice of the woman carrying on a one-sided conversation.

"It's about time you came," she said.

A silence. Undoubtedly the serving girl was making profuse apologies.

"So don't just sit there, bowing at me," said the loud woman. "Help me off with my sandals and take me where I can get some tea."

Another few seconds of silence.

"How much is a room for the night?"

Silence.

"How much? That's outrageous!"

More silence.

"Well, yes, just get me the owner of the inn. I want to talk to him about his prices. No, not now. First take us into a room and get us some tea."

In a few seconds the serving girl appeared back in the common room where Kaze was sitting. She seemed flustered and not at all sure what to do about her loud and assertive guests. Kaze was surprised to see that in fact there were three guests. In the lead was a woman old enough to be a grandmother, with hair shot with silver and pulled back in a bun. Across her forehead she had a white headband, and painted on the headband was the *kanji* character for "revenge." She wore hakama pants and a traveling coat just like a man. Stuck into her sash were a man's swords, and she strode into the room with all the power and arrogance of any real samurai.

Immediately behind her was a very old man. Where the woman was as sturdy as a sake barrel, the man seemed as ephemeral as a reed screen. His face was gaunt and cadaverous and his shoulders, elbows, and hipbones poked at his kimono. Kaze felt that he looked very much like a walking skeleton instead of a real man.

Immediately behind the old man was a young boy of perhaps fifteen or sixteen. On the back of the boy was a large wicker pack stuffed with cloth-wrapped bundles, and hanging on the outside of the pack was an assortment of pans.

The odd trio entered the room and occupied one of the corners of the common room. In politeness, Kaze shifted his position so that he was not looking directly at them. Under normal circumstances, Kaze's actions would erect an invisible wall between him and the other party, and he and the other party could each go about their business as if they were the only ones in the common room. This old woman, however, did not allow the invisible walls erected by polite Japanese society to deter her.

After ordering the old man and the young boy to sit in the corner, the old woman marched across the common room and actually tapped Kaze on the shoulder. Touching a stranger was extraordinarily rude, and Kaze considered how he should react. Should he treat her with the deference due to her because of her age? Or should he simply turn his back to her completely, snubbing her rude overture? Since he had been taught to indulge both children and old people, Kaze's distaste for being touched was overcome by his need to be polite to an elder.

"Yes, *Obaasan,* Grandmother," Kaze said politely.

"Are you the only other person in the inn?" the old woman asked.

Kaze shrugged. "I don't know."

"Well, have you seen a merchant?" the woman persisted.

"No, not at this inn."

"If you see a merchant, you tell me," the woman said.

"Any merchant?"

"No, of course not. The merchant we're looking for travels the Tokaido road, but you never know where such vermin may be found. We're on our way to the Tokaido now to see if we can find him. We are on an official vendetta. We have registered our grievance with the new Tokugawa government, and now we are looking for a certain merchant so that we can bring retribution and revenge upon his head."

"Those are two very weighty attributes for you to bring upon anyone's head, grandmother."

"I'm not here to do it alone," she declared proudly. "I brought with me my servant," she used her chin to point toward the gaunt old scarecrow, "and one of my grandchildren," she again used her chin to point, but this time at the young boy.

"Then surely that merchant must have a lot to fear and will not escape heaven's retribution."

The woman grimly nodded at Kaze's assessment of the ragtag trio arrayed against the unknown merchant. An official vendetta was no laughing matter. That meant the authorities had given the motley trio the power to hunt down and kill someone who had aggrieved their family. Before Kaze could get the details of the vendetta, the serving girl brought the owner of the inn into the common room, and the old woman focused her attention on the hapless inn owner.

The owner could barely get a greeting out of his mouth before the woman was assailing him on the quality of the accommodations and how he could have the effrontery to even charge one *sen* when weary travelers such as herself and her party were looking for accommodations more in keeping with what they were used to.

The flustered innkeeper bowed constantly, trying futilely to get a word in edgewise in the midst of the old woman's tirade. In desperation he looked at Kaze as if asking the samurai to come in as reinforcements against the old woman's assault. Kaze wryly shook his head, greatly amused at the scene playing out before him, but much too smart to get involved with this formidable woman.

Finally, in complete collapse, the innkeeper said that everyone in her party could stay at the inn for two sen instead of the normal five. The woman snorted that she would permit herself to take advantage of the inn's totally inadequate hospitality, but that even at two sen her servant and her grandson could sleep outside. She said it was the innkeeper who should be paying her for having to stay at such a flea-bitten hovel. The innkeeper retreated in disarray and confusion, leaving the servant girl to deal with his difficult guests.

Kaze enjoyed the spectacle but ate the rest of his dinner without talking to his weird companions in the common room. The trio did very little talking themselves, once the food was served. Kaze wondered what their vendetta was, especially since the woman's headband said revenge, but he had had quite enough conversation with the aggressive old crone and therefore did not ask for details about the vendetta.

As he was finishing his meal, the serving girl brought another guest into the common room. Before they had completely entered the room, Kaze was already on his feet with his hand on his sword.

"You!" the new guest screamed in anger.

The startled serving girl took a step back, and the trio in the corner looked up in surprise. Kaze simply gave a nod of his head.

The young samurai that Kaze had marooned on the island placed his hand on his sword hilt. "I demand a duel with you, and none of your 'no sword' tricks!"

Kaze studied the young man for a moment, then he said, "I'm sorry if I tricked you. It's in my nature to play such games." He dropped to one knee, taking the posture of a soldier reporting to a general. "I humbly apologize for offending you."

"You dog's offal! You coward!" the young samurai said.

Kaze made no reply. Instead he remained in a humble position.

"No, it's not good enough to apologize," the young samurai said haughtily. "I insist on a duel. You have not only insulted me, you have insulted the entire Yagyu school of fencing. Such an insult can only be washed away with a duel."

"All right," Kaze said, "But let's use wooden swords instead of steel. Since you want to demonstrate your swordsmanship, steel swords are not necessary."

The young samurai looked at Kaze with contempt, branding him a coward. Still, he said, "Fine! Wooden swords only. Let's do it right now and right here!"

"Let's do it outside," Kaze said quietly. He looked at the serving girl and said, "Fetch us two wooden staves, as long as katana. We'll be outside."

After looking at the two samurai fearfully, the serving girl scurried off to find two sticks of the proper length.

Kaze walked past the young samurai and made his way to the front of the inn. He put on his sandals and stepped outside into the dusty street. Behind him, the young samurai, the old woman, the servant, and the young man followed.

The girl quickly reappeared with the inn owner and his entire family in tow. She had two wooden sticks that she handed to each samurai with a bow. Kaze looked at his stick and took out his sword to cut down the handle into something resembling a real sword hilt. The young samurai took a strip of cloth and quickly tied up the sleeves of his kimono, crossing the strip across his back and looping it around each shoulder. He did this with a great deal of flash and panache, generating a few murmurs of approval from the small crowd. Smiling, he turned to face Kaze.

Kaze put his real sword into his sash and gripped his wooden stick with both hands. He took a formal fencing stance, with his eyes on the young samurai. The young samurai moved aggressively toward Kaze with a small shout, but Kaze stood his ground, his wooden sword not wavering.

The young samurai, a bit perplexed by Kaze's lack of reaction to his feint, stood for a moment, figuring out his next move. Suddenly, with a loud shout, he attacked with all the quickness and fury that youth can muster, bringing his stick down in a slashing blow. Kaze met the blow with his own stick, and both men executed a *kiri-otoshi*. With the kiri-otoshi, the blocking of the opponent's blow and the attacking counterblow are one motion, not two separate actions. The young samurai tried to counter with a kiri-otoshi of his own, jumping away from Kaze's cut.

After the clack of the wooden swords, the young samurai looked at Kaze with both respect and surprise. "You're a superb swordsman!" he exclaimed.

"Thank you," Kaze said with a short bow. "Is your honor satisfied now?"

"Well, it was a draw, but I supposed I can be satisfied with that," the young man said.

Kaze paused, then said, "All right then. Let us call it a draw."

"You don't think it was a draw?" the young samurai said.

"If your honor is satisfied, then that's what is important."

"Are you saying it wasn't a draw?"

"It was a draw."

"You are saying that, but do you believe it was a draw?"

Kaze said nothing. The young samurai threw his stick on the ground. "My honor is not satisfied," he said. "I insist we have a rematch, but this time with steel!"

"Please, let's not fight with steel swords. A rematch with wooden swords will do to settle the point."

"So you are a coward after all," the young samurai said.

"If you wish to believe so," Kaze answered.

"Fight!" The young man drew his sword. "Fight or I'll cut you down where you stand."

Kaze dropped the stick and drew his own sword. "I wish you wouldn't do this," Kaze said. Instead of answering, the young samurai advanced on Kaze, his sword held at the pointing-at-the-eye position. Once again Kaze stood his ground, waiting for the young man's attack. The young man came to within attack distance and warily watched the older samurai. He was waiting for a lapse in concentration, some momentary interruption that would give him an opportunity to push past Kaze's guard and strike a fatal blow. He saw none. The seconds crawled past, with the onlookers as mesmerized by the duel as the two participants. Suddenly, the young samurai attacked again, rushing forward with a great shout as he first raised his sword and brought it down in a blow designed to slash Kaze's neck.

Once again, Kaze did a kiri-otoshi, but this time the sword bit into the flesh of the young man. Surprised, the young man staggered back and looked down at his side, where a crimson stain was now spreading. He dropped his sword and clutched at his side, swaying slightly, then dropping to his knees from pain and weakness.

"Baka! Fool!" Kaze shouted. "You're too young to play with your life as foolishly as I do! You're also too stupid to play such dangerous games, challenging strangers to duels when you lack the judgment to see if you would win or lose in a mock conflict with wooden swords. The difference between victory and death in a sword duel is in the blink of an eye or the width of a finger. It's too fine a difference to judge if you have no experience. I pray to the Kannon that I haven't struck a vital organ with my cut. I tried to pull back so you would be wounded and not killed. I've killed enough in this district, and I'm sick of it. I especially don't want the killing of any more youngsters like you, who are too young and too stupid to know their own limitations and lack of skill."

Kaze looked at the landlord and the maid. "Take him into the inn and get him a doctor. He should live if we stop the bleeding now, so hurry."

The maid and the innkeeper rushed forward as ordered and helped the young samurai, now pasty white from loss of blood and shock, into the inn. Kaze wiped his blade on the sleeve of his kimono and stomped into the inn after them, with the old woman and her two companions bringing up the rear.

Kaze returned to the inn and picked up his bowl to resume eating.

The other three guests did the same, but this time the old woman was not anxious to disturb Kaze's privacy. At the end of the meal, as the servant girl was taking away his tray, she leaned into him and whispered conspiratorially, "That duel was superb! When all are asleep, I'll come to your room tonight. I still want to repay you for what you did for me."

Kaze made no reply, and the girl busied herself by gathering up the dishes on a tray and leaving the room. Kaze went to the room that was assigned him and found a futon already laid out on the floor, as well as a wooden head block, which was used as a neck rest. A single candle in a paper lantern lit up the austere room. As with every room in Japan, this one was laid out to a constant unit of measurement, the size of a standard rectangular tatami mat. He was in a four-mat room, which was small, but still large enough for one person.

Kaze sat for a minute and wondered if the room was big enough for one man and one serving girl. He leaned over and blew out the candle but didn't crawl onto the futon. Instead, he waited a few minutes until his eyes adjusted to the dark, and he stood up and slid open the shoji screen. He walked outside the inn onto a veranda and made his way to the corner of the inn where the men's urinal was.

The urinal was an area off the corner of the veranda with two bamboo screens. On the dirt floor fresh pine boughs had been laid. To use the facilities, a man stood at the edge of the veranda and made his water onto the pine boughs. Every few days, the pine boughs would be removed and fresh boughs would be added to keep the pine scent strong. Men only would use this facility, although Kaze was not too sure that he wouldn't be elbowed aside by the gruff old grandmother on the vendetta. Women would have to go to the privy, as would men when they wanted to do more than just pass water.

As he made his way back along the veranda, he saw two bundles sleeping on the ground behind the inn: the old woman's servant and young grandson. Kaze thought a moment, then walked over to the smaller of the two bundles and squatted down next to it.

"Sumimasen," Kaze said. There was a sleepy grunt of response.

"I've decided I don't want my room," Kaze said, "I'd rather sleep here in the fresh air. Would you like to sleep on a futon tonight, instead of the ground?"

"Oh, yes, thank you, samurai," the teenage boy said sleepily.

"Well, then, follow me," Kaze said, leading him back into the inn and to the room that he was supposed to occupy. "Just climb in the futon and stay warm," Kaze advised the boy, "and try to have a good night's sleep."

Smiling, Kaze slid the shoji screen closed behind him, walked outside, found a comfortable spot, and stretched out for the night, wrapping his kimono tightly around him and sleeping with his sword hugged in his arms.

The next morning, when Kaze went into the inn for his breakfast, he saw the old woman, the servant, and the young man already finishing up theirs. The woman was scolding her grandson.

"What is wrong with you this morning?" she said sharply. The boy looked up over his bowl of miso soup with a strange smile plastered across his face.

"Nothing, Grandmother," he mumbled.

"Well, you're acting most peculiarly," the old woman said.

The boy made no response but just continued to give a small smile.

As Kaze sat down, the serving girl came in and slammed a tray with his breakfast down before him. She had a look on her face that was both angry and accusatory. Smiling, Kaze tucked into his breakfast with a hearty appetite.

Before the strange trio left the inn, the boy came up to Kaze and thrust something into his hand. It was a scrap of cloth wrapped around something light.

"It's just *senbei*, rice crackers," the boy said, "But I wanted to thank you for letting me sleep in your bed last night!"

Kaze took the meager gift and put it into the sleeve of his kimono, where most things were carried, and forgot about it.

## CHAPTER 20

*A dead chick that had*
*no chance to preen or fly south.*
*Life's a precious gift.*

It was a fine day. The birds were singing deep in the woods, and a
light breeze ruffled the fragrant pine needles on the trees lining the
road. Kaze was walking slowly down the road, using his hunter's
senses to scan the periphery. He was looking for hoofprints that led
off the road or some other sign of activity.

It didn't make sense to him that anyone, human or demon, would
take the road from Suzaka to Higashi and then back to the crossroads.
Yet, he was also convinced that the man strapped to the horse of the
"demon" was probably the dead man he found at the crossroads.
The dead man was dumped at the crossroads, the timing was too
close to be otherwise, and the stripe of blood found on the dead
man's back, which ran parallel to his spine, could have been caused
by the body's lying over the back of a horse.

Kaze was convinced that something along the road from Higashi
to the crossroads was the reason for the roundabout route from
Suzaka to the crossroads. Maybe the demon met someone along this
road or maybe there was some other reason. Despite his desire to
push on to Rikuzen to see if his quest to find the young girl might
end there, he decided to spend the morning walking the road from
Higashi to the crossroads.

His careful examination of the road revealed nothing, and he was angry with himself for wasting time as he turned a bend in the road and saw the crossroads up ahead. Then he stopped. There, at the distant crossroads, was a tiny figure slumped in the middle of the road.

Kaze rapidly crossed the remaining distance to the crossroads but stopped short of the body. It was a young man sprawled facedown in the road, an arrow protruding from his back. It looked very much like the body Kaze had found at the same place just a few days before.

Kaze approached and leaned down to see if the man was dead. As he turned the man's head, he paused and gazed at the lifeless face, covered with dirt and in death contorted with pain. It was Hachiro, the young man Kaze had given life to twice. Hachiro's dead eyes stared back at Kaze, dull and clouded.

Kaze gently shut the eyes. He glanced at the arrow that cut the young life short and confirmed that it was the same type as the arrow that killed the unknown victim a few days before. He scanned the area around the body and saw the hoofprints of a horse. From the tracks of the horse, he was able to see that the body had been brought directly to the crossroads from Suzaka village. Why this time the body was brought directly to the crossroads, instead of by the indirect route through Higashi village, was something that Kaze couldn't fathom. In fact, why the body was brought to the crossroads at all was something that Kaze couldn't understand.

He looked around and found a sturdy stick. He picked it up and started scratching out a shallow grave, not far from the fresh grave of the previous victim.

When he was done burying the boy, he had carved another Kannon. When he had carved the statue for the bandits, he had had a hard time finishing the face. His encounter with the obake of the dead Lady had come back to disturb his tranquillity, and he wasn't able to finish the statue of the Goddess of Mercy. For this boy, he had no trouble. The familiar face of the Lady, beautiful and serene, appeared from the point of Kaze's small knife. Placing the statue over the shallow grave of Hachiro, Kaze clapped his hands twice and bowed deeply. When he straightened up, there was a look of weary sadness on his face.

Later that night, Jiro was making his evening meal when he heard a soft knocking at his door. He paused, not quite sure if he had actually heard a sound. The knocking was repeated. Jiro went to his door and said, "Who's there?"

"A friend."

Jiro reached down and moved the stick that prevented his door from being opened. He slid the door slightly, to make sure he was correct about whom the voice belonged to. He gave a small grunt of surprise and slid the door completely open. Kaze entered Jiro's hut and quickly shut the door.

"Sneaking unseen into a small village is worse than entering a lord's castle," Kaze remarked as he walked over to the cooking fire and sat down.

"What are you doing here? I was told you left."

"I did leave. Now I'm back. I want to spend a few days with you."

"Why?"

"I want to watch the village, and the best place to watch the village is from inside it."

"What for?"

Kaze sighed. "Something is not right here. It destroys my *ki,* my harmony and balance. I'm upset by it and want to restore that harmony."

"What are you talking about?"

Kaze smiled. "Let's just say I need a favor. I want to watch the village and the Magistrate and the headman Ichiro and maybe that prostitute, Aoi, too. If I'm caught here, it may mean trouble for you. I walked out on Lord Manase, and I'm sure he was upset. The fact that Lord Manase was undoubtedly upset about my leaving is why I slipped in here unseen. So the most powerful man in the District will not be pleased if he learns I'm back spying on the people in the District. He may also not be pleased with you if he learns I'm doing this spying from your house. It may be dangerous, and you could end up back in that tiny cage. If you say no, I'll understand."

Jiro turned back to his cooking. "You'll have to wait a few minutes for dinner. I wasn't expecting company, so I only cooked enough for one."

"Good."

The next morning, Jiro woke at his habitual time. The familiar darkness of his farmhouse wrapped around him. On the other side of the platform he could hear the breathing of the samurai, slow and regular.

Jiro got up from the platform, shrugging off the sleeping quilt. He stood on his feet, listening for the samurai once more, and moved toward the door, reassured that his guest was oblivious to his nightly sojourn.

Sliding back the door of his hut with exaggerated caution, Jiro slipped out into the cold night as soon as the door opening was large enough. He carefully slid the door back into place.

The velvet night nipped at his flesh with surprising sharpness. He thought briefly of slipping back into his hut to get a jacket but decided against it. He didn't want the samurai to know what he was doing any more than he wanted the rest of the village to know what he was up to. He felt ashamed by his nightly ritual, knowing that the others in the village would view it as a sign of weakness and something a real man wouldn't do, but he couldn't help himself.

The moon was a quarter full, so coming from the complete blackness of the hut, Jiro found it almost light enough to make out details on the ground. But Jiro didn't need to see his path. He knew it from countless repetition, over nine thousand journeys to the same destination.

He skirted the village and made his way up a nearby hillside. The pine trees gathered round him, but he knew the placement of every trunk and made his way rapidly up the path to the top of the hill. There, in a natural clearing, was the village graveyard.

Jiro went directly to a large stone flanked by a small stone. When he first started making this journey to the graveyard, he would worry about ghosts, but now it was as if the ghosts of all the past people in the village approved of what he was doing, and he felt safer in this place of the dead than in any other place on earth.

In front of the two stones, he squatted down.

"*Anata,*" he said tenderly, "Dear."

He reached out and touched the stone that memorialized his wife, now dead over twenty-five years. Then he tenderly stroked the stone that marked his dead son, who outlived his mother by only two days.

"How are you, Dear?" Jiro whispered. "The samurai has come back to stay with me. He's a strange one, but he has a good heart and I like him. I don't have much news to report to you. Things are more quiet in the village now that Boss Kuemon is gone, but I don't understand what the samurai is doing." Jiro shook his head. "Samurai! Always starting wars that kill peasants. Such a bother, *neh?*"

He stopped talking and felt the tears welling up in his eyes. The same tears that came every day for over twenty-five years, grieving over the loss of his wife and son. It was a weakness, Jiro knew. A man was supposed to bear it, showing strength in adversity. But Jiro couldn't help it. When his wife died, some part of him died, too. He felt incomplete without her, and the only time he felt whole again was when he was once more in her presence.

A rich man might have an altar in his house, to call the spirits of the dead to him with a fine brass bell. Jiro just had the stars and the pine trees and the two roughly hewn rocks to represent his wife and infant son. Yet somehow visiting his wife every day made him feel content and whole and ready to bear another unbearable day, until it was his karma to join her.

In the darkest shadow of the trees, Kaze stood watching Jiro. He was close enough to hear Jiro's conversation with the dead and knew what the two rocks meant immediately. He slipped back deeper into the forest, silently making his way back to Jiro's hut so he could seem to be sleeping when Jiro came back.

So the mystery of where the charcoal seller went every night was solved. Kaze didn't know if the dear one was a wife, mother, or mistress, but it was plain that Jiro was still linked to her in spirit. Kaze couldn't see Jiro's tears, but he could tell from the charcoal seller's ragged breathing that there were tears.

Kaze thought of his wife, killed along with his son and daughter when his castle fell to the Tokugawa forces. She died a samurai's death, killing her own children before they could be captured and tortured and then driving the blade of a dagger up under her chin and into her throat. The servants who escaped said she never hesitated when she realized all was lost. She retired to the castle's keep and did what she had to do, ordering the servants to set fire to the keep in a clear voice that never once wavered, according to the old family retainer who was instructed to report on her death to others, instead of joining her in death.

It was a fine death and a brave one. But Kaze wished she had been less the samurai's daughter and wife and more the woman. He wished she could have found a way to survive the destruction of their castle while Kaze was out fighting the Tokugawas. He felt tears forming in his own eyes, especially when he thought of the shining eyes of his children. Now, years later, Kaze found himself agreeing with the charcoal seller. Samurai were always starting wars, and peasants and other innocents were always dying in them. At one time it seemed so logical and sensible to him that bushido, the way of the warrior, was the natural way for a man to live. Now he wondered, especially when he dwelt on the losses that way had brought.

When Jiro returned to the hut, he found the samurai still sleeping soundly, breathing in a slow, gentle rhythm. Jiro didn't know that the samurai's breathing masked a sorrow as deep as his own and tears as bitter and salty as the ones the peasant shed every night in the forest. He drifted into a dreamless sleep.

Jiro woke early and stretched his stiff bones. When he sat up he was surprised to see the samurai already awake. Jiro nodded to the samurai and hoisted his heavy charcoal basket on his back. With another dip to say goodbye, Jiro left his hut to make his rounds, selling charcoal to the people who needed it. The activities in the village were no different from those on any other day, for nature and survival know no holidays, but with the elimination of Boss Kuemon the people had smiles on their faces and a lightness to their step.

Despite the gnawing danger of having the samurai hiding in his hut, Jiro, too, was especially loquacious that morning, actually trading small talk with several customers. By the time he returned to his hut, his basket was considerably lighter.

He entered the gloom of his hut and was surprised to see the samurai sitting in the lotus position, his eyes closed and his hands in his lap. He expected to find him gone or, at the very least, spying through the wooden shutters that covered the windows of the hut, looking at whatever it was that had prompted him to return to the village.

Kaze didn't open his eyes and made no move when Jiro entered. From the heavy sound of his footfall, he knew it was the old charcoal seller, still hauling his large basket. Jiro hesitated a moment at the doorway, then closed the door behind him and shrugged off his basket. He cleared his throat.

"Excuse me, samurai-san, but would you like something to eat?"

Kaze popped his eyes open. "Why are you getting so formal now? I already know how gruff and rude you are."

Jiro scratched his head and grinned. "You were so quiet and still that I wasn't sure I should disturb you."

"I was thinking. When I awoke this morning, I realized I was about to make a samurai's mistake."

"What's that?"

"Confusing activity with action. Sometimes thinking is action. I came here to observe the village, but I realized this observation was worthless without considering everything I knew and working up a strategy."

"What is it you're trying to observe?"

"That's what I should be thinking about. In the heat of battle, some samurai rush about like a school of fish, darting this direction and that, showing a lot of activity, but not killing too many of the enemy. The great Takeda Shingen would sit, holding his war fan and directing his troops. He would never move, even when the enemy was on top of him. He could do that because he would pick the strategic place to sit; the point where the entire battle would be decided. They called him The Mountain. He thought about the battle and knew where The Mountain should be placed. He didn't try different locations like a flea hopping across a tatami mat. If I'm going to be Matsu*yama*, pine *mountain*, I should take a lesson from Shingen and think about what I know and what I want to see. Then I can place the mountain at the spot where I'm most likely to see it."

"You say the strangest things. I can't understand you sometimes."

"That's all right. I can't understand myself sometimes. Let's have some breakfast, then I want to go back to thinking."

The charcoal seller and the samurai shared a simple peasant's breakfast of cold millet gruel and hot soup. After cleaning up, Jiro excused himself to go out and work in his fields. Kaze nodded and settled back into the lotus position, closing his eyes and thinking about what he had seen and heard over the last several days.

His breathing slowed and his entire being was focused on the meaning of the two bodies at the crossroads. In his mind he reviewed everything he had seen on the two bodies, carefully cataloging anything that seemed unusual or out of place. He tried to recall exact details, like a hunter examining the subtle turnings of grass blades or faint impressions on hard soil, searching out his quarry.

In his mind, he tried to replay every conversation he had had with every person he had met over the last several days, relistening to words and intonations and trying to recall minute changes in facial expression.

He also thought about his own actions, and he realized he had been hasty. He should not have eliminated the Magistrate as the first killer on the basis of a few arrows grabbed in panic on the night he played the trick on the village. The Magistrate could have several types of arrows. Boss Kuemon was also a possibility, perhaps killing the first samurai while someone else killed the boy. But was it likely that two different people would use the same type of high-quality arrow to kill? Even a woman could use a bow, and, if she was close enough, it would not take special skill or practice to hit her target. So Aoi was a possibility. Kaze knew Ichiro was probably capable of killing if provoked. Who knew what might provoke him if he or his family was threatened? So many choices to consider, and being hasty was not the way to consider them.

The sun climbed slowly to its zenith and started descending toward China. It passed behind the peaks of the mountains that ringed the village of Suzaka and caused the blue twilight that marked the time when the men and women trudged home from the fields. Before Jiro got home, Kaze opened his eyes. He said, "Good."

## CHAPTER 21

*Strange beast, with no eye
to perceive unripened fruit.
Some destroy the young.*

"**H**urry! Hayaku!" Nagato pulled the sniveling girl deeper into the forest. The girl hung back, tugging at his tight grip on her wrist. Nagato found it gave him a jolt of pleasure to cruelly twist the youngster's arm. She bent downward under the strain put on her limb and yelped in pain. He smiled. "You should be happy for what I'm about to do to you, you little whore!" he said.

He turned and continued to drag the eleven-year-old into the woods. Lust shot through him as sudden and hot as the desires of a sixteen-year-old. With the crying girl stumbling behind him, all his frustrations with Manase-sama and his wife and Boss Kuemon and the loss of money that the death of Boss Kuemon meant seemed to fade. He felt that he was truly a man after all, capable of conquering others, even if the other was just a young child and her peasant family.

Just a few minutes before he had been stomping away from the village, upset because of his latest fight with his wife and crone of a mother-in-law. His wife, as if sensing the fact that he was putting money aside for the purchase of a concubine, had been spending at a profligate rate. Nagato realized that money could buy power and that money could buy pleasure, and he was ready for either, but his wife seemed determined to deny him both.

Ideas came slowly to Nagato, and the idea that money could change his life had come equally slowly. But once the thought was planted, he embraced it with gusto. Unfortunately, it was Nagato's mother-in-law who had the money. He had not been clever enough to arrange for the assets of his father-in-law to be transferred to him upon death. As an adopted son-in-law, he inherited the position of Magistrate, but his mother-in-law still had the house, land, and money that should have been his.

Three years after their marriage, his wife had finally conceived a son, but soon after the birth of a Nagato heir, his wife had lost all tolerance for sex and started rebuffing him when he made his clumsy attempts to crawl into her futon at night.

Nagato, a man violent and bad-tempered with all underlings, was at a loss as to what to do about the abrogation of his rights in the marriage futon. Worse yet, his wife had told her mother about her new preference for sleeping alone, and the sharp-tongued old harpy had supported her daughter, threatening economic consequences if Nagato beat his wife or forced her to submit. This turned Nagato's world upside down, because he assumed it was the natural right of any husband to beat a wife who displeased him. That there might be consequences to this action befuddled and frustrated him, and he could think of no action to set his domestic world right except to find a concubine whom he could abuse and treat in a manner that he thought was fitting for a man to treat a woman.

The spring before, his interest had alighted on the daughter on the village headman, Ichiro. As was customary for all women and men in the village, during the hot months all the peasants worked stripped to the waist. Ichiro's daughter, Momoko, had just turned eleven, and she was helping the other village girls in the planting of the tender shoots of rice into the fetid water of the rice paddies.

This was a community effort, for no individual farmer could prepare the fields, plant the rice, care for the growing green shoots, and finally harvest and winnow the rice by himself. Some said this was why Japanese village culture was so close-knit and interdependent, but, to the peasants involved, acting cooperatively was the only way to survive.

The young women lined up along one edge of the field, and rice seedlings, which had been carefully nurtured from the best grains of the previous year's crop, were tossed to them in bundles, each bundle of precious shoots carefully gathered together and tied with a twist of straw.

The planting always started festively enough, but by the end of the day each woman was exhausted by the constant bending and tedious work. Some might welcome some of the gawking men on the edge of the paddy as potential marriage prospects. The crowd included men who had no real interest in the planting except to see all the young woman of the village lined up in one place. Nagato was such a man.

Many of the girls were fifteen or older and thus already married. Nagato didn't find these types appealing. Not because they were married, but because they looked too assured, too much like women. For some reason that made the Magistrate very uncomfortable.

Ichiro's daughter was joining the rice planting for the first time, and as such she was tentative and unsure of herself. She shrugged off the top of her kimono, letting it hang down from her waist sash. Since she was used to working and playing in summer with her chest exposed, she was not intimidated by the costume for planting. She was simply cognizant of the fact that her invitation to participate in the rice planting marked a passage for her, from the ranks of children into the ranks of the young women of the village.

Nagato found her hesitancy very appealing. He couldn't say why, but this quality made him have lustful feelings toward the child. That's why it seemed like an omen when Nagato, in a black mood after his fight at home, stumbled across the daughter of the village headman gathering roots at the edge of the forest. The child had the flat basket used for collection of roots in her hand. If she had a shallow round basket, she would be gathering mushrooms. She was with her mother, a woman Nagato dismissed as he did most of the peasant women in the village.

Nagato had been marching through the village to calm down from his fight and perhaps to find a peasant to yell at. He stopped when he spotted the girl and watched her with narrowing eyes. He carefully noted the way her body pushed against the cloth of the kimono and her innocent gesture of pushing her scraggly hair out of her face as she straightened up. She wasn't aware of the Magistrate, but her mother was.

Stepping between her daughter and the view of the Magistrate, Ichiro's wife bobbed in a low bow and said, "Good morning, Magistrate-sama!" Her voice was a little too cheerful, as if she was forcing herself to be bright and friendly, all against her better judgment.

The Magistrate said nothing and continued to stare past the woman at the child. The young girl had turned with the voice of her mother and was now looking at the Magistrate with surprise. It occurred to Nagato that he really didn't have to buy such a creature. As village Magistrate, he should be able to just take her. He stepped toward her.

"Would you like some freshly gathered roots, Magistrate-sama?" the mother said. Her words were innocent, but her voice took a sharp edge as she read the look on the Magistrate's face.

"Get out of my way," the Magistrate said as the woman further imposed herself between him and the child. Now the child had a look of fear on her face, and this incited Nagato's lust even more. She looked as if she was about to run away.

"Please, Magistrate-sama, won't you have some roots for your table?" the mother was pleading now, holding the basket before her like some offering. The words didn't match her thoughts, but it was plain she knew what was on the Magistrate's mind.

"I've told your stupid husband enough times what I want your daughter for, but he just doesn't seem to understand," Nagato told the woman. "Now I see it runs in the entire family. Now get out of my way. I am about to bestow a great privilege on that daughter of yours."

"Please Magistrate-sama! She's much too young! Take me instead. Please, Magistrate-sama! We can go into the woods right here and I can please you. The girl is still a child. She's too young for such things. Please!"

For Nagato, the woman's pleading evoked no pity. Instead, it quickened his need to take the child. He felt powerful and in control. His bluster, which so often crumbled when confronted with his new District Lord or his wife or the strange ronin, was now channeled into new and novel directions. He liked it and stepped closer to the child.

The mother imposed herself again, which surprised Nagato. The idea that a peasant might love a child and would want to protect it was one that had never occurred to him. Peasants were simply rice-producing machines: slow, stupid, dishonest, and untrustworthy. They had no human feelings.

The child was starting to run away, which enraged Nagato, and the mother had now dropped the root-gathering basket and dared to grab at his arm. "Please, Magistrate-sama! We'll go together into the woods, neh? You don't need the child. I can—"

Nagato struck her full force with his fist. The effect was even better than he had hoped. The woman crumpled to her knees, dazed. She released her grip on his arm, and it actually got the child to return to him and her mother.

"Please, Magistrate-sama! Don't hit my mother!"

Nagato smiled. "Come with me and I'll leave your mother alone."

"But Magistrate-sama—"

Nagato raised his fist to smash the now-defenseless woman kneeling before him. The child ran to him, grabbing at his arm. He reached over and grabbed the girl's wrist in a cruel clasp, twisting her arm and bringing a wince of pain to her face.

With her struggling to break free, he dragged her into the woods after him. Just before he stepped into the trees he looked over his shoulder and saw the mother staggering toward the village, her face cupped in her hands.

For once, Nagato felt powerful and completely in control. He actually smiled when he found a clear space in the woods and dragged the child close to him. He always knew he could kill any peasant with impunity, but he had never considered the other possibilities of what he might do.

He ignored the child's cries as he roughly stripped the kimono from her. Because she wouldn't stop struggling when he ordered her to, he gave her a backhanded slap that snapped her head back. He shoved her to the ground and fell on top of her, using his superior strength and weight to hold her down while he fumbled with his *fundoshi* loincloth.

He finally got his manhood free, but the child was still squirming and crying, and he coldly slapped her again. He wanted her chastened and subdued, but not unconscious. He found he enjoyed her struggles and the mewing pleadings that were coming out of her peasant mouth. He reached down with one hand to guide himself into her jade gates when he gave a large gasp. It was not a gasp of pleasure, it was a gasp of pain.

He reached behind to grasp the thing digging into the flesh of his back and felt the thing release its pressure. He brought his hand back to his face and was surprised to see it was covered in crimson. It took him a few moments to understand that his hand was covered in blood. His blood.

He rolled off the girl, the shock starting to ebb and the pain taking over. He could see Ichiro, the village headman, standing above him with a dagger in his hand. Nagato was astounded. A peasant in the village attacking him was unthinkable. The penalty for such an attack was the death of the peasant, the death of his family, and the death of at least four of his neighboring families. Collective responsibility extended beyond the need to cooperate to grow rice. It also meant collective punishment if one member of the village broke the laws protecting samurai and nobles.

Ichiro also seemed to understand the import of his act, because his weapon hand was shaking. His rage and need to protect his child had fueled his first thrust into the fleshy back of the Magistrate, but now, coming face-to-face with the consequences of his action, he realized he had murdered the child he wanted to protect, along with himself, his wife, and his other children. And for attacking a Magistrate, the deaths would not be quick ones.

Nagato made a bellow of anger at the sight of the village headman and reached for his swords, still tucked into the sash of his kimono, which he had not bothered to take off.

At the movement of the Magistrate toward his swords, the instinct for self-preservation took over Ichiro and he lunged forward, the sharp blade of the dagger catching the large man just below the breastbone, skittering downward into the soft flesh of his belly. Nagato clawed at the blade, roaring in pain and rage. He engaged in a desperate struggle with the smaller peasant, feeling his strength, blood, and life ebb away through the dagger wounds. Finally, still clawing at the weapon, he expired.

Ichiro's daughter had had her leg pinned by the corpulent body of the Magistrate during the entire struggle. The weight of the struggling Magistrate, the pain, and the shock of the attack had driven her to hysterics. She was pushing at the Magistrate's corpse, crying and not yet comprehending what had happened. Seeing his daughter's predicament, Ichiro dropped his weapon and helped the girl to push the large body of the Magistrate off her. Then, putting her torn kimono around her shoulders to cover her nakedness, he held his daughter to him as she sobbed and shook from her experience.

He tried to provide some comfort to her, but he had no comfort in his own heart. All he could think about was that he had killed them all with his rash act against the Magistrate. He racked his brain but saw no escape from the inevitable results of this killing. No one in the village would side with him, because his action had killed many of them due to the collective responsibility that samurai imposed on peasants. He couldn't run, because anyone who sheltered him would also be killed, along with their family, too. He couldn't plead that he was defending his daughter, because he had no right to defend his daughter, at least not from the village Magistrate.

His daughter was crying, and tears formed in his eyes, too. His daughter's tears were tears of shock and relief, but his tears were tears of despair. Through his tears, he saw a movement in the woods and, suddenly, standing before him was the strange ronin.

Kaze took in the scene in an instant. The half-naked girl being comforted by her father, the large body of the Magistrate with blood covering his stomach, the bloody dagger still impaled in the body of the official.

Kaze stepped over to the body and pulled the dagger out. He wiped the blade on the kimono of the Magistrate. For a second, Ichiro thought Kaze was going to administer justice on the spot, killing both him and his daughter for his crime. In a way, he almost welcomed this, because it would mean their deaths would be simple and quick. It would also mean that Ichiro would not be kept alive under torture so he could watch his wife and children and neighbors all killed before he, himself, also paid the ultimate price for his crime.

To Ichiro's surprise, Kaze extended the butt of the weapon to him. Taking one hand from his daughter, the village headman took the knife. He was confused about what Kaze was doing.

"It's terrible how these bandits have gotten out of hand in this District, isn't it? I guess one of Boss Kuemon's men took revenge on the Magistrate, mistakenly thinking he was responsible for Kuemon's death."

Ichiro heard the ronin's words but could not understand their meaning. He knew the samurai was strange, but now he thought that perhaps he was insane.

"What?" the headman said.

"I said it's terrible what the bandits have done. They're now so bold that they've killed the local Magistrate."

Ichiro still didn't understand. He looked up at the ronin in total confusion.

"I think you should say that the Magistrate was off for a walk, then later you saw a few of Boss Kuemon's men in the forest. You went to investigate and found the body. Keep the child in your hut for a few days and tell your neighbors that your wife slipped and hit her face on a rock. Don't mention you saw me. Now do you understand?"

"But why . . . ?" Ichiro gasped.

Kaze stared down at the shocked peasant, who was still holding his young daughter in one arm and holding the murder weapon with his hand. In a way, Kaze felt like a traitor to his class. His natural sympathies should be with the Magistrate, Nagato, because he was a fellow samurai. Kaze knew that there had often been peasant revolts in Japan and that the savagery and ruthlessness of armed peasants were exceeded only by the samurai who had been sent to suppress such revolts.

Yet, in the two years of his wandering, he had gotten to know the people of the land in a way no regular samurai could. They could be petty and venal and selfish. They could also be warm and generous and full of bawdy humor. More important, in two years of looking for the daughter of his former Lord, he had also seen the treatment of countless young girls and it was starting to disgust him.

In Japan they didn't indulge in the practice of exposing newborn girl infants as the Koreans and Chinese did, except in times of dire famine. Yet the life of a peasant girl was hard and often brutal, and Kaze sometimes wondered if life was such a precious gift when it was lived in these conditions. He wondered what the Lady's daughter had experienced in the two years she had been missing and what she would be like when he found her.

"Why?" Ichiro asked again.

Kaze looked at the body of the Magistrate. Kaze was now sure the Magistrate hadn't killed the samurai at the crossroads. The arrow he had shot at Kaze during the ambush was not like the ones that had killed the unknown samurai and Hachiro. Although the Magistrate could grab any arrow when startled at night, as when Kaze played the trick on the village, Kaze decided that the Magistrate would most likely use his best-quality arrow when he knew he would be killing men.

Still, the Magistrate might as well die for trying to rape the peasant girl as for some other crime, such as taking a bribe from a bandit. In fact, if Kaze had come upon the scene a few moments earlier, he might have killed the Magistrate himself. He had caught sight of Ichiro's wife rushing into the village, then of Ichiro running into the forest. Kaze had gone to investigate. The peasant wanted an answer for Kaze's actions, which turned his perception of class and the whole world upside down, but Kaze couldn't articulate one.

"Because it pleases me," Kaze finally answered. Kaze walked away, leaving the astonished peasant and the sobbing girl.

CHAPTER 22

*Red Fuji, caught in
the caressing rays of the
budding scarlet sun.*

**W**hen he was a boy, Kaze climbed trees and flew kites from the
treetops. He started by flying kites from fields, like other boys, but
found he preferred the intense sensation of flying a kite in a swaying
treetop. The leaves fluttered with gusts, and if the wind was strong
enough, the branches and trunk vibrated. Kaze felt like a part of the
kite, weaving with the wind and shaking high above the earth. In his
mind, the treetop was like another kite, tied to the real kite by the
thin twine in Kaze's hand, both kites dancing together in the wind.

The wind was a mystery and constant fascination to him. You
couldn't see it, but you saw its results in the bending grass, the fluttering leaves, and the ripples skimming the surface of a pond. If the
wind was strong enough, you saw grown men bending into it, fighting their way across a castle courtyard or down a country road. After
a particularly violent storm, you even saw trees uprooted or frame
and paper houses, held together with pegs and cunning joints, standing with tattered shoji screens and a forlorn, harshly scrubbed look.

Through the strings of a kite, you could interact with this unseen
force, playing the gusts and eddies to coax the kite higher and higher
into the sky. The force was invisible, but you learned to deal with

this force, conforming to the imperatives of the wind while using it to hold up your kite until you ran out of string or patience.

Kaze reflected that honor was like the wind. It was invisible, yet you felt it tugging at your conscience and impelling you in a direction that you might not want to go. You were buffeted by honor until you bent to its will, moving in the direction that it blew you.

As he grew older, Kaze stopped playing with kites but more keenly felt the effects of honor. If his karma was to grow old, he looked with anxious anticipation toward a time when he would again be near one end of his life span, this time the old end. Then he could have the luxury of playing with kites again.

Now the wind, insistent but not strong, forced him to hold his kimono a little tighter as it pushed against his chest and face. He sat in the dark outside Lord Manase's manor and waited until it was time to again visit the old blind Sensei, Nagahara. Since adding a nightly visit to the Sensei to his schedule, Kaze had devised a plan for entering Manase Manor that didn't require a snoozing guard.

The manor, as with almost all buildings of its kind, was built on a foundation of pilings resting on large rocks. This left a large crawl space under the floor, and this crawl space, plus the fact that the floorboards were not fastened down, made it rather easy for him to enter the manor anytime he wanted to. He knew the Sensei stayed up late reciting the books he was so desperate to retain, so he always appeared late at night, when the rest of the household was asleep.

Nagahara Sensei's energy appeared to be fading, but Kaze's visits seemed to revitalize him as he taught classes for pupils long since past. For his part, Kaze was learning about a Japan also long since past, a Japan where meat, not fish, was eaten in large quantities; where Buddhism was not a major religion; where people didn't bath for pleasure and ritual purification; and where beliefs were totally different from the beliefs Kaze held.

When the time was right, Kaze rapidly crawled under the manor, making his way under the hallway in front of Nagahara Sensei's room. When he was sure it was safe, Kaze displaced several floor-boards and climbed into the hall. Replacing the floorboards so there was no evidence of his entry, Kaze slid back the shoji and called out softly, "Sensei?"

"Hai." Nagahara's voice seemed weak. Kaze entered the room and found the old man reclining on a futon. The room was dark, because there was no need for a light with a blind man, but from the tiny amount of light that spilled in from the open door, Kaze could see that the old man looked tired.

"Perhaps it's a bad night, Sensei," Kaze said.

"Nonsense," the old man replied. "You're just trying to get out of your lessons so you can play with the other boys. Come in here immediately."

"Sensei," Kaze said gently, "Don't you remember? I am Matsu-yama Kaze, the samurai, not one of your youthful charges."

"Matsuyama? Matsuyama? Are you one of my pupils?"

"In a way. Remember? We have been talking about the age of Genji for the last few nights."

"The *Genji*? Shall I recite it for you?"

"No, Sensei, I'm just here to talk to you some more about it."

"What about the age of Genji?"

"Last night you were telling me about the time Genji went to see his paramour. Remember?"

"Genji? Oh yes. As you recall, it was the fourteenth of the month, so naturally Genji couldn't go to see his newest love directly. So instead he went to his good friend To-no-Chujo's and visited for awhile. After this visit, he then went to the Lady's house."

"But how did he know he had to do that?"

"Well, of course he looked it up. In a book. It's like today when we have feast days and extra months and other things on our cal-endar. In those days such things were on their calendar, in special books."

"And what about the things you told me about obakes in the road, Sensei? Did they learn that from books, too?"

"You learn everything from books," the old man said sternly. "In a sense, a book is like an obake, because it allows a person to speak to us long after death. But a young boy like you shouldn't concern yourself with things like obakes. Instead, I want you to recite the poems I gave you to memorize."

"Remember, Sensei? This is Matsuyama. I was not the one you gave the poems to memorize to."

"But if you're not the one . . ." The old man looked confused, then he gave a great groan.

"Sensei?" Kaze said, alarmed. He reached out in the darkness and touched the arm of the old man. It felt as skinny as a twig and as fragile as an old, dried leaf. "Are you all right?"

"It's . . ." The old man seemed to weaken suddenly, and his breathing became labored.

"Perhaps I should leave, Sensei."

"No. Don't. I feel so peculiar, it's like I was . . ."

"What is it, Sensei?"

The old man sighed. In the dark, it seemed like a sigh of contentment, not distress. "The sight of Fuji-san at dawn is the most wonderful thing I can imagine."

Kaze thought the old man was drifting again, but he was glad to hear a renewed strength in the old teacher's voice.

"Look there! See how the snow turns red with the rising of the sun? See how the entire mountaintop is capped in crimson!" The old man was pointing into the darkness, and Kaze realized that the old man was hallucinating in his blindness, seeing with his mind's eye and memory what his real eyes could no longer discern. "It's such a glorious sight, don't you think?"

"Yes, Sensei," Kaze replied.

"It's good that we can see such beauty, isn't it?"

"Yes, Sensei."

The old teacher gave another sigh. His arm dropped to the futon.

"Sensei?" Kaze asked, concern creeping into his voice.

"It's wonderful to see such marvelous beauty," the old man said softly. "Now I can die truly happy." A slow, prolonged hiss escaped from the old man. Kaze sat in the darkness for several minutes, listening for the old man's breathing. Finally, he dared to put his hand near the face of the blind teacher, but he felt no breath on his palm. Kaze sat in the dark silence for many more minutes, then he put his palms together and started reciting a sutra for the dead.

*Vain rooster, with plumes*
*of yellow and shining green.*
*Beware the sharp spurs!*

**H**e sat in a thicket, just as he had been sitting for several days. The last days of summer were gone, and it was starting to chill. He lived off the land, cooking rabbits caught in snare traps and roots and edible plants he gathered. At night he would sneak to Jiro's hut, stopping to get a pinch of salt or some miso to flavor his food. He still had the senbei he had received at the inn but decided to save it for a special occasion.

Kaze, by temperament and training, had more than his share of patience in a world filled with patient men. So he was not disappointed as the days passed and he didn't see what he expected to see. His long talks with the Sensei had convinced him that he had finally placed the mountain in the right spot. He was determined to be that mountain and not to budge from the spot until he saw what he expected to see.

Finally, after eight days, his patience was rewarded.

Instead of coming with his usual paraphernalia, he showed up dressed as a warrior. He jumped off his horse and unloaded his gear. He went to the trees and hung *marumono*, round targets, from low hanging branches spaced many paces apart. The targets were round coils of braided straw, whitewashed with a large black dot in the center. They hung from pieces of hemp twine.

After he finished hanging the targets, he shrugged both his outer kimono and white inner kimono off his left shoulder. He walked over to a quiver sitting on the ground and took out three arrows: brown arrows with goose-feather fletching, all of them of unusual quality.

He walked back to the targets and set them swinging back and forth in a smooth arc. Then he returned to his horse and swung easily up to the saddle. One arrow was fitted to the bowstring and the other two were held in the middle by his teeth. He swung around the meadow and urged his horse into a gallop, swinging by the first target at a distance of ten paces. He drew back the bow and let the arrow fly at the swinging target, hitting it near the edge. In a flash, he had a second arrow removed from his mouth and in the bowstring. He let fly at the second target, missing it, but not by much. Before he galloped past the second target, the third arrow was already fitted to the bow. As he approached the last target you could see the intense concentration in his face. Coolly drawing back his bow, he released his third arrow.

It flew in a path that intersected the swinging target, hitting it squarely in the black dot. The heavy straw target shuddered under the impact of the arrow. Kaze decided it was time for the mountain to move.

Lord Manase slowed his horse and briskly trotted back to his gear. He jumped off the horse and picked up a bottle of water. He was bringing the bottle to his lips when Kaze made his mistake.

"The last arrow was an excellent example of *kyujutsu*," Kaze said.

Manase dropped the water bottle and bent down to pick up his bow and a fresh arrow from his quiver, all in one smooth motion. Kaze anticipated that Lord Manase would have an interest in kyujutsu, the art of archery, but he didn't anticipate Manase reacting like a warrior. Kaze stopped his advance as Manase swung the bow around.

"The ronin!" Manase said, giving his irritating, tittering laugh. Kaze expected Manase to drop his guard, but instead the bow remained at the ready. Kaze had spoken too quickly. With Lord Manase at the alert, one, and perhaps two, arrows could be let loose before Kaze could cross the distance between him and the District Lord. Kaze put a smile on his face and took a step forward to shorten that distance. Manase raised his bow and drew back the string.

"No," he said. Manase's powdered face was as stiff and expressionless as a Noh mask.

"Is something wrong?" Kaze said, taking another half step before he stopped.

"You came back for a reason," Manase said. "I want to know what that reason is."

Kaze thought for a moment about the various answers he could give, and he decided that the simplest and best answer was the truth. "I actually never left. I've been spending most of my time here in the district."

Manase's mask-like face now showed a flicker of surprise. "You've been here ever since the day you disappeared?"

"Hai, yes," Kaze said. "In fact I've been by the edge of this meadow during most of the days. I saw you come several times to practice your Noh dancing. You really are a superb dancer, perhaps the best I've ever seen."

"Why have you been spending the entire time here spying on me?" Manase said.

"I haven't spent the entire time here," Kaze answered. "In the evenings I would sneak into your home."

Now Manase was very surprised. "Did you feel the need to spy on me at home, too?" he demanded.

"I wasn't spying on you. I was there to talk to Nagahara Sensei."

"That crazy old man? Why did you waste your time with him? He finally became totally useless. It was almost a blessing he died."

"He did slip in and out of reality," Kaze agreed. "But even when he was not aware of where he was, he wanted to talk about Heian

Japan. He was a great teacher, and all great teachers deserve our respect. Even when he imagined he was in past days, he still said many interesting things."

"Such as?" Manase said.

Kaze shifted his weight to a more comfortable posture. As he did so, he advanced another half step. "Such as the customs that our ancestors followed six hundred years ago. These are the kinds of customs that you try to follow, although I'm sure it's difficult to do so in the current times."

"I've told you I want to restore the customs of our ancestors," Manase said, "but that doesn't explain why you're still here and spying on me."

Kaze knew that he couldn't completely close the distance between them without Manase releasing the arrow, but he also knew that Manase's right arm must be tiring and that soon he would either have to release the arrow or relax the tension on the bowstring. If he could get him to relax the tension on the bowstring, that would buy more time to cross a few more feet, perhaps just the distance Kaze would need to get Manase to within a sword blade's length. Kaze assumed that he was going to die in that effort. Ever since he was a youth, bushido had taught him that death is a natural part of life. Through reincarnation, he would live again, so the thought of dying did not scare him. He was more disturbed by the thought of failure, of not killing Manase as part of his dying and failing to find the Lady's daughter.

"So what did that crazy old man say?" Manase demanded.

"I said he was a great Sensei and he still deserves our respect," Kaze said sharply.

Manase gave his high tittering laugh. "You come up with the strangest ideas," he said. "Did that old man say something that would cause you to engage in spying on me?"

"Actually it's something you said."

Once again Manase seemed surprised. "What did I say?"

Kaze smiled, shifting his weight and advancing another half pace. He could see Manase's bow arm had relaxed the tension on the string by a noticeable degree. "You said that when the Ise Shrine is dismantled every twenty years, they break up the hinoki wood and hand out pieces to the pilgrims who have gathered to see the ceremony."

Manase relaxed the bowstring even more, cocking his head in a questioning manner. While watching Manase acutely, Kaze was also thinking about the target practice he had witnessed a few minutes before. From the practice, he knew Manase was an excellent shot with the bow. Hitting a moving target from a moving horse was an extremely difficult task, requiring frequent practice and great concentration. There was something about that task, something important, that gnawed at Kaze's thoughts. It was something that his old Sensei could have told him immediately, and Kaze felt frustrated that such an important thing didn't pop into his head instantly.

"Why would that information about the Ise Shrine cause you to spy on me?" Manase demanded.

"It's very simple," Kaze said nonchalantly. "That first murdered man, the samurai, had a piece of wood on his money pouch instead of a proper netsuke. He was certainly prosperous enough to have a netsuke, so that piece of wood must have meant something to him. I think it was a piece of the Ise Shrine and it not only reminded him of home, but it was supposed to bring him good luck."

"Even if the man was from Ise, why would he have any connection to me?"

Kaze reached up and scratched his head, smiling. He saw Manase tracking the movements of his arm with the bow, and he knew what it was about Manase's archery that he was trying to remember. "That was harder," Kaze said, "but once I thought the man might be somehow connected to you and Ise, then I looked at things in a slightly different manner. For instance, those arrows you use are extremely high quality, much better quality than most people would typically use for hunting or even war. It's like many of the things you have:

only the best. The arrows are much too good for some bandit to have, and I suppose Boss Kuemon got some of them by robbing a shipment that was meant for you."

"He did rob a shipment," Manase acknowledged, "and I'm sure he used those arrows to kill that unknown samurai."

"But he couldn't have killed that young boy," Kaze said. "You see, I found the boy's body at the crossroads, too, and sticking from his body was the same kind of arrow that killed that samurai."

"That boy is of no consequence," Manase said. "He was not of the samurai class and therefore his death should have no meaning for you."

Kaze shrugged. "Perhaps you're right. But you see, I gave that boy his life back twice and it's very annoying that you took it."

Manase looked at him, puzzled, trying to fathom why the death of a peasant would concern Kaze. Kaze shifted his weight from one foot to the other and watched closely as Manase's bow followed his body movements. Manase's target practice was done while sitting on a moving horse and shooting at a swinging target. He was aiming at where the target would be, not where the target was. He had to anticipate the movements of the horse and the target and had to shoot the arrow to the position where the target would be when the arrow arrived. Kaze would use that knowledge.

"Of course, the most difficult part," Kaze said, "was trying to understand why you dumped the bodies at the crossroads. I was especially curious about why you took such a roundabout route to drop the first body off. I imagine the samurai was killed someplace near your manor, yet instead of going directly from your manor to the crossroads, you loaded him onto your horse, rode southwest to Higashi village and then northwest to the crossroads. To hide your identity, you put on a Noh mask of a demon and wore a demon's costume to frighten the peasants in Higashi village. The peasants didn't describe it fully, but I imagine it was the *hannya* demon's mask used in *Dojoji*. I know that's one Noh play you practice."

Manase made no response, but Kaze could see his lips tightening.

Kaze knew that he would soon have to attack or die where he stood. "That's where my conversations with Nagahara Sensei proved interesting. Even though he slipped in and out of reality, he still loved to talk about the Heian era. I'm sure you know that in ancient days a gentleman was proud of his skill at archery but would often hide the fact that he had skill with a sword. Very different from today, where the sword is the soul of a warrior.

"In those days they had many interesting customs that we don't follow today," Kaze continued. "For instance, I'm sure you know that in many tales there are times when a noble wants to visit a friend or lover, but instead of going there directly, he first goes to another friend's, stops there briefly, then goes to the person he really wanted to visit. That's because people then believed that on certain days, certain directions were unlucky. If the noble was trying to visit someone to the west on a day when traveling west was unlucky, he first traveled southwest to another person, stopped, then traveled northwest to his eventual destination. He never went directly west, so he was able to get where he wanted to go without breaking the prohibition against traveling west. That's exactly what you did.

"Nagahara Sensei said there are ancient texts that tell which directions are unlucky on which day, and I'm sure you have one of these books in your collection. On the day you killed the samurai, it was unlucky for you to travel directly west, so you went southwest to Higashi village and then northwest to the crossroads. On the day you killed the boy, it wasn't unlucky to travel west so you skirted Suzaka village and went directly to the crossroads.

"Why you wanted to leave the bodies at the crossroads puzzled me until Nagahara Sensei told me that in ancient days, people believed that obakes would get confused by roads. I know from personal experience that obakes inhabit roads. A crossroads would be confusing to an obake, because the roads branch off in all directions. To confuse the ghosts of the samurai and the boy, you left their bodies at a crossroads where many paths converge. Their ghosts couldn't find their way back to you, their killer."

Kaze decided that now was the time to act. Without warning, he quickly lunged to the left, pulling out his sword. Manase reacted immediately, pulling back his bow and letting loose his arrow. But before Manase did that, Kaze had already shifted direction. His move to the left was a feint designed to get Manase to shoot where he thought Kaze would be when the arrow reached its target. Instead of continuing left, Kaze simply leaned in that direction and then immediately shifted his weight to the right. Kaze's sword was out of its scabbard by the time the arrow neatly grazed the left sleeve of his kimono.

He closed the distance between him and Manase, expecting Manase to bend down to the quiver to grab another arrow or at least to pull out his sword. Instead, Manase, seeing his arrow had missed, dropped his bow and put up his hands in the universal gesture of surrender. Kaze's sword was already moving in a deadly arc, and it took effort on Kaze's part to stop the swing of his sword so it didn't cut down the helpless Manase.

"Take out your sword!" Kaze demanded. Manase backed up a step, his hands still up in the air. Kaze advanced, his sword at the ready and threatening. "Take out your sword and fight!"

Manase shook his head. "You killed five men by yourself with your sword. I'm no match for you. You're too strong for me."

"You killed General Iwaki at Sekigahara," Kaze said. "He was a good swordsman. There's no reason for you not to fight."

Manase shook his head. "I didn't kill him. During the confusion of the battle, my friend and I found the General and his bodyguard. They had all committed seppuku. They were dead when we found them. We dragged the General's body away from his bodyguards and cut it up so people wouldn't know he had committed suicide on the battlefield after his defeat. My friend lost courage, but I saw that this was my opportunity. I took the General's head to Tokugawa Ieyasu to get a reward. I think Tokugawa-sama was too wily not to be suspicious, and that's why he gave me this miserable little district as a reward instead of something grander. The samurai I killed was my friend from that battle. He returned to Ise and eventually heard about the reward I got for taking the head of General Iwaki. He came here demanding money, but I have no money. I've spent it all. I was even borrowing money from Boss Kuemon. That's why Kuemon started robbing shipments to me, to get his money back. My friend said he would tell Ieyasu what I had done and get his reward from the Tokugawa government for turning in a fraud. I had no choice but to kill him."

"And the young boy?" Kaze shouted.

Manase flinched, but, looking at Kaze's blade still glistening in the sun, he said, "My friend was stopped by Boss Kuemon. He told Kuemon that he was a friend of mine from Ise. Kuemon, thinking that my friend could get money from Ise to help pay off the loans I owed him, had my friend brought to me. That young boy was the person who led him to me. After you killed Kuemon, the boy showed up at my manor asking to be taken into my service. He could link me to my dead friend, and I decided it was better if he died, too. After all, although my friend was a samurai, that boy was just a peasant. His death was meaningless."

Kaze scowled. "We've had too many meaningless deaths over the last few years."

Manase shrugged. "Are you going to take me to the next district to present your case?"

"No," Kaze said softly.

Manase looked puzzled. "What are you going to do?"

"I'm going to execute you."

Manase sputtered, "How dare you! You're a miserable ronin and I'm a District Lord. I demand that I be given a proper hearing."

Kaze shook his head. "No. As you point out, I am a ronin and you are a District Lord. If I bring a case against you, it's impossible to know the results. I am sure that you won't tell the authorities in the next district the same story about General Iwaki that you told me. That fraud alone would carry the death penalty for you. You are a very clever man, Lord Manase, and by the time we got to the next district, I'm sure you would have developed an equally clever story that will put me in the wrong and you in the right."

"So you're going to kill me?" Manase said incredulously.

"Yes."

"I found a great deal of money at the bandit camp," Manase said hastily. "It's yours, all yours."

"This is not about money," Kaze said. "No amount of money can bring the dead back to life."

"This is ridiculous," Manase spluttered. "You can't murder a District Lord."

"No," Kaze agreed, "but I can execute one."

Manase stopped cowering and stood up straight. "All right," he said. "But I insist that I be allowed to commit seppuku—that is my right as a District Lord and samurai."

Kaze considered a moment, then said, "Remove your swords from your sash, and drop them on the ground." Manase did as ordered.

"Now step away from them," Kaze said. Manase walked four paces away from his swords with Kaze following him.

"All right," Kaze said. "You can commit seppuku, but you're going to do it right here and right now."

"Here, without preparation?"

Kaze gave a short bow. "I'm sorry. I don't mean to insult you, but the truth is I don't trust you. I think given enough time, you will find a way to get out of this situation. Therefore, if you want to commit seppuku, I'm asking you to please do it now. Otherwise I will have to execute you."

Manase gave his high laugh. "That's almost a compliment. You don't trust me."

Kaze gave another bow. "I've learned that your love of delicate and refined things does not make you any less a killer. I should not confuse a love of refinement with a lack of bushido."

"Fine," Manase said. "Right here and right now." He sat down on the soft green grass of the meadow, his legs tucked under him. He looked up at Kaze and said, "Will you be my second?"

Kaze nodded.

Manase looked about him. "I don't have paper to write a death poem."

"If you recite a poem, I will remember it," Kaze said. "When I have a chance, I'll write it down and send it wherever you want."

"To the shrine at Ise?"

"Yes, if that's where you want the poem sent."

"About the handwriting..."

Kaze understood. "I have a good hand, but if you're worried about that, I know a priest who is a master at calligraphy. I will have him write your death poem to send to Ise."

"Good," Manase said.

Kaze took Manase's short sword from the ground and handed it to him. Then he stood at the ready, his sword still and poised.

Manase paused, looking around at the fresh green trees swaying in the wind and then upward at the blue sky. He sighed. "It's a fine day to die, isn't it?"

Kaze made a noncommittal grunt.

"It's a shame I don't have ink, brush, and paper."

"You will not be embarrassed by the quality of the hand that writes it."

"It's good of you to be sensitive to my concerns. I mean no disrespect to you. I simply don't want the slightest possibility that someone may think that my death poem doesn't reflect the most delicate refinement."

Kaze nodded his understanding.

Manase sat for several moments, contemplating his final poetic statement in this life.

> *Graceful elegance*
> *Was no buffer from my death.*
> *Even flowers die.*

When he was done reciting, he looked up at Kaze. "Can you remember that?"

Kaze nodded, "Yes, I'll remember every word. It's a fine death poem."

Manase gave a curt bow of thanks. He shrugged his kimono and white inner kimono off his other shoulder, leaving his torso bare. He took the wakizashi Kaze had given him and put it in front of him. He did a quick bow, picked up the sword, and slid it out of its scabbard.

"I don't have any paper to wrap around this blade," Manase remarked.

Kaze looked around but saw no paper, so he took the sleeve from his kimono and ripped off a strip. He handed it to Manase. Manase took the strip of torn kimono and wryly said to Kaze, "You should have taken the new kimono I gave you."

He wrapped the strip of cloth around the blade of the short sword, right beneath the sword's *tsuba,* or guard. This allowed him to grip the short sword on the blade, so that the blade of the sword was more like a dagger. Kaze walked over and picked up the water bottle that Manase had dropped. He shook it to make sure there was some water left in the bottle. Then he took his sword, the blade facing upward, and poured a tiny amount of water on the blade down its whole length in a ritual purification. The water slid off the oiled blade in a silver curtain that spattered on the ground.

Kaze walked over to Manase, gave another bow, and handed him the water jug. Taking the jug wordlessly, Manase bowed back to Kaze and poured some water on the blade of his short sword, then he put the bottle to his side and grabbed the blade with two hands, holding tightly to the cloth wrapped around the highly polished metal. Kaze got in position to the left and slightly behind Manase, raising his sword blade at the ready.

"It's a shame all must end like this," Manase remarked. "Do you know I never once got to give a real Noh performance? If I have any regrets or harbor any animosity toward you, it's the fact that your disappearance robbed me of the opportunity to give a performance before an audience that would recognize and respect my talent."

"I'm sorry," Kaze said.

Manase made no reply but took a deep breath, holding the short sword at the ready. "All right?" he asked.

"I'm in position," Kaze answered from behind him.

Manase nodded once, closed his eyes, and plunged the sword into his stomach with all his strength. He gave a short groan of pain and surprise as the silver blade entered his flesh, but before he cried in agony or even drew the blade across his stomach, Kaze's own sword flashed down, neatly striking Manase's neck and severing his head from his body.

A red spray of blood gushed from Manase's severed neck, and his head hit the ground and rolled for a short distance as his body swayed and then collapsed to the earth. The eyes of Manase's head opened and the lids fluttered violently for a few seconds before they were finally stilled.

Kaze stood surveying the scene before him, breathing heavily, waiting for the tension to drain from his body, just as the blood drained from Manase's headless corpse. Kaze looked down at Manase's robes and decided not to wipe his sword on them, so he tore another piece of his kimono sleeve and used that to clean his blade before he returned it to its scabbard.

He walked over and picked up Manase's severed head by the hair and brought it back to his body. He took the body and rolled it over on its back, straightening its legs and putting its hands peacefully across its chest. He picked up the water bottle that Manase had placed on the ground and used the few remaining drops of water in the bottle to clean the dirt off Manase's head and to pat his hair back into place. Then he placed the head next to Manase's body. He got on his knees in the meadow and bowed deeply to the corpse of the District Lord, touching his forehead to the ground.

He sat up and looked at the lifeless face. The chalk-white makeup on the face didn't hide the newly gray pallor of the flesh underneath.

The eyes were looking back at him with the ridiculous painted eyebrows high on the forehead. Kaze reached over with his two fingers and closed the eyelids. Then he bowed once again.

"I'm sorry to bring trouble to your house and to end your life like this," Kaze said to the corpse of Manase. "But I want your spirit to know some things that I didn't care to discuss while you were still alive and there was a possibility that you could still escape.

"I was also a District Lord, just like you, except my district was several thousand times larger and I had every anticipation that, as my master prospered, I would prosper, too. My master, however, was loyal to the Taiko, Hideyoshi. When the war to decide who would succeed the Taiko occurred, he backed the Toyotomi forces and not Tokugawa Ieyasu. The battle that raised your fortunes, Sekigahara, is the battle that ruined mine. My Lord was defeated at Sekigahara, and I wasn't even there to die with him. Instead, I was leading an expedition back to his home castle that was under attack by an ally of the Tokugawas. I got there too late, and my Lord's castle was sacked.

"My Lord's wife and child were captured during the siege. I managed to rescue his wife, but not his child. As she was tortured, she was told that their daughter would be sold into slavery. The sorrowful fate of her child would eat at her like some tiny animal living in her heart. Because of the torture she lived only a short time after I rescued her, but she made me promise to find her child and free her."

Kaze bowed once again, touching his forehead to the ground. He sat up and said, "So you see, I'm sorry I brought misfortune to your house and caused you to commit seppuku. But the Tokugawa government, the government that now rules Japan, is not one that I can go to for justice. And I'm very sorry to have to say this, Lord Manase, but you were not a good ruler.

"Our beliefs tell us that harmony and balance must be kept if a Lord is to rule according to the natural order of things. Then peasants, merchants, priests, and other people can understand that there is a natural hierarchy to society and that the ruler is in place at the top of this hierarchy because of the benefits he brings to all, not just to himself. I'm sorry, but you forgot that principle and devoted your life to your own pleasure and interests, abandoning the people who depend on you to incompetent magistrates, bandits, and their own resources.

"That is why I decided to take action in this case, even though it involved only the death of one samurai and one peasant in a land where hundreds of thousands have died through wars and other types of injustices. I hope you'll forgive me." Kaze bowed once more, then he stood up. He took Lord Manase's horse and tied him to a bush on the road. When they came to look for the District Lord, they would find the horse and thus find the body in the meadow in the woods.

Kaze made sure his sword was secure in the sash of his kimono, then he turned and started walking down the road, starting his often-interrupted journey out of the District. He felt no elation over the outcome with the strange District Lord, but as he walked, breathing in the clean air, looking at the blue sky filled with small white tufts of clouds, he soon shrugged off his concerns.

He started humming an old Japanese folk song under his breath and stopped to examine the tattered sleeves of his kimono. As he did so, he found the bit of cloth with the senbei that the youth had given him at the inn and finally decided to eat it. He unwrapped the cloth and took a bite from the toasted rice cake he found inside. After all this time, it was a bit stale but still tasty. He was about to toss aside the scrap of cloth it was wrapped in when he froze, dropping the rice cake and holding the cloth in both hands.

There, on the inside of the cloth, was a mon with three plum blossoms. It was the mon of his Lord and Lady. It was the mon on the clothing of the girl he was seeking. Perhaps the cloth came from someone else in Kaze's scattered clan and perhaps it was simply a rag that had somehow come into the possession of the motley trio intent on revenge. And perhaps, just perhaps, it was a tangible link between that trio and the girl Kaze had been seeking for over two years.

The strange trio had a head start of many days on Kaze, but he knew where they were headed: the great Tokaido road.